MW00856919

Praise for *Detach*

"Twelve years after helping me build strong fundamentals in my personal and business life, Dr. Bob Rosen, in *Detach*, sheds a bright light on the path toward a life free of unnecessary and dangerous psychological dilemmas. Easy reading and impactful."

—Alessandro Valenti, CEO, Givenchy

"Bob is a great coach. Here, he shines a light on what's possible when people replace habits like perfection, which will get in the way of success, with behaviors like curiosity and lifelong learning, which will propel us forward."

—Brian Cornell, Chairman and CEO, Target

"I love this book. It's a revolutionary approach to improving your life. These concepts are so needed in our stressed-out world. In typical Bob Rosen fashion, the book is honest, real, and deeply human. His words and the stories of others will help you improve your health and well-being, experience more freedom in your life, and help you overcome your fears to live a life full of love. As a leader, I know these ideas help improve morale, reduce tension, and help people thrive through change. This is Bob's best book!"

—Linda Rabbitt, Founder and Chairman, Rand Construction Corporation

"Bob Rosen's *Detach* offers practical wisdom on how to merge Western ideas of personal fulfillment with Eastern insights about the release of personal attachments as the key to happiness. *Detach* includes data, personal stories, and insights drawn from Rosen's own career as an executive leadership coach. This book struck a real chord with me."

—Tim Kaine, United States Senator, Virginia

"An illuminating look at the obstacles that can keep even the most successful business leaders from experiencing a sense of satisfaction and well-being in their own lives. Through real-life examples and probing questions, Bob not only helps us explore our own relationship with the 'ten attachments' but also provides a pathway for moving away from them and into a life of greater purpose and joy."

—Mark J. Madgett, Executive Vice President and Cohead of the Foundational Business, New York Life Insurance Company

"Bob Rosen takes his many years as a practicing psychologist and organization consultant to weave his magic into every chapter. This is a great collection of wisdom not only from the author but from all that he gathered culled from others. He weaves a fascinating tapestry so that every reader can find nuggets to apply to their own life. This is a book you will want to recommend to many others for a variety of reasons."

—Dr. Bev Kaye, Author, *Love 'Em or Lose 'Em*; Thought Leader; Keynote Speaker; Consultant

DETACH

Also by Bob Rosen

Grounded

Conscious

Leadership Journeys

The Catalyst (Jeanne Liedtka and Robert Wiltbank)

Just Enough Anxiety

Global Literacies

Leading People (with Paul Brown)

The Healthy Company (with Lisa Berger)

DETACH

Ditch Your Baggage to Live a More Fulfilling Life

Bob Rosen

Matt Holt Books
An Imprint of BenBella Books, Inc.
Dallas, TX

Matt Holt is an imprint of BenBella Books, Inc.
8080 N. Central Expressway
Suite 1700
Dallas, TX 75206
benbellabooks.com
Send feedback to feedback@benbellabooks.com

BenBella and *Matt Holt* are federally registered trademarks.

Printed in the United States of America
10 9 8 7 6 5 4 3 2 1

Library of Congress Control Number: 2024050108
ISBN 9781637746455 (hardcover)
ISBN 9781637746462 (electronic)

Copyediting by Scott Calamar
Proofreading by Sarah Vostok and Ashley Casteel
Indexing by Debra Bowman
Text design and composition by PerfecType, Nashville TN
Cover design by Brigid Pearson
Cover images © Adobe Stock / K KStock
Printed by Lake Book Manufacturing

To those who carry personal baggage and aspire to lead
a more joyful life. That would be all of us!

CONTENTS

THE BAGGAGE WE CARRY

Why do we make life so difficult when it doesn't have to be that way? Every morning, we activate a switch when we open our eyes. We choose—consciously or unconsciously—how we want to live the day. We can choose the path of love, full of joy, curiosity, and freedom, or we can choose the path driven by fear, littered by worry, disappointment, and suffering. The choice is ours.

We all start out on the same journey toward the same destination. Our first attachments, if we are lucky, are formed early on with our parents. Hopefully, for us, our experience establishes a sturdy foundation for a happy, secure life. These attachments are essential to our healthy emotional development, providing us with security, pleasure, and the validation we need throughout our lives.

But, for many, something goes awry. We veer off course, finding ourselves distracted, seduced, or sabotaged by internal conversations that undermine our best selves. We develop attachments to ideas, people, ideals, and behaviors that weigh us down. They keep us from moving forward and inhibit our ability to live a full life.

What are these attachments? Where do they come from, and how do they develop? How do they poison our lives? And how can we confront and overcome them? Finding answers to these questions is central to living a good life—to experiencing joy, to being free, and to reaching our full potential.

This book probes these unhealthy attachments and how we can overcome them to live a healthy and fulfilling life, shedding those conscious and unconscious conversations we have with ourselves that keep us stuck in old patterns, shackled by dysfunctional habits. Convincing beyond belief and resistant to change, these attachments blind us from the truth and control how we live in the world.

Think of these attachments as baggage we carry around with us every day. Each piece of baggage represents an attachment in our lives. We can carry them in our heads, stuff them in our pockets, and drag them behind us in big sacks. They trip us up, drag us down, and wear us out.

Attachments come in many shapes and sizes. Some are simple thoughts and feelings; others are more elaborate philosophies about life, desires about the future, and ideas about success. As they develop, they grow like a cancer, like a dense, entangled psychological web, controlling our minds. One day, we wake up to find that we have created a compelling story that literally has hijacked our mind.

Our suffering occurs when we embrace these attachments and let them control our lives. When we worry about the past, become preoccupied with the future, or feel pressure to be perfect, we become shackled by sadness, anger, or guilt. Or, when we are dismissive of others or addicted to people and things, the result is suffering. The more we identify with our attachments, the more we suffer. By letting go of them, we become free of our suffering. Then, we can trade our disappointments for joy, worries for peace, and fear for love.

My name is Bob Rosen. As a psychologist and businessman, I have spent the last forty years helping top executives become better leaders and builders of great organizations. I have run my own company, met with more than 600 CEOs in 55 countries around the world, and have written eight leadership books. In my travels, I've had the great fortune of meeting thousands of people who have shared their life stories with me. As I look back on my life, I have had a great career and have met some amazing people on my journey. But this is just my public and professional life.

Like all of us, I have a personal and private life. So this time, I wanted to write a book about life, what I've learned from the people around me, and what it takes to be awake, joyful, and successful. I certainly don't hold my life out as a paragon of health. I've had my share of ups and downs, illnesses, mistakes, and accomplishments, and suffered from anxiety and addiction. Fortunately, I've had my husband and life partner of forty years by my side. Yet this time, I wanted to write a book about successful living and working and our common search for meaning and happiness in our lives.

As a student of Eastern and Western philosophy, I find myself deeply influenced by the psychology and spirituality of both traditions. Eastern psychology, especially Buddhism, teaches us about change and suffering, how our attachments are the source of this suffering, and what we can do to release ourselves from this bondage. Western psychology teaches us about aspirations and the power of ideals and the importance of positive thinking. By aspiring to higher goals, we can fulfill our potential and awaken our best selves. Both perspectives are central in this book.

We also live in a world of paradox where we find ourselves sitting on both sides of the fence of life. We learn to aspire for more *and* grasp for less, to improve ourselves *and* accept who we are, to dream of tomorrow *and* live in the moment. To help us succeed, we must draw on the philosophies of both the East and the West. This paradox is one of the most important lessons of my life.

WHY THIS BOOK NOW?

We live in a world of uncertainty. Like all times in history, we have our unique challenges *and* opportunities, making it difficult to stay calm in a world of chaos. Geopolitical instability and rapid climate change provide the backdrop for this angst. Diminishing trust, prejudice, and polarization infiltrate our relationships. Closer to home, work pressures, gun violence, addiction, and family conflicts exacerbate the stress, anger, sadness, and worry we face. A systemic and pervasive anxiety hovers over all of us, and many lack the agility, adaptation, and resilience skills necessary to thrive in these conditions.

As I look across the landscape, I see two primary areas of angst simmering inside of people. The first is the growing disconnection people feel toward others and their organizations and communities. This lack of meaning and belonging isolates people and creates high levels of loneliness in society.

The second area of angst is the growing level of anger and cynicism among the masses. Inflammatory rhetoric, intensifying vitriol, and affective polarization between groups of people are commonplace. Whether in politics, business, religion, or the media, people resent more and trust less.

The result of this internal turmoil is that people are less comfortable in their own skins, less engaged with others, and more fearful about the direction of the world.

At the same time, we are entering a new age of health and prosperity. Digital intelligence is accelerating the pace of our lives. Greater diversity and hybrid work arrangements are enabling more flexible living. And, democratizing power and information are giving more voice to the people.

We are also coming out of the recent pandemic with different feelings about ourselves, our families, organizations, and society. These deep psychological shifts are shining a light on our holistic selves, fostering a renewed search for well-being and quality of life. It will take years to figure out the full impact of this worldwide health crisis.

As humans, how we manage these challenges and leverage new opportunities will make a huge difference. We have a choice. We can live with too little anxiety—the face of complacency—by blindfolding ourselves and pushing problems under the rug. Or we can live with too much anxiety—the face of chaos—where rising stress levels, exhaustion, and frenetic living are the norm.

There is a better way, but it requires more evolved people, those willing to unlearn old ways of thinking, feeling, and acting and embrace new mindsets and skills. When this happens, we become physically and emotionally healthier, happier, and more fulfilled, and we're more likely to reach our potential and perform better.

By letting go of old baggage and our attachments, and practicing a new way of living and working, we can rise above this angst and move forward. *Detach* is the antidote and the source of what's possible.

THE TEN ATTACHMENTS

What are the ten attachments? How do they poison our lives? How can we *overcome* them?

1. The Attachment to Stability

We are all part of a big delusion: We believe that we can create stability and safety in our lives. But there is no such thing. Every time we breathe, the world changes. This is true of our brains and bodies, our companies and economies, and the planet we live on. We love the feeling of stability, but it's simply not sustainable. Scared of uncertainty, we deny this truth. We flee from or get hijacked by change, and we risk becoming too attached to stability. If we learn to accept uncertainty as the true nature of life, we can become more agile and free from this fear of uncertainty and change.

2. The Attachment to the Past

Every day is a gift, filled with potential. Yet many of us are living in the past, trying to make sense of what's already happened. We idealize or demonize our memories, becoming immobilized by old emotional scars, neglectful parents, relationships that didn't work, or business deals that went sour. We are haunted by thoughts of loved ones who have died or partners who have left us for another. By not facing the truth about times gone by, we risk becoming attached to the past, replaying old stories, and missing out on today. If we can practice acceptance and forgiveness and let go of our emotional baggage, we can face reality head-on and move on with our lives.

3. The Attachment to the Future

Conversely, many of us are preoccupied with the future, striving for more, obsessing over what is missing in our lives. Whether it's finding the right job, the right mate, the right degree, or the right house, we keep trying to fill life's cup that is always half empty. We're never satisfied with who we are or what we have. We let day after day pass us by. We never take vacations, so we'll have money for the future. When we hold out for the perfect partner, we miss the wonderful person in front of us. We save everything and buy little. By fearing that something is missing in our life, we risk becoming too attached to the future. But, if we can live in the present moment and learn to appreciate what we have and who we are, we can live a wonderful life—today.

4. The Attachment to Control

From early childhood, we are taught to shape our environment. We learn to minimize our weaknesses by maximizing our strengths. Over time, we develop the confidence and courage to try to control our own destiny.

We take charge. We plan things meticulously. We cleverly maneuver our way through situations or manipulate people to get what we want. We fail to see that many things in life are simply outside our influence, like managing the stock market, moderating another's emotional reactions, navigating rush-hour traffic, and guiding our grown-up children. Determined to control the uncontrollable, we create havoc in our lives. In trying to hide our vulnerability, we risk becoming too attached to control. If we learn to trust ourselves and the mystery of life, and let ourselves be vulnerable, we become free from our controlling nature.

5. The Attachment to Perfection

People are imperfect by nature. Yet, how many of us are ruled by the need to be perfect? We're the ones who can never make a mistake, who must be right or smart or good all the time, and who get publicly embarrassed when we admit a weakness. Keeping this quality to ourselves would be bad enough, but we tend to impose our perfection on the people around us—from parents to kids, spouses to partners, and bosses to associates. Why can't we just acknowledge reality and laugh at ourselves? By fearing to look inadequate, we risk becoming too attached to perfection. In learning to be gentle with ourselves, we can fall in love with our imperfections.

6. The Attachment to Success

Everyone dreams of success. Who doesn't want to be the best? But when our desire for success turns into a compulsive need for achievement, then we've got a real problem. Suddenly, we find our dreams dictating our lives. Whether we define success by how much money we make, or by being a great parent, a tireless advocate, or a moral person, we give up a piece of ourselves when we can't distinguish "who we are" and "what we do." We end up defining success from the outside in, based on other people's expectations and society's standards, and not on our own definition of success. Our fear of failure drives our attachment to success. But if we are authentic and comfortable with ourselves, we can learn the true nature of success.

7. The Attachment to Pleasure

Many people are attached to the pleasures in their lives. But that's the point, right? Well, partially, but not when your desire is driven by dysfunctional grasping that undermines your health and performance. Alcohol, drugs, food, and sex are the best-known addictions. Less obvious obsessions include exercise, workaholism, religion, and being in love. Oddly enough, these obsessions are driven by an inability to experience pleasure *and* pain and to be alone in our own skin. By fearing our difficult feelings, we risk becoming too attached to pleasure. But if we learn to experience the full range of emotions and sit with our anxiety, we can enjoy life's pleasures without being hijacked by them.

8. The Attachment to Youth

The Japanese have a commendable concept for aging called "wabi-sabi," meaning there is beauty in all living things, whether growing or decaying. There is no question that our society idealizes youth, ignoring its older citizens. Nowhere is this process more insidious than in our own heads. Rather than appreciate our aging minds and bodies as facts of beauty, we spend thousands of hours and dollars trying to reverse this natural process. We ignore the many benefits of aging: more maturity, wisdom, independence, and freedom. By fearing the aging process, we risk becoming too attached to our youth. By accepting our natural state, we can allow ourselves to age gracefully.

9. The Attachment to Self

We are, indeed, alone in the world, living in the inner sanctum of our minds. Some of us are simply too attached to ourselves, preoccupied with our own needs, thoughts, and feelings. With a sense of entitlement and self-interest, we are seduced by our inner experience. Under the guise of taking care of ourselves, we withdraw from others and rarely find our needs met, often avoiding the very people who could give meaning to our lives. There is another way: experience the world and become more conscious of it. This path is full of empathy and compassion, caring and service. By fearing intimacy and connection with others, we risk becoming too attached to ourselves. When we can practice generosity, we can lead our life loving others and making a difference in the world.

10. The Attachment to Life

All things die. It's plain and simple. Why do we have so much difficulty accepting the natural process of growth and death, whether it's our natural surroundings, our jobs and retirement, human relationships, or simple beliefs that change over time? And, why is it so painful to think about death and dying? Are we simply scared of these life changes, the pain and suffering that might come, and our not knowing where we might go afterward? Or are we afraid of leaving our past behind—or departing the world not having made any lasting contribution? Wouldn't it be great if we could make peace with these questions of beginnings and endings? By fearing death or even loss, we risk becoming too attached to life. But, if we feel gratitude and appreciation for each day and a life well lived, we can see life and death as inevitable and just part of life's evolution.

So there you have it, the ten attachments. Each one is driven by *fear* in a vicious cycle of negative beliefs that activates destructive emotions and leads to sabotaging behaviors.

Fear comes in many forms, from being hurt to feeling loss, from being unworthy to feeling failure, and from pain to insignificance. If we continue to hold on to these attachments, we amplify these fears and end up infecting our lives and undermining our health and happiness.

Attachments are part of our unhealthy self, a self that can be arrogant or cynical, ignorant, or scared. When grasping and clinging behavior become engrained, we become asleep at the switch of our own lives.

There is another way. We can live our lives motivated by *love* and a virtuous cycle of affirming beliefs that lead to positive emotions and nurturing behaviors. Rather than clinging to one of the ten attachments, we can let them go and step onto an alternative path of positive aspirations for the future.

That path leads us to our healthier self, one full of wisdom and flexibility, joy and generosity, mindfulness and abundance, and forgiveness and gratitude. By replacing our attachments with positive aspirations, we free ourselves to live a joyful, liberated, and more successful life.

Wait a minute! Don't we need some stability in our lives or some ambitions to motivate us to succeed? How about our memories from the past or our dreams for the future? Don't they matter? And what about our first attachment with our mom and dad, or the love we have for our partners, or even our friends? Aren't these attachments important to living a good and prosperous life?

And while we're at it, what about the idea that people are motivated by fear *or* love? Can life be that simplistic? Don't we all experience fear *and* love throughout our lives?

All of this is true. Admittedly, there is a healthy side to these attachments. Some degree of stability and ambition is motivating. Memories and dreams can be wonderful. As social animals, we need our emotional connections with others. And we all experience both fear and love over the course of our lives. But, when our attachments become preoccupations, obsessions, even addictions, we turn our lives over to fear and limit our capacity for love.

That all sounds great. So where do we start? How can we begin to rid ourselves of these attachments and step out on the path of aspirations toward true health and happiness?

Let me give you a personal example of how this process works. For a long time, I struggled with an attachment to the future. As a dreamer and planner, I always looked ahead to imagine my future and the path forward. Much of this planning was motivated by my need for success and my fear of not being "special." Coming from a broken home, I was thrust into my newfound independence and my desire to control my own destiny. But, when I looked ahead, I sometimes found myself dissatisfied with who I was and where I was at the time in my life. What was I missing? How could I obtain it? Was I with the right partner? Was my career moving forward? As you can imagine, this path was littered with worry and anxiety about the future. To complicate matters, I had come from a lower-income family and was insecure about not having enough money for my future life.

The upside of this attachment resulted in my working hard and having a job since I was ten, getting a full scholarship to college, and getting my PhD at age twenty-five. Yet, as I examined my attachment more closely, it became clear to me that much of my motivation was driven by my fear of financial insecurity and not getting what I wanted in life.

Fortunately, I began to examine my attachment more closely, accept the impact it was having on my life, and separate myself from the attachment itself. Rather than seeing my life from a position of scarcity, I began to practice the power of abundance. Meditation helped me appreciate the present moment. I tapped into my gratitude for the great things in my life—my family, my career, my health, and daily happiness. Slowly, the attachment to the future evaporated, and I began to live more fully in the present.

Some scar tissue still emerges from time to time. Yet today, I feel more grounded and conscious as a person and executive. Being grounded helps me stay centered in the face of life's challenges. Being conscious keeps me aware, agile, and adaptive so I don't get hijacked by these demons.

THE POWER OF SELF-AWARENESS

The key to moving from attachments to aspirations is deep self-awareness, and the only way to achieve this stage is to look at ourselves in the mirror. Regardless, many of us live in a world of delusion, a kind of psychological avoidance. We avoid the mirror at all costs, and we do this to avoid discomfort and anxiety.

Our natural tendency is to look outside ourselves for answers to life's problems. In a counterintuitive way, our peace of mind really comes from the inside. Indeed, many of our problems are self-imposed, and the only way to put an end to our suffering is to deepen our self-understanding. By turning inward, we can find true joy and freedom. Otherwise, we are left with faulty thinking and disturbing emotions and the attachments that weigh us down.

As human beings, we have enormous capacity for change. Our brains rewire through neuroplasticity; our minds adapt through self-discovery and self-development. By listening to our inner voice, questioning our assumptions, and looking for patterns, we can let go of the way things are and create a new picture of ourselves.

Why then, do so many of us have trouble with change? Fear of uncertainty and vulnerability is a major reason. Some people run from these deep feelings and remain complacent. Others ignore the resistance that lurks under the surface. Some of us don't like to give up what feels good and will do everything we can to avoid withdrawal. Other times, it is merely inconvenience. And even if you want to change, your partner, peers, or family can expect and reinforce the opposite behavior.

The result of this resistance for many is a fear of losing our current life, whether changes in ourselves, our relationships, or our health and well-being. But for most, we believe our busy, hectic lifestyles don't afford us the luxury of looking inward.

THE TEN ASPIRATIONS

The secret to letting go of our attachments is to replace them with more powerful aspirations. Tapping into our hopes and dreams provides the direction to live a better, more productive life.

Turning your attachments into aspirations is a lifelong process. Faulty thinking can appear at any time and can last a lifetime. And just when we think we've mastered the transition, the attachments raise their ugly heads and come back to torment us. As true keys for change, our aspirations unlock those mysterious shackles and shine a light on our healthier selves.

As you read the ten attachments, each one has its own attendant aspiration. The key to an attachment to stability is the aspiration of agility. We release the attachment to the past by accepting and forgiving old demons and facing the truth with honesty and compassion. The attachment to the future is lifted by living in the present moment. By practicing trust and making friends with vulnerability, we can eliminate the attachment with control. When we accept our shortcomings, we can befriend our imperfections and loosen our attachment to perfection. The attachment to success is remedied by the aspiration of abundance. By experiencing pain, we can help eliminate our attachment to pleasure and find peace and comfort in life's ups and downs. By practicing acceptance, we can reduce our attachment to youth and allow ourselves to age gracefully. By loving generously, we can avoid the attachment to self and feel true intimacy and connection. And by feeling grateful, we can lessen our attachment to life and move through it with grace, flexibility, and conviction.

Detach is designed as a personal guide for achieving this freedom. By letting go of old baggage and practicing a new way of living and working, we can rise above our angst and move forward. We literally can save ourselves from ourselves.

Remember, each day is the first day of the rest of your life. By knowing yourself, being yourself, and loving yourself, you can achieve the three goals of life: to feel joy, to be free, and to reach your highest potential. The choice is yours.

HOW TO READ *DETACH*

I have written *Detach* with three priorities in mind. First, I hope that the book presents a fresh psychological approach to successful living and working and blends Western and Eastern philosophies.

The search for health, happiness, and success is not new. Philosophers, writers, poets, psychologists, and spiritual leaders from all traditions have spoken and written about these issues for thousands of years. It's part of being human. But that doesn't make the search easy.

As humankind has evolved, we have increased our ability to think, reason, and plan. We have developed a deeper understanding of our emotional lives. Accordingly, we have also increased our capacity to sabotage our own efforts—blinded by our biases, misconceptions, and faulty logic. And we've become vulnerable to being hijacked by our attachments. We take three steps forward and two steps back.

More of us today are searching for the good life—a life that has meaning, brings joy and freedom, and makes us happy and successful. People in all walks of life are determined to control their own destinies, creating the lives they want.

Conversely, many feel challenged by this goal. We are asking ourselves what success really means to us, as many of us have lost our sense of who we are and where we're going.

With its psychological foundation, *Detach* offers a way to reflect on how you might be standing in the way of your own success. It allows you to ask yourself hard questions and know you're not alone.

Second, the book unfolds its message through the personal stories of real people, sharing the secrets of how they have mastered and struggled to overcome their attachments.

I have a long history of talking with people about their troubles and triumphs. In my career, I've used what I've learned to help leaders at all levels become better equipped on their life journeys. I've also found that shining a light on real people, with deeply honest stories, is the best way to communicate new ideas. It's a great way to show how those ideas affect people's day-to-day lives.

In *Detach*, I tell the stories of the special people in my life, how they are grappling with their own attachments, what they are good at, and where they are still struggling. These are folks who work (or who have worked) at all levels in business, government, and nonprofit organizations. They are men and women, young and old, from diverse backgrounds, countries, and cultures. I also weave my own story throughout the book. How could I not, after asking you to reveal your attachments and aspirations along the way?

One final point: *Detach* is purposely written as a practical guide. I've included concise sections for easy reading, added supporting science when appropriate, offered tips and advice, and listed quick quizzes throughout. Reflection questions complete each chapter.

I hope you enjoy the book.

ONE

THE ATTACHMENT TO STABILITY

- Do you naturally shy away from change?
- Do you consider yourself rigid, controlling, or highly organized?
- Do you feel the need to live in a stable environment?
- Are you someone who procrastinates in the face of change?
- Do you get anxious when your world is uncertain?

In 2020, our world underwent traumatic uncertainty during the Covid-19 pandemic. For the next three years, distress pervaded every household with fears of contagion, illness, and death. Unsettled and confused, we were all living with the same questions: "Where did it come from?"; "Who is at risk?"; and "How can we combat the menace?" Those questions plagued people daily and aroused a deep feeling of anxiety that many had not felt for years. What people didn't realize was that Covid brought to the surface the same uncertainty that exists in our lives every day.

In fact, everything is changing around us at record speeds all the time: from technology and demography, to geopolitics and climate, to lifestyles and marriages, the list goes on. The challenge is that the world is often changing faster than our ability to adapt.

Many of us are unprepared for these accelerations. Reacting too slowly as new challenges confront us, we get overwhelmed by problems and ignore opportunities. Sabotaged by outdated thoughts, misguided principles, and inflammatory relationships, we face uncertainty with fear and mistrust. Stress and burnout undermine our ability to live up to our full potential, casting a pall on our efforts to steady our environment, keep things on an even keel, and maintain some semblance of balance. At a time when we must stay nimble and learn faster, our minds, in their current state, are unprepared for this new reality. It was that way with David.

David has lived a successful life. Yet a black shadow has haunted and hovered over his psyche. For years, he suffered from a deep attachment to stability and security—at home, with friends, and in his career and romantic life. With time and hard work, he found a way to shed light on that shadow and release his attachment. Today, he lives a joyful and agile life. This is his story.

David recalls his earliest years: "I was born in a nursery and stayed for six months until I was adopted. I left with an emotional scar of isolation, separation, and alienation. Then, I entered 'the perfect family.' At least, that's what my father wanted. The epitome of the American success story as a prominent university president, he was all about image. My adoption was swept under the rug until I was four, so I never had an opportunity to process it. From my perspective, it was a horrible flaw in my life, and my job was to live up to self-imposed expectations to repay them for taking me in.

"So, my life was all about security: making sure I had a roof over my head, enough money to live on, and a career where I couldn't get fired. I sold myself out to my attachment."

Eventually, David graduated from the University of Miami and became a lawyer. Off he went to the federal government for his new-found career and security. He moved to Arlington, Virginia, and bought a house. "My home was my castle. I was meticulous and controlled everything in that house. It gave me a sense of security; it was my sanctuary where I could retreat from the outside world.

"With my friends and relationships, I kept everyone separate from one another. I never allowed anyone to get too close to me, for fear of exposing myself to emotional attachment that threatened me. I lived a controlled, single life."

From the Department of the Treasury to the Department of Commerce, and back to the Treasury, where he worked in the Office of Foreign Assets Control, David flourished. In his job, he discovered a real aptitude for organizing and managing people and things. David jokes, "It was my early practice as a kid collecting shells, coins, stamps, and rocks that were immaculately labeled and organized." He put his attachment to stability to good use.

After twenty years in government, he quit his job suddenly, a move that was completely out of character. David recalls, "I resigned as a matter of principle. I wasn't going to work for someone who sabotaged the career of a woman who did nothing wrong. There I was, leaving my job without an income and living two years off my retirement." For David, quitting was a huge accomplishment that catapulted him into a sea of uncertainty. But he did it.

Then he got the call to become the next assistant secretary of commerce for export enforcement, his reward for being agile and flexible in his life. "I always thought being gay would be a professional liability, but there I was under the Obama administration being considered because I was gay and had deep managerial experience." There, David spent seven years successfully managing two hundred special agents who wore badges, carried guns, and made arrests. David finished his career at

Citigroup as general counsel and managing director for economic sanctions and anti-bribery.

"Back in 1997, I was challenged by my mentor and enneagram teacher, who saw my attachment to stability. He told me, 'David, go out and expose yourself to life, especially to heartbreak. Boy, did that hit home. I'd been guarding my heart for years. I never accepted people into my life who were available, and always ended up feeling empty and disconnected from others."

Years later, "there he was at a party. Adam appeared in my life, and it scared the hell out of me. He was available and represented a lot of the qualities that I knew addressed my underlying fears and my attachment to stability—loyalty, commitment, duty, and trustworthiness. Compatible and complementary, our new relationship helped me take the last step to weaken my attachment to stability in my personal life. Today, we've been happily married for nine years."

As we look back on David's life, he has shed important parts of his attachment to stability—at work, with friends, and with Adam. His house is still organized meticulously and his vast library of books are all cataloged properly. David still loves his stability and security, but the dark shackles in his mind don't own him anymore.

THE ATTACHMENT TO STABILITY

Let's face it. Stability is an illusion; uncertainty is reality. Every time we breathe, the world changes. In fact, I believe the idea of stability is a human construct that we created by necessity to help us feel safe and secure in our lives. Many of us long for stasis, striving to find the perfect, stable life. However, this mindset is limiting and keeps us mired, slow to adapt, risk averse, and undermines our overall agility. We want to believe that we will find comfort in the predictable, but it doesn't always exist. We need to develop the ability to navigate in a world of uncertainty and change.

Wait a minute. Let's be honest here. Everyone needs some stability and security in their lives that allows them to take a breath, relax and reflect, enjoy the present moment, and cultivate a sense of peace. Who doesn't like a vacation, some downtime from an intense project, or a night with yourself? Naturally, we want to keep good things alive without changing them. Stability is also important during unpredictable times, when we need safety and security from threatening people and events.

But what we want and what exists can be two different things. As Heraclitus observed, "No man steps in the same river twice, for it's not the same river and he's not the same man [or woman]." The Buddhists also get it right here: change causes suffering when we resist it or ignore it.

Uncertainty can become our undoing if we are not open to what's around the corner, whether new ideas and experiences or the latest resentments or disappointments. During a state of uncertainty, we must learn to be comfortable with being vulnerable. Although the idea may seem counterintuitive, vulnerability is a strength, not a weakness. Allowing yourself to be vulnerable says you are willing to take risks, be an imperfect person, and accept reality, whatever it may be.

WHERE ARE YOUR SHADOWS?

Being unaware can be a big problem. There is a growing gap between those who are awake in the world and those who are asleep. The faster the world changes, the bigger the chasm becomes. In my previous book, *Conscious,* I wrote about some reasons why we sabotage ourselves when we need to change. We get:

- *Too shallow:* We are often too superficial in our thinking. Spending too little time in self-reflection, we stay stuck in our personal stories about change, shackled by old baggage with little understanding of ourselves.

- *Too narrow:* Biased and closed-minded, we are often encased in steel bunkers with no way out. We ignore facts, harbor faulty assumptions, and make uninformed decisions, causing us to rely on fixed mindsets with unconscious biases.
- *Too safe:* Many of us approach the world too cautiously. Afraid of change, we prefer to avoid the uncertainty around us. By being too safe, we atrophy and fail to evolve and transform, leaving us standing in place as the world turns.
- *Too small:* If your view of yourself is too small, you won't see connections, possibilities, or solutions. Staying small and never stepping up is sure to lead to future regrets that will undermine your personal power and potential.

Without self-awareness, we pretend our lives are stable and secure, when they are not; like a stone in a swiftly moving stream, change eddies around us.

HOW OUR BRAIN RESPONDS

Modern science tells us that our "adaptive brain" is an integrated, interdependent network of electricity, chemicals, thoughts, and emotions. Its primary mission is to respond to threats and challenges and adapt to changing circumstances. This adaptive brain developed out of millions of years of evolutionary pressure.

Our brain constantly strives to achieve homogeneity and stability. But, with our internal and external worlds constantly changing, it's impossible to achieve that outcome. Fortunately, our brain has an incredible capacity, called neuroplasticity, that allows it to rewire itself and enables itself to grow and adapt. This ability of the brain sustains our feeling of stability that is actually a psychological and neurological illusion.

As Brigham Young University neuropsychologists suggest, "our very survival depends on our ability to respond quickly to advantageous and threatening events. The more our brain can predict potential outcomes with different courses of action, the better it can adapt to the future. And by linking past and present threats, we can activate our survival circuits and avoid dangerous situations."

Deeply connected to our bodies and the outside world, our brains don't operate in isolation either. In fact, our emotions, thoughts, and social bonds, which provide acceptance, connectedness, and a sense of belonging, all have evolved together to help us survive and adapt.

As you know all too well, as part of being human, the "slings and arrows of outrageous fortune" can happen at any time. And when our extraordinary brain network doesn't function as planned, this assault increases our negativity, with anger, moodiness, worry, insecurity, and dissatisfaction. These emotions ultimately accumulate when we get too attached to people, places, and things.

When our physical body goes into fear mode, it prepares us for the uncertainty lurking around the corner. Our emotional circuits label our experience with feelings, like pain, worry, and anger, concurrently tapping into our memories from similar situations. Our thoughts create context for the sudden upheaval, fabricating a story that helps us understand what is happening. Unfortunately, it can also lock us into belief systems that deceive and delude us from seeing reality for what it is. Most often, it's our anxiety that sends us the message that it's time to pay attention.

THE THREE FACES OF ANXIETY

My mind raced as the ambulance sped through traffic. Lying on the gurney and listening to the siren, my heart pounded, and my anxiety skyrocketed. I was a healthy forty-five-year-old guy. I worked out. This wasn't supposed to happen. But there I was, headed for the hospital with a diagnosis of atrial fibrillation.

A year or so later, I was hospitalized again—not once, but twice—for a bowel obstruction. Soon after, I underwent surgery to correct a congenital growth in my small intestine. A couple years later, I was confronted with unexpected surgery to repair a herniated disk that ruptured while I was sitting on a Canary Islands beach. And just four years ago, my back herniated again, this time at the typical L5 joint that required surgery. You would think that would be enough. Just recently, my heart, after years of the original diagnosis, required a pacemaker. I'm hoping that's it for a while, and I remain in "good shape."

With each health crisis, I found myself face-to-face with the uncertainty of life and my anxieties about illness and death. And with each crisis, I had to make a choice: Was I going to let my emotions shut me down, or could I find a way to understand and manage them? I decided to embrace my anxiety.

In 2004, tapping into my own experience, I decided to write a book called *Just Enough Anxiety* to help explain how we all experience and manage uncertainty in our lives. Its primary premise asserts that:

> Anxiety is a fact of life. How you use it makes all the difference. If you let it overwhelm you, it will turn to panic. If you deny or run from it, you will become complacent. But, if you use anxiety in a positive way, you will turn it into a powerful force in your life.

Everyone said it was a great title, yet the book had a mediocre showing in the market. I remember my niece called me while traveling after she bought a copy in an airport bookstore. "Really interesting, Uncle Bob," she said, "but I'm hiding the cover so people don't see what I'm reading." At that moment, I knew we had a problem.

YEARS OF FAULTY THINKING

Here's the catch. Dealing with change can be a slippery slope. The confusion goes something like this: change creates uncertainty and makes us anxious; anxiety is bad, a sign of weakness, something to avoid. This view comes hardwired into our brains from centuries ago, when we had to cope with hungry lions lurking in the savanna. Back then, change was truly dangerous, even life-threatening. So we as a species learned anxiety, equating it automatically with danger.

Today, that mental model is often viewed as a mental health issue. Yet now, centuries later, the complexity and pace of our daily lives change at a moment's notice. Consequently, when we encounter these changes, we get hijacked by our innate anxiety from years past. We're afraid that we can't manage the anxiety, so we avoid it, resist it, run away from it, or medicate it. Pushing the anxiety away only compounds the situation and makes us feel worse.

Understandably, anxiety has gotten a bad rap. But think about it another way. Like other emotions, anxiety is a form of energy. Paradoxically, this energy has two sides and can act as a wake-up call, a ping on our built-in cell phone to the brain, signaling our bodies and minds to pay attention and act as a positive force for growth.

Because anxiety travels with change and uncertainty, it can give us the boost we need to deal with the ups and downs of life. Managed effectively, it can encourage us to take advantage of unforeseen opportunities or help us confront difficult issues. We just need the right amount of it.

Of course, not all anxiety is healthy. Instead of helping you cope with a situation or spurring you to action, it can cloud your good judgment, scatter your thinking, and interfere with healthy functioning. Left unattended, unhealthy anxiety can lead to physical and psychological illnesses and require professional help.

It's time to shake off our outmoded beliefs about change. Let's rethink our understanding of uncertainty. And let's reframe our perspective about anxiety.

TOO LITTLE ANXIETY—THE FACE OF COMPLACENCY

The easy option is to live an insulated life—to enjoy the status quo, avoid change, and limit new possibilities. In a protected bubble, we are spared challenges and upheaval, sheltered from the complexity of the world as we know it today.

Understandably, people who have their heads buried in the sand do not witness the volatility of modern life, yet they miss out on anything new. Perhaps early in life they may have been spared difficulty or learned how to protect themselves through denial or complacency. This attitude is like wearing a self-imposed blindfold that restricts the opportunity to learn and keeps us from enjoying the excitement of life. In my travels, I have observed different ways that people express too little anxiety in their lives.

- *Idealistic people live in a fantasy world:* Driven by their need to have things work out favorably, they tend to ignore reality and gloss over bad news.
- *Cautious people are frightened by the world:* Driven by their fear of change and uncertainty, they overcompensate by trying to avoid everything.
- *Detached people isolate themselves from the world:* Driven by the need to protect themselves, they operate best on their own or with minimal interaction.
- *Overpleasing people live in other people's worlds:* Driven by the need to make everyone happy, they are uncomfortable with conflict and avoid their power to influence others.

I'm sure you know people who might fit into these categories. They're not always the easiest friends, or you may have trouble working for, with, or managing them. You may even want to ask yourself whether you are a "too little anxiety" person? Consider these questions:

- Do you focus on the positive while downplaying the negative?
- Do you analyze everything to avoid making mistakes?
- Do you seek comfort and security whenever possible?
- Do you try to give everyone what they want?
- Do you believe everything will be OK or resolve itself?
- Do you find it hard to get in touch with your emotions?
- Do you naturally shy away from conflict?

TOO MUCH ANXIETY—THE FACE OF CHAOS

Many people are far too familiar with too much anxiety. Today's frenzied world makes it difficult to avoid this lifestyle of turmoil. Caught up in their need to be right, in control, or high achieving, too-much-anxiety people can easily become overly attached to success. Their anxiety is born out of fear of being inadequate, insignificant, or vulnerable, and these feelings can become internalized and habitual. Often out of touch with themselves in the moment, they are held hostage by their emotions of anger and resentment and end up broadcasting their negatively charged feelings at home or in the office.

Here are some types I've observed over the years:

- *Egotistical people want the world to revolve around them:* They are driven by two needs: to be admired and to protect themselves from their feelings of inadequacy.
- *Perfectionistic people try to orchestrate the way the world works:* They are accomplished micromanagers. Underneath the surface, they are driven by the fear of failure or not being good enough.
- *Volatile people believe the world is against them:* Driven by the desire to win at any cost, they wield their power like an

emotional saber cutting down whatever and whoever gets in their way.

- *Suspicious people are mistrustful of the world around them:* Their own suspicious nature leads them to believe that people are inherently dishonest.

So, what are your reactions when you bump up against these people? Do they pull you into their drama? Do you respond defensively? Or do you cower in their presence? Maybe ask yourself: Are you a "too much anxiety" person? Consider these questions:

- Do you know what it feels like to be anxiety free?
- Are you broadcasting to the world that you are tense, upset, or a powder keg ready to blow up?
- Are you suspicious of other peoples' motives?
- Does your impatience prompt you to react too quickly?
- How important is it for you to be respected or admired?
- Do you wear your emotions on your sleeve?
- Do you worry about being taken advantage of?

JUST ENOUGH ANXIETY—THE FACE OF SUCCESS

Turning anxiety into a positive force is key to living a life of balance and success. For instance, compare your life to a seesaw where there is tension between weights on either end. Your job is to balance the seesaw. Under stress, some of us are drawn to too much anxiety as the seesaw tilts, and we become vulnerable to chaotic energy. At other times, we may lean toward too little anxiety that produces ineffective energy, so we retreat into complacency where we feel safe. A rare few of us are poised to live in the middle.

That's why we must maintain a consistent level of tension with just enough anxiety that allows us to balance the seesaw of life without resistance, giving up, or being overwhelmed. Allowing this anxiety unleashes positive energy and helps us stretch ourselves so that we become the person we truly want to be.

Anxiety is contagious too. Our brains are hardwired to pick up cues from our environment, including from other people. We unconsciously monitor tone of voice, facial expressions, body language, eye contact, attentiveness, and other nonverbal cues. We interpret people's behaviors, sense their intentions, and feel their feelings. And they feel ours. We are simply hardwired to be connected to each other.

So there you have it. The world is constantly changing and uncertain all the time. We use our entire brain to understand and modulate these changes. Having just the right amount of anxiety protects and guides us through these transitions. And we are all different in how we manage these changes.

THE ASPIRATION OF AGILITY

In the tapestry of nature, I find few creatures demonstrate the art of adaptation quite like the chameleon, a master class in versatility and survival. The chameleon, in truth, stands as an emblem of resilience.

This remarkable reptile traverses tree branches at a leisurely pace, yet it strikes with a tongue speed unmatched in the animal kingdom—a testament to nature's ingenuity. Imagine a tongue that could propel from a standstill to breakneck speeds akin to a racing car achieving 60 mph in a mere blink of an eye.

Besides their astonishing speed, chameleons boast a visual prowess unprecedented among vertebrates. Their eyes operate independently, offering a 360-degree panoramic vista, coupled with the ability to perceive both visible and ultraviolet spectrums.

Color change, their most famed trait, is surely their craft of camouflage, but it's also a form of silent communication, a vibrant display mirroring their internal state. Far from being duplicitous, each shift in shade is an honest expression, like a mood ring.

As humans, we don't see the chameleon as our rival, but its wisdom is undeniable, signifying the adaptive qualities we treasure: transparency, vigilance, and the capacity to flourish amid flux. In these creatures, we find not only ecological marvels but also a silent mentor, reminding us of the virtues in embracing change wholeheartedly.

If you embraced uncertainty and dedicated yourself to living a life that was intentionally agile, much like the chameleon, what would it look like?

THRIVING IN THE UNKNOWN

Imagine you work in the US Army Special Operations Command, providing survival training to army generals, lieutenants, and airmen entering danger zones around the world. It's my nephew's job to teach these soldiers how to survive, evade, resist, and escape back to safety. "I'm not here when they are shot down," Michael says, "so I need to make sure they can think out of the box, thrive in uncertainty, and stay agile in the face of reality." Like Michael's students, we all experience our own version of uncertainty training.

On my fiftieth birthday, after a speech in Bangkok, I treated myself to a short trip to Angkor Wat in Cambodia. Surrounded by the majesty of temples and the whispers of the rainforest, I pondered the wisdom of Pema Chödrön, a Buddhist nun, and her teachings on embracing the chaos of life.

In that momentous solitude, I sat reading one of her many books, *Comfortable with Uncertainty*. Her counsel to relax amid upheaval resonated deeply, etching in me a powerful truth: accept life's constant flux while trusting in our own resilience. This serendipitous encounter with Chödrön's words above Cambodia's sacred ground was a catalyst for growth, a testament to how life's greatest teachings often find us when we're most receptive.

THE PATH TO AGILITY

Here's a road map to guide you through uncertainty and change and to help you weaken your attachment to stability and accelerate your agility into the future.

Go Deep—Harness the Power of Introspection

Consider that your mind is like a mirror that often reflects blurry perceptions, confusing emotions, and distorted thinking. These distortions prevent us from seeing a clear picture of ourselves and opening a path for the future. "Going deep" opens your mind and exposes shallow thinking. By opening your mind, you can see your strengths and shortcomings, get comfortable being uncomfortable, and thereby confront your attachments.

"Going deep" also helps you expand your awareness of reality and dispels those illusions that we all carry within our minds. Its benefits are seeing yourself and others more clearly and providing a strategy that leads eventually to self-discovery. Being flexible and agile is key, as you respond to sudden events that activate anxiety and retreat to a "safe" place.

Susan David, psychologist at Harvard Medical School and author of *Emotional Agility*, explains why flexibility is key to navigating events of uncertainty. Having "emotional agility" is a process that doesn't ignore difficult emotions and thoughts. Instead, it holds those emotions and thoughts loosely, faces them courageously and compassionately, and then moves past them to make big things happen in your life.

So change your relationship to change. Move from clinging to stability to embracing uncertainty, a process that requires new tools like resilience, anxiety management, confidence and courage, and the ability to accept reality.

It's also important to upend your mindset from seeing "change happening *to* you" to seeing "change happening *for* you." The first is a victim's no-control perspective; the second is to regard change as a natural resource, happening for a reason, even if you cannot see its benefits at the time. You have changed before, and you can do it again.

Think Big—Imagine a World of Possibilities

An agile mind is a self-transforming mind, requiring ingenuity and imagination. You must dig deep for new data, act with instinct and intellect, and ask challenging questions of yourself and others. This process can be more difficult than you think.

Daniel Kahneman, Nobel laureate and author of *Thinking, Fast and Slow,* highlights a critical cognitive blind spot: our tendency to focus on what we know and overlook the "known unknowns" and "unknown unknowns"—those areas where we lack information or can't yet perceive its importance.

The task then becomes to push beyond these mental boundaries. As a mental experiment, ask yourself: If you knew that you absolutely could not fail—money was no object, and no obstacles stood in the way—what would you do for the rest of your life? Consider what changed for you when you remove all restrictions. What became possible? Many of us don't think that way because we assume there are too many obstacles in our way.

By learning to think expansively, we open a myriad of possibilities that beckon us to be more, to dare with ambition, and to envisage various futures without being confined by our usual patterns of thought.

To adopt a mindset of boundless potential, it's necessary to sidestep the trap of narrow thinking that so often limits us. "Thinking big" is an accessible tool for everyone, unlocking a vision that empowers us to take on greater challenges. It begins with a simple yet profound act: opening our minds to the vast landscape of opportunity.

Get Real—Be Intentional About the Change

Much of life is spent on autopilot. That's good, because life is complex, and if we had to interpret every perception, thought, or feeling, we would be overwhelmed with data. Every day, we are exposed to fresh facts and new information that gets stored in our brains and morphs into a preexisting story that we tell ourselves, stories that stabilize us in our ever-changing environment. Over time, these stories become the lens through which we see our current existence. Consequently, our story becomes ingrained in our psyche, and we fail to see a new pathway to change.

To grow as a person takes work and getting real with the stories you tell yourself. You must "get real," otherwise you can get caught up with the indelible thought patterns that keep you safe. The antidote to being safe and too comfortable is to be intentional about how you move through life.

The first step is examining the lens that you might not realize is there and revving up your internal drive to improve the story. Intentions can be positive or negative, depending on whether you are working with verified facts or assumptions that may or may not be valid.

Seeing, thinking, feeling, and acting with a new lens demands a dash of optimism and just enough anxiety to motivate yourself from your all-too-familiar plotline. Learn to be optimistic and realistic at the same time. Use just enough anxiety to propel yourself forward. Becoming a change agent in your own mind also requires introspection to see the accelerators and hijackers that can either propel or impede our progress.

Accelerators fortify us with courage, drive, optimism, and, most of all, the resistance to backtrack and head for the stable place. Lurking in the shadows of our fabricated story are the hijackers that sabotage us, keeping us entrenched and triggering our most difficult emotions. Fixed mindsets, cynicism, prejudice, and our attachment to stability all lie in wait, ready to resist new ideas, fresh experiences, and change! With the right modicum of anxiety, you can move out of your "stuck" place and move forward into the world of uncertainty.

Step Up—Act Boldly and Responsibly

Being unaware of what we are feeling or thinking by default leads us to behave on cruise control, resulting in walking a cautious path through life. But that path doesn't always get you where you want to go. You must "step up" to enter the mysterious morass of riskiness and stay conscious as you walk on the hot coals of uncertainty. Just think: If you could increase your level of awareness by 1–2%, you could move from seeing life in black and white to seeing life in color. "The unexamined life is not worth living."

Linking being aware with acting boldly releases an inner power and allows introspection to jump-start new ideas that, in turn, changes your behavior and enables you to disengage from your attachment to stability. Stepping away from our unconscious behaviors catapults us into a bigger version of ourselves that speaks our truth, challenges our status quo, and takes more risks. In that mindset, we not only surprise others, we amaze ourselves.

A STORY FROM STABILITY TO AGILITY

"Sometimes we make choices because we want stability, security, and safety. But those choices can diminish our lives. Yet if we're really connected to who we are, life might not be easy, but it will be more fun." These are the words of Amir, who grew up in northern India and came to the United States alone at the age of seventeen.

"I moved around a lot as a child. My father made financial choices, so we lived in lots of different neighborhoods. We were well-off for a time, and then I saw my father and uncles blow everything—gambling, mismanagement, alcoholism. Today, my dad has limited options, and I support him. I also find myself holding on to my financials so closely because I saw my dad lose them.

"So I left and came to the US to go to college. Everybody came here to create a better world, and the education was promising. But I always felt like a migrant without deep-rooted friendships and family. And that lack of grounding made it difficult to ride through periods of change.

"After my studies, I entered religious life. There, I found my life secure and loving with a real community of friends. But after some years, the experience was less than fulfilling and too secure. I felt like I was retiring at age twenty-eight with too much stability and not enough change. As one author said, 'When there's too much stability and no change, your heart line is flat, like your heartbeat is dead. That's how I felt.'"

So Amir left the religious community and entered the business world where his attachment to stability started to show its ugly head. He shared some examples. "When I heard we were going through a merger, my gut sank into my need for stability and security. It was a visceral response. Thoughts that I wouldn't have a job and the change would cause me pain invaded my mind. I felt the same about my finances. I had set a goal and then worked anxiously, obsessively toward my goal, sacrificing other things in my life. That tape operated in my head constantly; it was quite scary.

"I realized life happens, things change, but my way of dealing would be to overanalyze everything, and sometimes, it was silly and took up a lot of time and energy. I went into hyperproductive mode. I didn't have panic attacks, but I analyzed the situation to death. It was my way of controlling my fear about change. I felt alone and without options. But, when push came to shove, I followed my heart and searched out the challenge in an adaptive way.

"Ninety-nine percent of the time now, it works out well for me. Post-merger changes expanded my role and responsibilities, and my paycheck increased. Psychologically, I can articulate that, but that is not the tape running deep inside me. It's my monkey brain saying monkey things. In your mind, you're trying to be safe and secure, yet you know you want to change. It's a real polarity."

Given that turmoil, Amir now is clear where he wants to be in three to five years. "I want success in my career with adequate income, doing meaningful work that is bettering the world. I want a broad network of close friends, surrounded by people whom I love, and they love me. And I want an ongoing reflective, spiritual life. So, I work hard, take time to reflect, and try my best to manage the issue of stability."

Amir has a mild psychological trauma based on his experiences with his dad and uncles in India. His overall self-awareness is striking. He lives with productive anxiety on most days and too much anxiety on others. Amir knows there is a kind of disconnect in his life between how he lives his life and the story he tells about his life. At times, he holds on to his story built on stability, loneliness, frugality, and security. Yet his life is full of risks, and much *has* turned out well. In Amir's case, he might even unconsciously trigger his own trauma, so hopefully, with conscious awareness, he can reprocess it and demonstrate to himself that he is not his father.

Being able to shift from external to internal work is vital. Amir's goal is to feel stable and secure in his core self. His strength is his intellect, but the real work is deeply emotional. How can he proactively rewrite his story so it's more consistent with how he lives his life? Fortunately, Amir continues to do great work of shedding the difficult part of his attachment to stability while savoring a life of agility and change.

Reflections

- Where does your attachment to stability come from?
- What areas of stability and security are you willing to give up?
- What risks have you taken in your life and how did it work out?
- Are you a "too little," "too much," or "just enough" anxiety person?
- How well do you thrive in the unknown?
- Do you consider yourself an agile person and why?

TWO

THE ATTACHMENT TO THE PAST

- Do you sometimes feel stuck in the past?
- Do you often feel resentful during the day?
- Do you have trouble letting go of things?
- Do you have trouble feeling happy and joyful?
- Do you find it hard to forgive others?

remember my first days as a psychologist in training. Our small class of nine PhD students was learning how to conduct clinical interviews. We took turns doing intake interviews with new families coming in for evaluation. Cocky and anxious to show off my stuff, I volunteered to be the first while my fellow students and the professor stayed behind and observed me through a one-way mirror.

There, I found a pleasant Jewish family of four—middle-aged parents and their two lovely children. I wasn't in the room but for twenty seconds when the rather outspoken, controlling mother spoke up. "So, Mr. Rosen, you look awfully young. What experience do you have treating families?"

I don't know what happened, but the words just came out of my mouth. "Well, ma'am, let's put it this way; you're not the first Jewish mother I have met." Obviously, I was referring to my own at the time. In retrospect, I probably was a bit defensive, but we all laughed and continued the conversation.

When I got back behind the curtain, I was greeted by nine mortified faces, all probably wondering what surprise they would find in their own interviews. But it was my professor who had the last word. I remember it to this day. He said, "A dysfunctional family is a redundancy." We all have *mishegoss*—Yiddish for "insane," "nuts," "crazy," or "loony." The message was simple: we all have our own attachments to the past.

I was the best little boy in the world—president of everything—student council, honor society, senior class, you name it. Extroverted and popular, I got along with everybody, including their parents. We lived in a small apartment, without much money, and I supported myself with cash that I earned as a busboy and caddie at the nearby country club. Sure, I had my fun side, partying and drinking alcohol and drugs, but I was hiding a big part of me that was most scary and uncomfortable. I was gay. I stayed in the closet, ran away from my feelings, and lived alone inside myself. I knew I was different. And the only way I knew how to cope with my anxiety and sense of loss was to compensate by overachieving and getting out of town.

Back then, I saw my parents like many teenagers, with their flaws and imperfections. No doubt, they loved me, yet my mother's narcissism and my father's insecurity and lack of confidence made it difficult for me to fully embrace them. With good therapy and hard work, I was able to escape those deep feelings about my past and create a new reality for myself. I learned to practice acceptance and forgiveness by acknowledging that my parents were not perfect. They did the best they could at the time. I soon recognized that I got my mother's courage and toughness and her willingness to stretch and take risks. My father shared his warmth, authenticity, and sense of humor. Eventually, I took what I valued from them and rejected what I didn't want.

I still have my mother's bad spine and my dad's anxiety, but I also have my gym workouts, my meditation, and much less attachment to the past. I spoke to my parents a couple times a week until they died—my dad in 2014 from a car accident at eighty-seven and my mom in 2021 from Covid at eighty-five. In time, I fell in love with my gay self in my early twenties and have lived a wonderful life ever since.

THE PAST IS ALWAYS PRESENT

Your past is always with you. Who you are and where you come from are with you forever, its recollections providing context for your life, a kind of story that connects yesterday to today. It also helps you make sense of yourself and the world. While you can't disconnect from your past, with hard work and time, you can rewrite your story.

Through your memories and dreams and the stories and narratives you tell yourself, you remember the milestones in your life: birthdays and family reunions, report cards and graduations, your first walk, bike, date, and kiss.

Some of these memories—full of joy—bring smiles to your face. Others remain quite painful, potentially causing havoc in your life, like your memories of rejections, failures, and addictions, and deep-seated prejudices, phobias, and abuses. You can get hijacked by your most difficult emotions of pain, fear, worry, loss, and anger. Often, these memories are embedded in your psyche, too deep to access, hidden from your conscious awareness. In fact, the past is hardwired inside you: physiologically, neurologically, and psychologically.

THE GAME OF LIFE

Playing the Game of Life deals out four major "cards" in your hand: your genetic makeup, your personal development, your life experiences, and your personality. Ultimately, you can play your cards as they have been dealt, or you can choose to trade them in and opt for new ones. Of course, each card holds built-in risks and rewards. And, sometimes, your cards choose you—especially the life experiences. Examining each card can reveal which ones you will hold or replace for a better hand. Let's look at each:

- *Genetic makeup*: Genes determine your physical vulnerability to stress and diseases. DNA establishes a "set point" for anxiety and stress—which makes you either reactive and sensitive, agile and resilient, or somewhere in between. While living with your genetic makeup is mandatory, allowing it to define you entirely is your choice.
- *Child and family development:* This card creates memories that shape your identity. Early in life, most of your experiences, while unconscious, send messages that become deeply imprinted in your young brain. In your teenage years, unless your parents are evolved people, chances are that you picked up some bad habits.
- *Life experiences*: As you set out on your path through life, you encounter obstacles along the way, take detours, and accrue positive and negative experiences. How you deal with these ups and downs makes all the difference.
- *Our personalities*: As an aspiring adult, you begin to solidify your personality, those deep-seated beliefs and feelings that morph into self-fulfilling prophecies and become hardwired into our brains. Psychologists call this process "sense making," those stories you create to understand your life or rewrite to improve your life.

THE OPTIMISTS VS. THE PESSIMISTS

Are you an optimist or a pessimist? I ask because both perspectives give you a unique lens on viewing your past. Whether you see life's cup as half-full or half-empty has a huge influence on your health and well-being. Consider the benefits to both.

Hope and optimism are powerful partners that help you stay positive and motivated, to push past obstacles and strive for something bigger and better. Being optimistic projects a picture of what can be—what's possible. It's a refreshing tonic that can lower levels of depression, anxiety, and stress.

However, it can produce a feeling of what social psychologists call "illusory superiority," because this mindset may contain a large dose of overestimating memories, achievements, and capabilities. Believing that the future will be better than the past also underestimates the occurrence of bad outcomes. Optimists may acquire a "bias" that they are good problem-solvers who can march bravely into the future, undaunted. Sometimes inaccurate, their "optimism bias" derails their handling of the present circumstances.

Pessimists, on the other hand, may have an extra advantage when dealing with the world and its exigencies. Some researchers suggest that pessimists see the world more accurately than optimists, certainly giving them an edge in life. They evaluate what's working and what's not and rectify the solution faster.

I have always been intrigued by the fact that moderately depressed people may actually see the world—and their lives—more accurately than healthier people.

As Jonathan Haidt, author of *The Happiness Hypothesis,* observes, "the human mind reacts to bad things more quickly, strongly, and persistently than to good things." It takes at least five good actions to atone for one damaging act. The pleasure of gaining a certain amount of money is offset by the anguish of losing the same amount. Consequently, persistent pessimism can threaten your well-being and self-esteem.

By being aware of the benefits and pitfalls of each powerful motivator, we can navigate our lives in a balanced way.

THE MAESTRO TAKES THE STAGE

Years ago, I had the opportunity to meet James DePreist, the six-foot-three conductor of the Oregon Symphony who lived with polio. As I watched the maestro at work, I realized that he existed physically in two realities: the present, conducting, and the future performance. While paying attention to every note and all sections of the orchestra, he imagined the music as Beethoven intended.

"This goes on simultaneously," Jimmy said, "and I'm changing the performance based on the feedback I'm getting from the musicians. Where is the performance falling short? Where is it exceeding my expectations?" In real time, he noted the cues from his orchestra, while forecasting the "future performance."

I learned the power of being realistic and optimistic at the same time from Jimmy. Being honest about what's working or not working keeps us in the moment but acknowledges that the moment can also enrich the future. Examining the pain and memories of the past can fuel your courage and confidence in future endeavors. When exploring the attachment to your past, both optimism and pessimism figure into the process.

THE POWER OF ADVERSITY

Understanding adversity and our reaction to it is the second way to examine our attachment to the past. We all experience the pain of coping with a broken relationship, the recovery from an accident or illness, the loss of a friend, or making sense of a bumpy childhood. How you responded to those events makes all the difference in your ability to develop resilience—a stronger, more capable you.

Adversity actually can be an asset. Your handling of challenges often reveals a strength you might not know you possess. It can help you recognize others' vulnerabilities and reassure yourself that you have a strategy to cope with your attachment to past events.

Studies confirm that resilience can be learned. Researchers say that learning resilience tames your stress-response system. As your fight-or-flight reactions diminish, you learn to harness your positive emotions. With careful curating, your brain becomes stronger and more accustomed to handling adverse challenges.

Learning resilience also results from repeated exposure and trials. Research with adolescents and young adults (ages fifteen to twenty-five) suggests that young people need some form of crisis in their life to prepare them for adulthood. In learning how to deal with adversity, they are less vulnerable to the stresses and uncertainties of middle age.

THE POISON OF TRAUMA

To understand the most difficult challenges with our past, we should investigate the topic of trauma, where some of the most exciting research lies.

Bessell van der Kolk, author of the bestselling book *The Body Keeps the Score,* has been at the forefront of trauma research and clinical practice for over thirty years. In a recent conversation, Bessel observed that "trauma is ubiquitous in our society. One out of four Americans reports having been left with bruises after being hit as a child; one out of five was sexually molested, one out of eight has witnessed severe domestic violence, and a quarter grew up with alcoholism and drug addiction." Trauma can even be transmitted across generations. This intergenerational trauma shows up in Holocaust families and in racial trauma, like slavery.

"New insights into our survival instincts help us understand why traumatized people experience incomprehensible anxiety. Traumatized people stay on hyper alert; they feel chronically unsafe, in danger, and have problems feeling calm and enjoying the moment." Simmering inside us is devastating fear.

Van der Kolk warns that "trauma affects the entire human organism. Exposure to trauma secretes stress hormones, wreaks havoc with our immune systems, and our body organs. Trauma survivors are also vulnerable to a host of medical issues and chronic pain syndromes, insomnia, drug and alcohol addiction, depression, obesity and lack the capacity for self-regulation and self-care."

Fortunately, there is tremendous hope for the future. Van der Kolk states that "recent advances in brain science, attachment research, and body awareness can free trauma victims from the tyranny of the past. By activating the brain's natural neuroplasticity and counteracting the helplessness and invisibility associated with trauma, both adults and children can reclaim ownership of their bodies and lives."

The only way that we can change the way we feel is to become aware of our inner experience and befriend what is going on inside ourselves.

So, whether you're an optimist or pessimist, dealing with adversity, or battling with deep-seated trauma, you must have the confidence and courage to face your attachments to the past.

THE ATTACHMENT TO THE PAST

As the executive vice president and member of the executive committee of a Fortune 50 company, Richard makes tough business decisions every day. You might be surprised to learn that Richard was paralyzed making decisions as a child. But it's true.

Richard remembers: "I had a very tough childhood. When I was ten, my older brother died at age twelve. As you can imagine, it made for a lonely childhood. My father was a tough guy, a severe narcissist who took it out on me. He had reason to find fault with everything I did, and I would receive his constant reprimands. My dad was one of the five smartest people I knew. And I will admit I got two invaluable gifts from him—his love and appreciation for music and his mantra that stuck with me my whole life: 'anything worth doing is worth doing well.' But he wasted his gifts by being self-absorbed and judgmental.

"At some deep level, I knew early on that his criticisms were wrong. My values were different, and I wanted to prove to myself that I could be successful despite his unforgivable behavior. My first love was music; I wanted to be a conductor. In typical fashion, my dad ridiculed my thinking as stupid and silly. To this day, I wish I had become a conductor. Instead, I became the youngest managing director at a renowned Wall Street bank.

"The best thing that happened to me in my life was meeting my terrific wife, Vivian, and marrying into a healthy, close-knit family who gave me the love and support I needed. During those early days, I naturally thought, when things went wrong, it was my fault, and I tried to improve the situation with my dad. But it was like watching an old movie I'd seen before. With the help of a great therapist, I was able to detach from him and my ugly past."

Richard's story is not uncommon among hard-driving executives. With strong, controlling narcissistic parents who set high expectations of them, these people grow up to be highly successful executives. Yet, deep inside, they never feel good enough.

It doesn't have to be that way. Richard examined his past and accepted the reality of his situation. Today he gets judgmental at times, modeling the behavior he learned from his dad. But by working to detach himself from the old scripts in his head, he has become a kinder person, makes better decisions, and experiences greater contentment.

WHY WE CLING TO THE PAST

We all have stories from our past. You might be someone with mostly positive stories to tell: a warm family life, wonderful friends, a great career, or a terrific partnership with someone you love. Others of us are not so fortunate. Much like Richard's story, difficult, deep-seated experiences weigh us down, like baggage, and generate lots of pain in our lives. The more we cling to these stories, the more we suffer. And, when we get too attached to anything—people, places, or things—we create distress that can haunt us for a very long time. So, why do some people get so attached to the past, while others don't? I think there are several reasons:

- We minimize or ignore our emotional lives—the ups and downs, losses and separations, the full range of our feelings—because we think our difficult emotions are too painful to experience.
- We delude our minds with mental traps and cognitive distortions that confuse our reality and blind us from seeing the truth. (See the box about common thinking errors on page 49.)
- We get stuck telling ourselves past stories about difficult people, unhappy events, or painful circumstances, and we can never let go of them.
- We live with our head in the sand and have trouble noticing how our attachment to the past shows its ugly head in the present moment.
- We misinterpret setbacks and adversity, not realizing that these events are there to make us stronger. You know the saying: "no pain, no gain."
- We become hypervigilant to certain cues, people, and situations that constantly bring the attachment to the surface.

When we practice one or more of these dysfunctional strategies, we put ourselves at risk and stay stuck in the morass of our attachment. And there are no shortages of attachments. We're all too familiar with the life events that can haunt us: from bad parenting, death of a loved one, and bullying at school to flunking, acne, drugs/alcohol, and growing up poor. Early childhood trauma can take its toll, too, just like discrimination, layoffs, obesity, and gender dysphoria.

COMMON THINKING ERRORS

Here are some mental traps that distort our way of seeing the world.

- *Overgeneralizing*: Interpreting our past as a regular pattern that shows up all the time
- *Magnifying or minimizing*: Exaggerating the importance or belittling the significance of problems and mistakes based on our past experiences
- *Personalizing*: Assuming inappropriate personal blame for situations or events that may have happened in the past, even those unrelated to your current situation
- *Disqualifying the positive*: Rejecting positive reactions and experiences today, insisting they are isolated and inconsistent with who you are or your memories of the past
- *Labeling*: Ascribing to yourself broad labels from a single event or one person's opinion, like interpreting a mistake into feeling like a loser
- *Catastrophizing*: Expecting that the worst-case scenario will happen and will have a devastating effect on you
- *Shoulds and should nots*: Advice from others or advice you give to yourself that is unnecessarily restrictive and takes away your freedom

When we put a face on these events, the pain can get worse: the controlling father who pushes his perfect son to be obsessed with success;

the unpredictable alcoholic mother who drives her overpleasing daughter to worry all the time; the emotionally detached coach who feeds and fuels the self-critical athlete; or the so-called friend who controls everything in your life.

So, let's look more closely at the difficult emotions that keep us mired.

THE FIVE DIFFICULT EMOTIONS

There are five challenging emotions that form the backdrop for our attachments to the past—pain, fear, worry, loss, and anger. They develop out of the four cards in the deck of life. Let's look at each one:

Pain

Pain is a complex, strong emotion that comes in all shapes and sizes. Whether physical or psychological, it's a multifaceted syndrome that affects our entire body. Some believe that life should be pain-free. Others think pain is inevitable, repeating itself at every turn. Many are quick to turn to others to assume responsibility for taking our pain away.

One of the most common reactions to pain is to eliminate it as fast as possible. An entire pharmaceutical industry exists, with all its pain remedies, with just that goal. Yet, Mel Pohl, MD, the author of *A Day Without Pain*, says that 80% of pain is emotional—and suffering is the main cause of excessive pain, with all its accompanying emotions like fear, sadness, anger, and loneliness coming to the rescue.

An ancient Buddhist parable explains that pain can come in two parts: the first arrow of initial injury and the second arrow of suffering. The two work in tandem. For example, physical back pain disables us, followed by an abiding fear of chronic disability. More insidious is feeling loss, failure, or rejection that ignites the self-inflicted, secondary sadness or anger. The second arrow becomes the story that we tell ourselves as a result of the first real infliction.

To the Buddha, there is no relief from the first "real" arrow; it hurts. It's what we do with the second arrow that's important. Healthy people embrace discomfort but protect themselves from the second arrow. While pain is inevitable, *suffering* is self-imposed. It's a deliberate choice.

Fear

Fear is one of our deeply seated emotions, the foundation upon which many of our other emotions are built. And there are many fears that perpetuate our attachment to the past.

- *Fear of the truth*: Reluctance to face the past, who our families are, where we live, and how much money we have
- *Fear of places and things*: Scared of snakes, heights, dogs, blood, injections, confined spaces, rats, thunder, and germs
- *Fear of social connections*: For instance, intimacy, public speaking, social get-togethers, traveling, and flying
- *Fear of people*: The rich or poor, diverse races/ethnicities, abusive parents, dead people, phobias, and religions
- *Fear of difficult emotions*: Shame, sadness, anger, anxiety, guilt, deceit, hostility, and obsessiveness

These fears hibernate quickly within your memories. In no time, they become an insidious attachment to the past. As their cues surface in your current life, they emerge as bursts of anxiety that can sabotage you.

The key is not to keep your fears hidden; they only grow larger. Your simple acknowledgment of the fears helps to calm them. Remind yourself that you've mastered similar frightening situations in the past. Don't be afraid to confront what's most frightening to you. Run toward it, not away from it. With time, familiarity will reduce your suffering and breed confidence.

Worry

Worry is a normal part of life. We worry about teenagers who arrive late at night; we sweat over work deadlines imposed by our boss; we fret about thunderstorms, flooding, or excessive heat on the evening news; or we agitate about a traffic jam or today's volatile stock market. These are common occurrences in life.

Yet, when our worrying becomes excessive, persistent, and uncontrollable, we have a problem, for our negative thoughts, feelings, and actions take over, creating excessive anxiety about potential threats that haven't even happened yet. When we become obsessed, our anxieties activate our more deep-seated attachments from the past, and all hell can break loose. How about the wife who worries that her husband is cheating on her? She gets angry, pushing him away without any corroborating data. Suddenly, she feels horrible about herself. The next day, she's convinced that she rejected him. Believing that she's a failure, she decides that she deserved the rejection all along. This entire scenario is exacerbated by a long-standing story about men who rejected her in the past.

Loss

Lose a close friend. Get fired. End a relationship. Develop a disability. Lose a political campaign. Suffer sexual dysfunction. These common losses in our lives often come with sadness and a feeling of separation. Learning the nature of loss is critical to understanding your attachments to the past.

Judith Viorst, author of *Necessary Losses,* shares her wisdom on the subject. "Losses are an inevitable and necessary part of life. Through the loss of our mother's protection, the loss of the impossible expectations we bring to our relationships, the loss of our younger selves, and losses of our loved ones through separation and death, we gain deeper perspective, true maturity, and fuller wisdom of life."

A dear friend of mine lost his parents when he was twenty. At the time, it was too painful to fully examine the depth of his loss. Like many people, he buried the grief, guilt, and depression deeply into his psyche. Experiences like these, often minimized outside our conscious awareness, can cause lasting psychological damage.

Recently we had a conversation about his loss. He explained that "the pain inside made me very cautious and raw for a long time, in terms of taking risks in relationships, friendships, family, and even potential partners. The death of my parents really weighed me down for years." With meditation and therapy, he confessed, "I started to stick my toe in the water and allow myself to be vulnerable. I learned there's no perfect person in the world, including myself." Today, he's married and in love, feels like he has fully processed the death of his parents, and claims, "It's better to have loved and lost than to have never loved at all."

When we experience loss early in our lives, as my friend did, we can reactivate our awareness of the larger losses throughout our lives. Some of us hide in a cocoon to protect ourselves from pain and disappointment. Others believe that they deserved the losses and are responsible for what happened. Regardless of your story, you can't hide from loss. It always simmers under the surface. If you do hide it, don't be surprised that you end up becoming a sad, melancholy person your entire life.

Anger

When was the last time you got angry? If you're like most people, it's a common result of frustration, irritation, or hostility. Underneath the surface, we are typically afraid, offended, and rejected, or trapped, abused, or treated unfairly. Whatever the reason, it's not unusual to be defensive and want to fight back. Some do that aggressively, others passive-aggressively, and a few of us learn to express our displeasure in healthy and assertive ways.

Expressing frustration is a normal part of life. It's when our feelings become intensified that we can become resentful, the negative reaction to being mistreated, typically leading to our inability to let go or forgive another person.

From my experience, resentments incubate over a long time. If you don't deal with them directly, they can quickly become an attachment to the past. It's the guy who can't stop thinking about the person who feels superior to him, or the woman in a traffic jam who can't let go of her anger and trails the car in front of her too closely, or the college student who nurses grudges toward his friends. These "microaggressions" are brief, verbal, or behavioral slights that are conscious or unconscious and have the effect of making the situation worse.

By repressing these experiences over time, you set out on a journey to become an angry, resentful person who harbors negative energy that envelops your whole being. You start taking things personally, create internal arguments that you were right, and attack quickly when anyone asserts themself.

THE ASPIRATION OF LETTING GO

Grace, a successful IT program manager, shares her feelings about her success story: "I'm good at my career and I'm the type of person who never gives up. I've built a lot of discipline and perseverance over the years. Success is important to me."

Yet, Grace harbors a secret: "It's my fear of being alone, and this is very scary for me. For years, I felt very lonely in life; something was clearly missing in my life.

SELF-TALK—MY NEGATIVE PAST ATTACHMENTS

- I am who I am, and I'm not changing.
- I'd rather not think about it right now.
- There's nothing I can do about it.
- I will never be free from my past.
- If I stay a little longer, he will stop drinking.
- My parents caused me to be this way.
- I must reject my past to be free.
- I'm just an anxious and depressed person.
- My mother blamed me, and I always feel bad about myself.
- I never will be happy, ever.
- Don't tell me how to think; I know about my past.
- You see, this always happens to me.
- I caused my own problem.
- I should have a much nicer life by now.

"The way I see it: Many of my fears came from my mom. I never really had an intimate relationship with her. While I was growing up, my parents got divorced, and she was off living her life. When she then moved to Florida, I was more alone than ever.

"Since then, I've been clingy and needy over the years, too dependent on others, and not very free from the deep-seated feelings from my past." As Grace's story unfolded, there was a clear connection between being alone as a child and feeling alone as an adult. Grace developed a deep-rooted trauma with a special kind of fear-based anxiety. Because her relationships lacked firm boundaries, anything that smelled of rejection scared her.

Grace describes a trip to Europe with her husband some years back. "When we went to Rome, Italy, my husband was cold and detached for a couple days. Every little thing I did felt like I was walking on eggshells. I was in another country and felt vulnerable and scared, scared of being alone, without him.

"When I returned, I really hit rock bottom, lying in my closet one night at three in the morning, filled with pills, cocaine, and alcohol, flat out on my back, feeling helpless.

"Suddenly, this warm flowing water overcame my entire body. God was present in my little closet. For the first time in my life, I admitted to God that I couldn't do it anymore. I had to admit that I was powerless, ready to give up control. I walked into the Light that night with peace and comfort."

Today, Grace's faith in God and her spirituality have helped release her fear of being alone and her attachment to the past. "I was not raised with faith, nor was I raised with the word 'God.' But I found something real, something personal and attainable, something consistent, and all loving. It raises my spirit, comforts my fears, and gives me a reason for being.

"A lot of people get stale and stagnant after they find the Light, so, I try to make this part of my daily discipline. I read scripture every day. And my husband and I work a lot on our marriage, going to church together, taking our daily walk, and strengthening our faith together. With newfound boundaries, he tries to comfort me, and I try to stand up for myself."

Like many people, Grace's fear of the past influences her fears of the future. "I consider myself a good mother, yet I've always been afraid of losing my kids. I remind myself that I am not my mother. I've always been interested in my kids. I'm around them often. And I have never moved away. I may get controlling at times, and they are the first to warn me about that. But it's all a reaction to the fears from my past and my anxieties of the future.

"Sure, there's some scar tissue that raises its ugly head. Life isn't perfect. Yet I always have the presence of God by my side."

FIVE STEPS FOR LETTING GO

Attachments can be quite sticky and difficult to discard. Without facing them directly and letting them go, these attachments can stay glued to our sense of self and influence our entire lens to the world. Consider these five steps for rejecting them.

Get Comfortable Being Uncomfortable

Discomfort is a catalyst for growth and change. Sounds counterintuitive, but it's true. Without discomfort, you have neither the motivation nor the desire to fix anything. Fortunately, you are far more capable of handling discomfort than you think you are. The more aware you are of your pain, the more you can address it.

- Accept yourself as imperfect by nature; get comfortable being vulnerable.
- Allow yourself to fall down, feel the pain, put a bandage on your knee, and try walking again.
- Learn resilience skills. You will gain more confidence and courage to walk through the coals by yourself.

Discover Your Deepest Emotions

Most of the time, when we get stuck on our journey, trying to let go of our past, we are too lenient on our emotions. Whether it's pain, fear, worry, loss, or anger, we often take a superficial approach. When we

cover up our most painful feelings and keep them hidden from ourselves, we end up never addressing the true attachment to the past.

- Label your emotions, so you can distinguish one from the other.
- Lean into the pain and continue to lean into the pain, until
  there's no pain left to lean into.
- Be tough and gentle with yourself. At some point, you may feel
  a rush of energy as you begin to ease your pain and your attachment to the past.

Learn to Surrender and Let Go

Dr. David Hawkins, in *Letting Go: The Pathway of Surrender*, says "Letting go involves being aware of a feeling, letting it come up, staying with
it, and letting it run its course without wanting to make it different or
do anything about it. You have the feeling without resisting it, venting
it, fearing it, condemning it, or moralizing it."

- When letting go, ignore all your thoughts. They are just clouds
  moving with the winds in a motionless sky.
- Watch as your thoughts rationalize and reinforce the attachment in your mind.
- Become your own witness to your thoughts and then let them
  go. Your thoughts are often the main cause of your suffering.

Forgive Yourself and Others

Forgiveness is the engine for letting go of your past. Some of us are naturally forgiving and live happier lives. Others hang on to our grudges and
resentments, putting us at risk for heart attacks, high blood pressure,
and a variety of stress disorders.

Dr. Karen Swartz, director of clinical and educational programs
at the Johns Hopkins Mood Disorders Center, shares how it works.

"Forgiveness is an active process in which you make a conscious decision to let go of negative feelings, whether the person deserves it or not. As you release the anger, resentment, and hostility, you begin to feel empathy and compassion for the person who wronged you."

- Make an intentional decision to forgive. Let go of your expectations.
- Develop compassion and empathize with the other person. And don't forget to forgive yourself.
- You don't have to forget or excuse the harm done to you. But if you do, it can bring peace that allows you to move on.
- Remember: Forgiveness is contagious. So don't be afraid to say, "I'm sorry." It often inspires others to forget their own grudges.

Rewrite Your Story

Everyone has a story. You are the author. These stories come from our day-to-day experiences, are housed in our memories, and retold during the day in our minds and in our dreams while we sleep. There are good stories and bad ones, typically comprised of our senses, thoughts, and feelings. When we are attached to the past, our story is typically based on a troubling scenario that we can't discard. By rewriting our past stories, we free ourselves from the shackles that tie us up and keep us down.

- Sit quietly with your eyes closed. In your mind, capture your past story with all its context and color, self-talk, and interactions with others.
- Notice the thoughts and emotions of your story, how it begins and ends, and what are the consequences.
- Now, frame a more positive story with different intentions and outcomes. Be aware of your changing thoughts and emotions.
- Practice telling the story to yourself and others. Give it a title. Write it down and reread it every day.

SELF-TALK—MY POSITIVE ASPIRATIONS

- I can change who I am.
- I am quick to forgive myself.
- I avoid getting tripped up by difficult feelings.
- I accept the whole story of my life.
- I want to forgive others.
- My dreams provide interesting information.
- I allow myself to feel all my emotions.
- I am hopeful and realistic about my life.
- I bounce back quickly from adversity.
- I am a naturally good person.
- I look at my fears head-on.
- I'm aware how my mind can fool me.

Reflections

Here are some questions to deepen your understanding of the attachment to the past. Find some quiet time to reflect on these questions.

- Why are you feeling resentful today?
- What stops you from feeling happy and joyful?
- Why do you have trouble letting go of painful situations?
- What is keeping you stuck in the past?
- Why are you having trouble forgiving others?
- Do you get hijacked by pain, fear, worry, loss, or anger?

THREE

THE ATTACHMENT TO THE FUTURE

- Are you focused on achieving, becoming, or chasing something?
- Do you get anxious when people don't return your calls and emails?
- Do you worry about how events will turn out in the future?
- Do you spend time comparing yourself to others?
- Do you have trouble living in the present moment?

first met Andrew playing poker in 1988. His keen intellect and charismatic personality touched me right from the start. We drank a lot of beer that evening as he proceeded to win most of the chips on the table. Sometimes you just meet people, and your gut says you're going to become fast friends for life. Well, that's how it was with Andrew. Over the next thirty years, he became my attorney and my friend.

Today, Andrew is a successful guy. As a partner at a prestigious law firm, he is one of America's leading business attorneys. Author of twenty books on the legal and strategic aspects of business, Andrew has advised dozens of Fortune 500 companies and hundreds of emerging growth companies. Yet, like most of us, there's a story behind his story that teaches us about the attachment to the past and the future.

Andrew grew up in a wealthy suburb outside Philadelphia, but he and his family were different from the rest of the neighbors. "We grew up in modest means and were poor compared to other people," Andrew told me. "My dad had a lot of different jobs. Many of them didn't work out. My parents divorced because of these financial pressures, and I knew when the time came for me to develop a profession, financial stability would be at the top of the list."

Andrew's past had a major influence on how he pursued his career. "I entered the professional world believing that I would have to work twice as hard as the next person." Book after book, client after client, Andrew worked hard to overcome his past. But, he reflects, "At what point do you ever overcome your past. I don't know whether I will ever declare victory. I look at each day as if I could go right back to where I was. I know I'll probably declare victory when I retire. By then, it's too late."

At the law firm, there's a huge poster of Rocky hanging on his office wall. "That's me up there on the poster," he says. "I'm that street fighter from Philly who overcame the odds to get to the top of the art museum stairs. I don't assume anything. I've got to prove myself every day. I don't have degrees from super fancy schools or family connections. So, every day, I try to let the past remain, not as a chip on my shoulder, but a reminder of where I come from.

"It's almost like a survivor mentality. You never really know when your next meal is coming." But he's learned to deal with it by protecting himself from falling backward. "I keep lots of projects going on at once, and I have difficulty saying no. If I have one hundred projects and I lose seven, I still have ninety-three. But, if I have one project and I lose it,

I'm out on the streets. Having all the balls in the air gives me a sense of security."

However, there are consequences. "I have trouble being fully relaxed," Andrew laments. "I get up at three in the morning, sometimes thinking about a client problem. Now, I live on three or four hours of sleep at night, but it does come at a cost. Some years ago, the light bulb went off, and I realized there was more to parenting than being just a provider."

Andrew clearly has an attachment to the past, the good and the ugly, the anxiety and success. And he has even turned that situation into an advantage. "I feel lucky to have been born in America. It's the one country where you can redefine yourself, wake up in the morning and change your attitude, paint a new picture, and literally rewrite your life's storybook." At least that's true for some people.

Today, as Andrew enjoys his life, it's the attachment to the future that really haunts him these days. "I've changed major law firms six times in search of the best environment for me and my business. Every time I reach a goal, I raise the bar on myself. It's my own internal battle against apathy and complacency. I worry about taking things for granted and getting too soft."

As Andrew continues to strive, he proudly admits that "our lake house gives me a place of solitude, and having a grandson forces me to live more in the here and now." But he can't help himself. Part of Andrew will always live in the future. He asks, "Will I be at my grandson's high school graduation? Will I be lucky enough to see him married? Will I ever meet his kids? I guess I'm still living in the future, not just for business reasons, but for personal reasons too."

Like Andrew, if you fear that something is missing in your life, you risk becoming too attached to the future with all its accompanying worry and angst, never fully enjoying the present moment. Just ring up Andrew in the middle of the night when he wakes up with the idea for his twenty-first book.

THE FUTURE IS HERE

We humans are one of only a few animals in the world who think about the future, and those thoughts have many benefits. The future is the source of our dreams, goals, and achievements, giving us the opportunity to spot trends and be bigger and better every day. It's the CEO who forecasts the future to avoid being disrupted by technological forces; it's the parent who teaches a child how to prepare for adulthood; and it's the artist who imagines a work of art on the canvas before even touching the brush.

To understand the future better, let's look at human science to see how three prominent professions—the futurists, the economists, and the psychologists—help us understand human behavior.

The Futurists See Signals and Patterns

Of course, nobody can predict the future, but the futurists have found ways to come close. As they gaze into the future, they help us paint pictures of alternative scenarios. They start by seeing a VUCA world: volatile, uncertain, complex, and ambiguous. Their goal is to create some understanding and clarity to make sense of our unpredictable future.

The Institute for the Future has led the way for many years. Says Bob Johansen, Distinguished Fellow at the institute, "The future doesn't just happen to us. We have agency in imagining and creating the kind of future we want to live in, and we can take actions to get us there." Bob suggests some well-studied guideposts. Forget about predictions and learn to look backward from the future. Focus on signals and patterns. Voluntarily engage in fear. And link your hindsight to your foresight to get fresh insights.

Hindsight—the thinking and feeling we tell ourselves about the stories of our past—is anchored in our past experiences. Foresight identifies those forces that disrupt us and the patterns and possibilities we identify looking into the future. Our insights are those special moments when you create a new story in your mind about the future with fresh connections in your brain. "It's all about linking today's way of doing things to tomorrow's way of doing things."

The Economists Assess Behavior

Traditional economists view people as purely rational actors with self-control who naturally pursue their long-term goals. But, there's a new breed of economists who combine economics and psychology to understand how people behave in the *real* world, subject to their emotions, impulses, and circumstances. These newer behavioral economists believe people often behave in irrational ways *against* their self-interests, *with* biases, blind spots, attachments, and difficult emotions.

You know the people: the man who avoids or delays investing in his 401(k); the woman who overeats and refuses to exercise when she knows she's at risk for heart disease; or the house-hunting couple who pays a lot more for a home when all the area brokers claim the house is significantly overpriced. In each case, these folks are overconfident in their abilities, more afraid of losing than winning, and more likely to pursue short-term benefits over long-term gains. Instant pleasure wins out at the expense of their overall well-being.

By observing these unpredictable, irrational behaviors, these modern-day economists are helping today's marketeers manipulate people's choices and decisions. They're also shedding light on how some people can get so attached to the future.

The Psychologists Explore the Psyche

Psychologists call "prospection" that ability to envision and think about the future. This psychology approach digs deep into the psyche to study memories, imagination, and our ability to project into the future. As humans, when we can mentally transport ourselves forward and imagine situations that don't exist yet, we generally project our present selves into the future so that we can ensure that we feel pleasure or prevent pain.

Not surprisingly, we each carry our own subjective lens into the future. By seeing ourselves as unique and special, we tend to cling on to both the positive and negative stories in our lives, ones that shape and distort how we see the future. We also have the capacity to misperceive the past and the future, but we always remember *how* we feel about each one.

Thinking about the future can be pleasurable or unpleasurable, even healthy or unhealthy, primarily because most of us have blind spots, and we tend to saturate these blanks with our emotions. Dan Gilbert, Harvard psychologist and author of *Stumbling on Happiness*, has a lot to say on the subject. He describes our psychological immune system, a protective system in our brains that defends against painful experiences, much like the physical immune system defends the body against illness.

Dan believes that "when most people daydream about the future, they imagine themselves achieving and succeeding, rather than fumbling or failing. A healthy psychological immune system kicks in and finds a balance that allows us to feel good enough to cope with the situation, but bad enough to do something about it." He warns, "We need to be defended—not defenseless or defensive—that's why people often seek opportunities to think about themselves in positive ways." When we think positively about the future, we tap into our positive emotions. We anticipate good things happening and look forward to positive surprises.

Positive emotions are naturally hardwired into everyone, stimulating our parasympathetic nervous system that reduces heart rate, muscle tension, and stress. Yet we all differ, depending on our experiences, upbringing, genetic makeup, and circumstances. These emotions also may be shaped by a crisis, good parenting, or a rich spiritual life. In fact, spirituality and all religions have a deep psychological basis rooted in our positive emotions.

Here's a list of the most common ones. We talked about the difficult ones in the attachment to the past.

- *Hope*: Our ability to imagine and invest in a better future
- *Joy*: Our feelings of positive intent, and our triumph over suffering
- *Love*: Our ability to feel intimacy, passion, and commitment
- *Generosity*: Our empathy, kindness, and compassion for others
- *Gratitude*: Our ability to be thankful and appreciative with others
- *Forgiveness*: Our capacity to let go of resentment and anger

By practicing these positive emotions as we think about the future, we can improve our well-being, foster compassion with others, make prudent decisions, and achieve our goals.

LIVING IN THE GAP

"Mind the gap" booms over the loudspeaker repeatedly in the London Underground, reminding everyone—especially tourists—that there's a space between the train platform and the train they are boarding. Life is spent living in the gap—the gap between our current reality (station platform) and our desired future (train). During these microtransitions, you must learn to be comfortable being uncomfortable and experiment with new ways of seeing, thinking, feeling, and acting. You must also learn to be vulnerable, allow yourself to make mistakes, and believe that you can cope with adversity.

The future can hold positive and negative feelings simultaneously. Because the positive ones set the stage for *anticipatory pleasure,* you can tap into your inner reserve of hope and faith. Conversely, your difficult emotions set the stage for *anticipatory anxiety* that projects fear into the future. It's these fear-based emotions that terrorize us in the gap, where our attachment to the future shows its ugly head.

ATTACHMENT TO THE FUTURE

Like other attachments, most of us who are attached to the future know it. We are too attached to a certain situation or are fearful of the outcome. The outcome could be anything, of course, but often we find ourselves obsessing over an event and worrying about the unknown consequences. This behavior is grounded in anxious striving for the wrong reasons, like searching for more and better or obsessing over what's missing in your life: always judging, comparing, complaining, and worrying.

Whether it's chronically reaching for a better job, more money, the perfect partner, or anything upsetting in your life, the attachment to the future keeps you in a state of angst. Some of us are haunted by past events and the fears of repeating them in the future, like having an accident while driving at night. Others are frugal savers who never buy anything and refuse to go on vacation. So, the more you sit in judgment of yourself, the more pain and unhappiness you will feel.

Numerous studies show that the more you try not to think about something, your mind forces you to think about it even more. Whether it's worrying about a rejection of a loved one, the fear of upcoming surgery, the panic of an uncontrollable virus, or simply making the wrong life decision, you become obsessed with the outcome you most fear. While nothing is wrong with dreams, goals, and making improvements in your life, it's a slippery slope when you don't meet your expectations, or they preoccupy you.

A smart twentysomething colleague of mine is a good example of someone attached to rejection. As a self-conscious woman, when she goes to a social event, she starts to think about how she will be received even before she arrives. At the event, she observes her behavior in real time, and she leaves questioning how she came across in conversations. The next morning, feeling isolated and lonely, she harbors self-doubt within a faulty belief system. She questions whether she embarrassed herself by piling on self-deprecation.

Many folks call this "monkey brain," a chaotic oasis of troubling thoughts and feelings. I remember the monkey forest on a visit to the city of Ubud in Bali, where there are hundreds of monkeys everywhere—on the ground, in the trees, on your shoulders, in your face trying to steal your purse or sunglasses. It's just like your mind full of gnawing monkeys, having your thoughts and emotions swinging randomly in all directions. Your mind simply can't remain still. When this chaos persists, you become too attached to the future, like a rat chasing food on a roller coaster where it's hard to gain perspective, and you are left with a story, full of anxiety, and no positive ending.

Eckhart Tolle, author of *The Power of Now,* sums it up nicely: "Many people live with a tormentor in their head that continuously attacks and punishes them and drains them of vital energy. It is the cause of untold misery and unhappiness, as well as disease. The good news is you can free yourself from your mind. This is the only true liberation."

At this point you might want to ask yourself some additional questions:

- How aware are you of your emotional life? Honestly?
- When was the last time you laughed so hard, you cried?
- How do your emotions shed light or cast shadows on the people around you?
- How did your family handle emotions? Did you laugh, scream, cry, or just avoid each other at dinner?
- What kind of people make you smile, and who in your life makes you angry or frustrated as hell?

- How easy or difficult do you find it to forgive others? To feel compassion? To find joy? To be hopeful? To express love?
- Are you a worrier who is always anticipating problems? Or do you believe that things will turn out for the better and that you can make a difference?

A LIST OF COMMON ATTACHMENTS TO THE FUTURE

Are you worrying about:

- A budding relationship in the early stages?
- Whether or not you're going to have a boy or a girl?
- Winning a close election that matters?
- Waiting for a raise, bonus, or new job?
- Receiving your college exam score?
- Getting a desired or undesired text or email?
- Your retirement money in the stock market?
- Giving an important speech in public?
- Your in-laws coming to visit for two weeks?
- Planning and having a great vacation?

THE YIPS KEEP ME UP AT NIGHT

What happens when our attachment to our future success and the elaborate stories we tell ourselves converge to derail our progress? We all watched the 2020 Olympics when everyone expected Simone Biles to run away with the gold in gymnastics, yet she got a case of the "twisties" and failed to land several events. This syndrome in the golfing world has long been known as the "yips," a tremor-like condition when the hands shake at the most inopportune moments—namely on the putting green when an accurate putt can earn millions!

Years ago, Jim Hardy—now the successful CEO of Plane Truth, the world's largest international training and certification company, which has 260 golfing instructors from 18 countries, 2007 PGA Teacher of the Year, and ranked regularly in the top ten on *Golf Digest*'s list of greatest teachers—was living out a nightmare on the golf course, plagued by the yips.

I met Jim when I was sixteen and on the golf team at my high school in Philadelphia. After my mother introduced us, he asked me to caddy for him during the Philadelphia Classic. Quickly, he became a mentor and a friend. However, little did I know that Jim was miserable, feeling that his life had little purpose, tormented by what he perceived as a failing or weakness. He was plagued by a recurring dream that, during the Masters Tournament, he would botch a three-foot, right-center putt and "never make it to win." Every day on the golf course, he would live out that self-defeating thought and defeat himself. That dream of failure became his truth. Fear, not joy, drove him until he finally quit altogether.

While Jim had a fierce desire to excel, he realized that he had to overcome this overpowering fear of future failure and fix the roadblock to success. At the time, part of his problem was the universal belief that the yips were a player's inability to "control his nerves." In other words, it was "all in his head." He drank, having figured that alcohol would quiet the tremors, and equated beating himself up with such thinking as "you're gutless, something's wrong with your mental approach and you're not manly, you're not a warrior, whatever crap we want to throw at ourselves."

Then, when pros and amateurs sought him out as a teaching pro, he slowly regained his balance, putting more effort into instruction. To his surprise, "I liked teaching. It gave me a higher purpose, something more meaningful and satisfying than prize money. I could kind of go, 'You mean I don't have to try to make $100 million and satisfy everything and everybody in the world? Woo-hoo, this is kind of fun!'" Jim found a way to replace his attachment with a more pleasant alternative, while enjoying the present.

In addition to replacing the fear with joy that emerged from teaching, the "it's-all-in-your-head" explanation dissolved when, seventeen years later, he discovered that the yips were, in fact, neurologically based, not psychological failings. Dubbed "essential tremors," they are genetic in nature, resembling Parkinson's, run in families, and are fired and intensified by adrenaline, which, of course, releases in situations when people experience pressure or stress—like the eighteenth hole of the Masters.

Learning that his tremors were not caused by mental weakness was immensely liberating. He could now trust his newfound self-awareness about what was important. He became emotionally stronger and healthier. "I understood that it's more about personal mastery than how I stood with competitors or other people. I started to have peace with myself."

Today, Jim has developed a unique approach, centered on teaching students how to discover their own strengths and weaknesses. Students have flocked to him, including numerous tour pros. Jim's detachment from his fear of future failure has transformed his life, and the yips no longer haunt him in the early hours of the morning.

JIM HARDY'S PATH TO SANITY

Here are four possible steps Jim Hardy might have used to detach himself from the yips and his attachment to the future.

Step 1: Attachment

Jim took the first step when he realized how fearful he was of missing the potential Masters putt. He expanded his fear to all short putts and labeled them "the yips." He then started to become aware of the full range of his limiting thoughts and emotions. By deepening his insights about obsessing over the outcome, he acknowledged the truth about himself. He was ready to go to the next step when he identified his specific attachment to the future.

Step 2: Acceptance

In this phase, Jim began to accept how his attachment was hijacking him. By digging deeply into why and how it was causing him to suffer, he slowly gained awareness of his angst, dissatisfaction, drinking, and his lack of desire to play golf. He began to see himself as separate from the attachment and cultivated compassion for himself. You are ready to go to the next step when you realize that you are NOT your attachment.

Step 3: Aspiration

Here, Jim eventually stopped clinging to his attachment and started talking about it with others. He saw the connection between his feelings and the attachment, and by substituting healthy thoughts and emotions for unhealthy ones, he began to retrain his mind. Jim started to see alternative explanations for the yips as tremors and sought out new career options. Jim was ready to move to the next step when he clearly understood what he had to do to overcome the attachment.

Step 4: Action

Jim's final step was to make the commitment to discard the attachment. He actively pursued his dream job—teaching golf pros and students—that led to a variety of entrepreneurial ventures. Not only was he recognized for his great work, but he was able to rewrite his story and apply his aspiration in different situations. Jim forgave himself for harboring the attachment, using it as a teaching opportunity for others.

THE ASPIRATION OF LIVING FULLY IN THE PRESENT

We live in an attention-deficit world with excessive amounts of information, not enough time to process it, and the desire to get as much done as possible. For many of us, we have trouble focusing on what matters and find it difficult to integrate our work, family, and personal interests. The consequences are real: hectic, stressful, and unfulfilling lives.

For over four decades, Ellen Langer, psychologist at Harvard University, has influenced the field of positive psychology. She reveals that by paying attention to what's going on around us, instead of operating on autopilot, we can reduce stress, unlock creativity, and boost performance. Ellen says, "Life consists only of moments, nothing more than that. So, if you make the moment matter, it all matters."

The present moment is here and now. It's about being mindful of what is happening at this very moment, not distracted by intruding thoughts or emotions. This stance helps you cut down on worrying, keeps you grounded and connected to yourself, and enables you to make better life choices.

Mindfulness is a state of active, open attention to the present moment. With its roots in Buddhism, Taoism, and Native American traditions, you are not your thoughts from moment to moment, nor are you grasping for them or pushing them away. You are awakening to the present, a practice that takes intentionality and allows you to watch the passing drama of your feelings, which forces you to stop overthinking, getting lost in your mind, or worrying about the past and the future.

Recent research provides strong evidence that practicing present-moment awareness (mindfulness) changes the brain. Meditation affects two parts of our brain: the anterior cingulate cortex (ACC) located deep in the forehead and associated with self-regulation, and the hippocampus buried inside the temple and associated with memory and emotion.

Practicing mindfulness affects body awareness, introspection, pain tolerance, and emotional regulation. It also helps you label your feelings, monitor your behavior, and exhibit self-control. Simply put, mindful people are happier, calmer, and more empathetic to others.

MEDITATION TIPS

- Find a quiet place and sit comfortably with your back straight.
- Focus awareness on your breath; ignore anything that comes to mind as a distraction.
- Notice any negativity that arises. Don't resist, overanalyze, or judge it. Feel and accept it and view it as a helpful sign, telling you to pay attention.
- Consider doing a mindful body scan and relax each part of your body.
- Repeat a mantra/sound to focus your attention and avoid distractions.
- Go deep to ponder the causes of your angst and anxiety. Try to find the fear that drives your most difficult emotions.
- Allow yourself to admit mistakes, befriend your vulnerability, or walk into the unknown.
- Don't just do something, sit there. Be grateful for where you are at this moment. As your attention turns to the here and now, you will feel a sense of warmth and peace.

At dinner parties, my partner, Jay, and I like to facilitate a wonderful conversation on the topic. We ask our guests to cite a percentage out of one hundred on how much time they spend thinking about their past, present, or future. It's amazing that most people spend their time primarily in the past or the future and would actually like to live more in the present. The folks who linger in the past tend to be sadder or angrier. The guests who live more in the future tend to be anxious and worried. Bottom line: everyone yearns to be in the present moment.

Meditation is a good place to start. Some of you who are veteran meditators can teach us a thing or two about your experience. Others are novices and need to start at the beginning. Wherever you are on the spectrum, we all start from the same place: quiet and empty your mind; concentrate on the here and now. Twenty to thirty minutes per day is a great commitment.

PRESENT MOMENT IN ACTION

What about the other fifteen and a half hours we are awake? How do we live in the present moment during these times? While it's certainly fine to reflect and ponder the past, or dream and plan into the future, we just can't get stuck there. Why not practice mindfulness throughout the day? I like to call it "awareness in action." How can you see clearly, think openly, feel positively, and act constructively? Moment-to-moment awareness during the day reduces anxiety and impulsivity. You can also stay focused on what matters, avoid being distracted by passing thoughts and feelings, and avoid unhealthy behaviors.

Staying mindful during the day improves your relationships too. How many times do you get angry with your partner or a colleague, feel hurt when someone ignores you, feel guilt or shame for making a mistake, or worry about deadlines or sick kids? When does burnout influence your interactions with others?

It is in these times when we need mindful action in the moment. When you confront these situations, take time out to look around. Take some deep breaths. Open your eyes and ears to what's really going on around you. Get up on the balcony, take the high road, and show up with a positive demeanor. Disengage from the drama of others, shedding their microaggressions. *The Four Agreements* reminds us that 98% of things happening in the world have nothing to do with you. They have to do with the other person.

Most importantly, don't beat yourself up. Yes, you are imperfect just like the rest of us. But be grateful for who you are and what you have. Remember, this is a great time to know yourself, be yourself, and love yourself in the moment.

MINDFUL ACTIONS

- Take a walk, ride a bike, take a shower, sit in the sun, eat a favorite food.
- Keep a journal of your daily positive experiences.
- Take frequent breaks and spend time away from your phone and computer.
- Engage in mindful movement—yoga, tai chi, and Pilates.
- Stimulate your endorphins with aerobic and anaerobic exercise.
- Get totally absorbed in something—singing, reading, writing, teaching.
- Keep a gratitude journal.
- Brainstorm ways to solve problems.
- Practice deep breathing in the moment.
- Avoid multitasking; not only does it not work, but it can also be quite stressful.

MINDFULNESS IN THE MILITARY

Jeanne has always been a self-sufficient woman. She remembers that "as a kid, I learned how to change a tire, replace a spark plug, mow the lawn, and do electrical, primarily because of my father. My parents told me that I could do anything I wanted; I just had to learn to take care of myself." So, when she chose to enter the Air Force Academy, it really wasn't a surprise to anyone.

"I was always conscious of the fact that there were a lot more men in the academy, from the time I was seventeen until I retired from the military. I never saw it as a 'woe is me,' but just as the cards I was dealt and situation I found myself in."

Yet, for Jeanne, fellow female officers, and women in other workplaces, it certainly wasn't a cakewalk. She remembers, "Some guys would say, 'I just don't know why women are here, why they're in the military.' But there's nothing I could say or do to change their worldview. I could just do my best and earn a place here."

Jeanne recalls a poignant story: "I was a swimmer growing up, and we were doing water survival training. Here, I found myself not just keeping myself afloat; I'm keeping two other people afloat. No 'attaboy' or 'good job!' If a guy did it, they would say 'really cool.' As girls, we were always expected to do as good or better, never expected to be as good, and if we were on par, they would say we were average or less. Sometimes, it felt hurtful. We were a bunch of seventeen- to twenty-five-year-olds, and we would get frustrated and irritated. There were even times when I didn't want to be there. But you did your best and moved on."

As Jeanne graduated and entered the Air Force, her mind matured, but the demographics didn't. "Sometimes I'm the only female in the conference room, or there may be two to three of us in a room of twenty. Now, we're in the same career field, and we've gone through the same education, and the men need to explain it to me, as if I didn't go through the same training. And I would think *been there, done that*.

"I don't want to speak to their motivation, because I don't know what it is, but I think it's ego. They just forget we do things the same way they do.

"Don't get me wrong. I spent time now and again sitting in the pity pot. Everybody's allowed five minutes on the pot, but you can't wallow and take up residency there. You just pick yourself up and ask: 'What can I control in this situation?' and then you march forward."

Recently, Jeanne retired at forty-eight as lieutenant colonel with a successful military career behind her. As a foreign liaison officer, she was responsible for the foreign defense attachés and foreign senior defense officers. Today, she works in a consulting firm and lives with her husband, also an Air Force Academy graduate.

Why did I include Jeanne's story as an aspirational solution to a potential attachment to the future? Namely, she could have gotten all tangled up by dwelling on sexism in the military, but she chose to live in the future *and* stay comfortable with herself in the present moment. Confident and courageous, she rarely got sidetracked by the possibility that military culture could have impeded her career progress. Rather, she followed a handful of principles that protected and guided her on her journey. Consider these actions:

- Take care of yourself first.
- Distinguish what you can and cannot control.
- Have confidence in your ability to manage your attachments.
- Determine who is dealing with what personal issues.
- Go to the pity pot if you need to, but don't stay too long.
- Be vulnerable with your friends who take care of you.
- Practice present-centered mindfulness.

Reflections

Here are some questions to ponder as you explore your attachment to the future.

- As you think about the future, what kinds of experiences get you most excited?
- What events or situations in the future cause you to feel the most anxious?
- What future decisions do you find most difficult to make?
- What kinds of people do you want to avoid in the future?
- How do you practice mindfulness and live in the present moment?

Finally, let me leave you with the wise words of Mark Twain about the future: "I have known a great many troubles, but most of them never happened."

FOUR

THE ATTACHMENT TO CONTROL

- Do you like to control people and situations?
- Do you find yourself criticized and controlled by others?
- Are you a natural people pleaser?
- Do people call you passive-aggressive at times?
- Do you see yourself as cynical and mistrustful?

I magine you are a thousand feet in the sky, looking down. There, you see a man walking his dog on a leash. The dog stops, glances around, squats and drops something, and walks away without a worry. The man stops in his tracks, reaches into his pocket, pulls out a bag, and then bends down and picks something up from the ground. They walk away as if nothing happened. Who is controlling this relationship? I sometimes ask that very question.

We first met Cassie, an adorable border collie, on the streets of Dallas when we were coming back from the gym. With no apparent destination and wearing no tags, she seemed completely at peace with herself. Dutifully, we took her to the animal shelter, but for two days, we couldn't stop thinking about her big brown eyes and infectious smile. So, we returned to the shelter, signed the papers, and off we went back home to the nation's capital where Cassie became the new member of our family.

Despite the strange surroundings, Cassie was clearly in control. She was confident, independent, and quite capable of taking care of herself. We figured that she had developed that trait surviving on the streets, alone. When she met her new brother Chocco, our chocolate Labrador retriever, it was clear she was the alpha dog. Although considerably smaller, there was no question who was in charge.

Underneath this affable kisser was a canine totally attached to being in control. Cassie would never lie on her back. Now, most dogs like tummy rubs, but not Cassie. She was unwilling to give up control. She was also very jealous of Chocco. Every time we gave him attention, she would shove her little butt into the middle of the conversation, push him away, and demand that she be front and center. Vulnerability was simply not her thing.

But it's amazing what a little love will do. In time, Cassie learned to roll on her back to get her daily tummy massages. She also shared the limelight with Chocco at dinner parties and hovered under our legs for protection during thunderstorms. As she learned to trust us, she became more vulnerable and gave up her controlling nature.

For his part, Chocco was the big baby in the household. We immediately discovered that at puppy parties when he adventured a few feet away from me, he then doubled back quickly, jumping on my lap for safety. As he matured, he learned more manipulative behaviors like excessive barking for food, thinking we didn't notice. He was also irreverent and passive-aggressive. To wake us up, he had an entire routine going: first, he stared at us, then he whined, barked, pulled the sheets off, and gnawed at our hands with rapid bites—in that order. We loved him dearly, but he certainly had a different way of controlling us.

Years later, Queen Tessa, our Saint Bernard mix, arrived on the scene. Mature, loving, and wise right from the start, she was playful and gentle, yet independent, and quickly became everyone's best friend. When you met her gaze, she immediately went on her back with her legs up in search of connection and affection. Confident yet vulnerable, she understood the true benefits of being in *and* out of control.

Just like dogs, people have different relationships with control. Some love being in charge, and at times can be aggressive; others like being controlled by others; and still others have difficulty expressing their feelings, directly or adaptively. This chapter explores these types of relationships.

THE POWER OF AGENCY

"Agency" is the sense of control you feel in your life. It's your capacity to influence your thoughts and behavior. It's the faith you have in yourself to handle a wide range of situations. And it's your ability to master and shape your environment.

You need this sense of control for important reasons: Agency provides you with safety and protection from perceived danger. It also helps you connect with others and build relationships. This faith in yourself helps manage your anxiety as you travel into the unknown with comfort and competence.

Naturally, we are attracted to people with agency. They're the ones who project confidence. They cope well with life's stresses, set boundaries, and make things happen. They are simply happier, healthier, and higher-performing people than the people who lack agency.

There are three essential tools for tapping into your own power of agency: self-efficacy, self-control, and self-mastery. Let's look at each one:

- *Self-efficacy*: Agency starts out with a belief that you can succeed in life and work. With confidence and courage, you actively learn, expand your capacity, and develop new skills. With this inner confidence, you believe in your ability to accomplish things: managing your time, executing key projects, exercising and eating well, and advocating for yourself. By observing others who succeed and surrounding yourself with people who believe in you, you get that extra boost of self-esteem.

- *Self-control*: We all live in a world of constant interruptions— kids, schedules, work, health, and our partners. Nothing is more important than developing an inner sense of control to balance out these external disruptions. This internal self-control helps you think clearly, manage your emotions, and stay even-keeled. You believe that control comes from within, and you have control over what happens to you. Hence, you're more likely to take responsibility and be accountable for your actions.

- *Self-mastery*: By having confidence and an inner sense of control, you make things happen in the world. This stance requires vision, discipline, energy, and the courage to act. With self-mastery, you make life choices, negotiate conflicts, and manage difficult people. Authority, leadership, and decision-making power come with the territory. Without self-mastery, you stay doubtful, restless, and passive. You obsess over details, procrastinate, and worry excessively. And, you lack the confidence to take risks.

Combining self-efficacy, self-control, and self-mastery produces a healthy, fulfilled, and productive person. But, in the Game of Life, you might not start out with the best cards.

You might find yourself genetically wired as a controlling, impulsive person, developmentally controlled by a depressed, dependent parent. Or, you may be reactive to a life trauma that caused deep sadness or loss.

Maybe you survived an alcoholic dad who shut you down and taught you to be conflict averse and passive-aggressive.

Some of us see ourselves as controllers, others as fatalists or victims, and still others have plenty of agency without all the baggage that comes with excessive or diminished control. Let's examine our most common attachments to control.

THE ATTACHMENT TO CONTROL

In my travels, I've noticed four types of people who struggle with an attachment to control. For each, control plays a central role in how they live their life. Whether it's with their spouse/partner, their children, friends, or their boss and coworkers, the issue of who has control and who doesn't creates a host of people and relationship problems. Public and private boundaries are inappropriately crossed, fears of separation and connection fuel the tension, and all parties feel they aren't getting their needs met.

Those Who Control Others

Controlling people often admit that they feel the need to exert control over others. Some controllers become completely aware of their behavior, often stunned when they realize what they have done, and they feel guilty that they've hurt someone they love. Others are completely oblivious, unconscious of their motives and actions, and they don't see the insult until someone brings it to their attention. Many others simply believe they have done nothing wrong and react defensively during moments of objection.

Controlling others comes in all shapes and sizes. The most innocuous type is *benevolent control*, like offering unsolicited suggestions, taking over household responsibilities, or driving from the back seat, which all have best intentions at heart.

Directive control has a deeper underlying agenda. Often motivated by anxiety or resentment, the controller micromanages, assumes his/her own opinion is always right, or takes credit for others' achievements. They may even be seen as kind and thoughtful by others, but the coals are kindling inside.

The third type is *oppressive control*, motivated to shut down the other person and make them feel dependent. Examples of this behavior might include giving orders, constant criticism, verbal abuse, or isolating the other person.

The last type of control is downright *dangerous control*. Here, the controller can show rage by throwing objects, exhibiting physical abuse, demanding sex, or stalking someone.

On the surface, controllers see themselves as strong and independent. To them, life is a contest with a strong need to win or be right. Fearing feeling inferior and helpless, they pride themselves on controlling their environment.

Some controllers are driven by other attachments. An attachment to stability can drive someone to control their environment. Those attached to success can control others to improve their own performance. And the perfectionists who control others reduce their anxiety by confronting the imperfections they see around them.

Here's the catch. Underneath the surface of all these examples, controllers fear vulnerability yet have a deep desire for connection. Authenticity is their Achilles' heel. Fearful of their own feelings of dependence, they hide this part of themselves from others. Their desire to control others and cultivate dependency allows them to feel connected and less vulnerable, especially as they get more and more separated from others.

Neurosurgeon Takes Charge

"I'm a take-charge, dominant woman, and it just comes naturally to me," says Isabella, who lives a hectic life in a downtown metropolitan area. "I grew up in a high-pressure home with a commanding mom who had very high expectations." With that background embedded in her psyche, Isabella took to her controlling nature like a fish in water. She is the master of her world.

Moving at rapid speed and living on the edge is her speedometer. Controlling, at times quick to anger, Isabella finds it difficult to relax and stay centered. Then, she found her ideal job: Isabella became a neurosurgeon with all the fast-paced, high-energy action she thrived on.

"I am in charge of life-and-death decisions every day, like flying airplanes inside storm clouds, and controlling everything around me, from brain tumors to herniated discs, powerful drugs, and complex machines, even the entire medical staff. It's been the perfect job for me." But there are consequences. "I can get burned out from all the intensity, yet I love the work."

Isabella readily admits that she "can be arrogant and haughty at times and push people too hard with my assertiveness, penetrating personal boundaries that alienate others. Some even say I feel better than the other physicians."

Her family is the recipient of her controlling nature too. Isabella proudly admits that "I am in charge of most household decisions: the money, our weekend time, and our vacations. The bills must be paid on time, the beds must be made by morning and the dishes out of the sink by evening." Even her husband and teenage kids get tired of her controlling nature and "they are quick to remind me that they can make up their own minds and don't like to be told what to do. I listen, but it's still hard to give up my controlling nature."

Isabella knows when she needs to back off. She must learn to trust more, set healthier boundaries, and allow herself to be more vulnerable. Like most controlling people, she has a strong need to get things done. Yet, it's the fear of losing control and her connections with others that drives her controlling behavior.

Her story is tame in comparison to the story I heard several years ago during a business dinner in Berlin. I sat next to the ex-wife of a business executive of a large electronics company who spent the evening telling tales of her ex-husband and his abusive, controlling ways. I remember her saying that "he was so angry all the time, ranging from cold, aloof silent treatment to sudden outbursts of rage. He controlled what I wore, how much money I had in my bank account, and often warned me not to talk back to him. The put-downs were constant, complaining I was fat, criticizing me in public, and telling me I was worthless. It took me five years to get out, and I promised myself never to date an abusive, controlling guy again."

CONTROLLING BEHAVIORS

- Questioning people's motives
- Never showing appreciation or compliments
- Controlling money and budget
- Constantly correcting other people
- Overplanning your partner's life
- Trivializing the concerns of other people
- Exhibiting verbal or physical abuse
- Demanding sex when you want it
- Finding fault in other people
- Giving orders to others

Those Who Are Controlled by Others

We all get a taste of losing control when we travel through airports. With little control over the weather, mechanical breakdowns, and delayed departures, we must accept reality and detach ourselves from our hopes and expectations. If we don't, we can make ourselves sick.

Most people don't like to be controlled because it makes us feel powerless, interferes with our ability to act using free will, and brings forth feelings of shame, anger, negative self-talk, and poor self-esteem. Accordingly, motivation wanes, trust is destroyed, fear is activated, and relationships are tarnished.

If we are controlled by others, we get stuck in an alternative reality and end up living in another person's world. The controllers attempt to define us by their needs and perceptions, rather than our own. Then, psychic boundaries are crossed, reality is blurred, and we lose ourselves and live a life foreign to who we are.

As we lose confidence, we set aside our own experiences and take on the other person's experience of us. We lose our ability to respond to our own needs and feel overt and covert attempts to control us. They can be simple gestures like "take out the trash," "feed the dog," or "clean your room," or more elaborate commentary that criticizes or castigates you.

Reactions to being an object of this kind of treatment can create multiple psychological results. Many people struggle to be heard and then fight back; others disconnect, feeling fearful, lonely, and exhausted. Some even feel erased and think they deserve the abuse. It's amazing how a powerful, demanding, and selfish person can manipulate, confuse, and diminish another human being. Lamentably, it happens on a regular basis.

For some of us, the lack of control becomes ingrained into our personalities. Victims believe they have little control over their work, life is predictably negative, and people and the world disappoint them. They live life blaming others. Fatalists have a different lens, believing that life is beyond their control, everything is constantly changing, and nobody can predict the future. They live life tossed around by uncertainty.

In all these situations, we lose our confidence in self-efficacy; lose our self-control by relinquishing our power to another person; and diminish our self-mastery by behaving in a passive, dependent manner. This abuse of power can be seen at our dinner tables, inside our teams, with friends, and through our institutions, like the church, politics, and the media.

It's important, though, to remember that sometimes those being controlled by others cause their own problems by not taking responsibility themselves. When this happens, all parties are angry, and these resentments can simmer under the surface for a long time.

A College Student Discovers His Career

"Today, I feel very fulfilled about what I'm doing at work and where my life is going, but it wasn't always that way," says Matt, a doctor in physical therapy.

"My parents are both engineers with a practical mindset. When I was getting ready for college, they immediately pushed me into the field of engineering. They stated emphatically, 'If we're going to pay for your college, we want you to start supporting yourself and making money.' I tried to talk to them about alternatives, but I felt that I was being controlled.

"As you can imagine, I didn't like my engineering major, and I approached my parents several times to change it. We had numerous arguments, but they kept insisting that, after I graduated, I would get an engineering job, and everything would be just fine. Despite my preferences, I felt guilty because they were paying for my education. But, boy, was I miserable and resentful toward my mother because she kept pushing me on this path. It was ruining our relationship."

Matt got out of school and worked for two years at a natural gas company, doing bridge design work. "I didn't like the job and felt like I was wasting my time. You have eight hours a day to do what you want to do. That's a third of your life, why not do something that brings you joy, passion, and fulfillment. Fortunately, I had a 'second job' doing CrossFit training and loved thinking about how the body works and manages pain. I decided what I really loved was physical therapy.

"I remember telling my mom on the phone one night that I had signed up for PT school. That conversation did not go well. In fact, it was a really, really upsetting argument. She went off on a familiar rant: 'You're going to have to quit your job; you're going to be poor; you might be homeless. I paid for you to go to engineering school, and we wasted money on PT?'

"Now, my mom is a good woman, but she couldn't help herself. My dad was an alcoholic, and I could never understand how much his alcoholism was affecting her. She fought for years to control my dad's drinking, and she wanted to make sure my brother and I had secure jobs and that we were always safe and happy in our lives. But, I reacted to her, just like she reacted to me, without reflecting on myself. As I look back on that now, I see the situation totally differently. Then I decided to see a therapist.

"Once I got to PT school, she was like, 'Wow, you really like what you're doing,' and she saw how much happier I was. I was doing something that was really fulfilling and that totally changed our relationship. I think she got in touch with the fact that she was also an engineer, had an engineering job, didn't like it, and quit, and went back to school to become a teacher. Today, she loves teaching."

Matt has learned a lot as the person being controlled in this situation. "I learned that I control what I control, and I must let go of the other things. I can't control how people react to me, but I do have the capacity to control my own life. Going back to PT school allowed me to do something for myself instead of for someone else. I took my life back. In retrospect, I wish I had done things differently and had taken control of the situation earlier."

Despite her blind spots and best intentions, Matt's mother was controlling him. To get out of the cage, Matt had to reach deep inside himself to follow his heart, tap into his inner truth, and develop the agency, confidence, and personal power needed to protect his boundaries and free himself from her handcuffs. Only then could he feel joy, be free, and reach his highest potential.

The Passive-Aggressive Folks

Passive aggression is one of the more popular forms of control. Because it is easy to express and hidden from sight, you don't have to take responsibility for it. Not a bad deal. However, it can create havoc in relationships at home and work.

In contrast to direct control, this type of control is seemingly innocuous and understated, yet it expresses real negative emotions and aggressive motives in indirect ways. And it can show up as verbal language, nonverbal behavior, or physical actions.

So how do you recognize it when you see it? It's there when your spouse pouts, withdraws, and punishes you with silent treatment. It is manifest when your son doesn't clean his room, procrastinates, and makes excuses for his behavior. It raises its claws when your girlfriend, who is nice to your face, talks behind your back. Or it's obvious when the neighbor who denies feeling upset about the fence then acts out physically by slamming the gate and turning up the music to annoy you.

At work, we are all familiar with our passive-aggressive colleagues. They're the ones who drag their feet on projects and miss deadlines; they withhold information and sabotage the work of others. Or they complain about being wronged and keep score in the office.

Some people learn this behavior from their family upbringing; others develop these habits along the journey of life. In all cases, direct emotions are usually discouraged, feelings are not shared, people learn to be conflict averse and avoid difficult conversations with others. This chronic behavior typically erodes trust and puts extra pressure on relationships so that they cannot thrive.

The psychology behind this behavior is clear: folks are uncomfortable with difficult emotions, even though they carry lots of resentment. They're afraid that if they let these feelings out of Pandora's box, the emotions will not be validated by others, or they will overwhelm people with their anger.

Conflict Averse and Passive-Aggressive

"My father was full of bluster, quick to anger, and often crossed the line and hurt people, including me," laments Scott, a middle manager at a large manufacturing firm. As a result, "I tend to be conflict averse and not a big risk-taker. I'm also known to be passive-aggressive at times. I adjust to others' needs and probably don't get everything I want out of life.

"I find myself lowering the bar on my career expectations and swallowing my feelings to avoid confrontation. I do accomplish a lot in my life; I just do it indirectly at times." Most people know passive aggression as anger directed at another person; but as Scott illustrates, indirect anger can be directed at yourself, too, and can undermine your own control.

"I love to tease people with cutting comments and sarcasm. It's not unusual for me to get quiet, withdraw, pout, and shut down. It's meant to tease out an issue without any significant collateral damage.

"Today, I live a balanced life. I set realistic goals. I guess I've never been a fan of people overly dedicated to their careers. I have more money than I ever thought, but I do know my lowered expectations have affected my career success.

"One thing is true: I'm especially good at relationships. I have great friends, and I'm sensitive to others. And I have a special kind of intuition that serves me well in life."

Scott is a good guy. His relationship with his father likely influenced what we see today. Parental anger is difficult for children to process. They often feel responsible and respond with obedience or learn to shy away from conflict and avoid confrontation altogether. But the anger must go somewhere or be swept under the rug for another day. It's only natural for these conflicts to show their ugly heads through passive-aggressive actions.

TIPS FOR THE PASSIVE-AGGRESSIVES

- Ask yourself why you are angry or resentful toward others.
- Notice the behaviors that express your resentments indirectly.
- Practice more assertive behaviors that communicate directly.
- Access feelings of forgiveness toward those you are angry at.
- Take the high road and be more collaborative in situations.

TIPS FOR THE RECIPIENTS OF PASSIVE AGGRESSION

- Recognize the signs of passive-aggressive behavior.
- Manage your feelings and avoid blaming others.
- Take control over what you have control over.
- Give people the opportunity to share their direct feelings.
- Share the mutual consequences if the behavior continues.

The People Pleasers

A type of control that can be particularly damaging to the psyche is developed in early childhood when children learn to get what they want by being a people pleaser. Sensing unrest, mistrust, or conflict, children, being especially vulnerable, desire a happy environment and want to make everyone happy. They learn from an early age to please others and often use their own power to manipulate the people around them. Eventually, most people pleasers subdue their identity, losing a part of themselves.

People pleasers can also find themselves stuck in a psychic-neurotic lock with their partner. In this insecure or codependent relationship, each partner brings his/her own neurotic thinking and behavior into the dyad. As a result, both parties never get their needs met. One familiar example is the push/pull scenario where one person chases and grasps for more intimacy and connection while the other partner feels smothered and runs for the hills.

Often, these kinds of relationships become repeating patterns, either modeled first by your parents or copied from previous relationships in your past. Let's meet Brian, whose people pleasing led to a serious drinking problem.

How Control and Pleasing Led to Drink

"My job was to keep people happy. And my happiness was completely tied to the happiness of the people around me. It became ingrained in me," says Brian, a successful healthcare executive who was able to keep this secret hidden from the world—until the red wine nearly destroyed his life.

"I had a crappy childhood," Brian remembers vividly. "My father was an alcoholic, and we were always walking on eggshells, waiting for his temper to explode. His unpredictable verbal criticisms led me to believe that I was never good enough.

"When I was fourteen, he decided to leave us, and I was the one who had to tell my mom he was going to divorce her. I'll never forget that responsibility. I quickly became my mom's surrogate spouse—and the middle person between them for the next ten years. In retrospect, I learned my controlling behavior from my dad."

At work, Brian exceeded everyone's expectations. "You would see the best employee you've ever met. I worked hard, worked weekends, whatever was needed. People say that I was a great father, too, until I started traveling.

"I was always raising the bar to make people happy, driven to control everything and everyone around me. I liked to say I was playing chess; I had twelve moves at any time. My challenge was that I was always searching for my own happiness and never felt good enough as a person." Later, Brian would find out this mindset was at the expense of himself.

Overwhelmed by these internal pressures, Brian shares that "I started drinking, which lasted twenty years, the last three were the absolute worst. I never had a real deep understanding of relationships, and as I got more isolated, they grew increasingly transactional.

"Everything was about red wine when it finally took over my life. I went to wine dinners and wineries. I wrote wine blogs. I collected wine in my basement; today there's still fifty thousand dollars of bottles sitting idle downstairs. It didn't take long before I would feel empty and vulnerable. Nobody reacted the way I wanted them to act anymore. My strength—my people pleasing, controlling nature—became my vulnerability." This realization prompted the beginning of the end for Brian's old life.

With deep self-awareness, a commitment to the Serenity Prayer, a search for his own happiness, and not raising his hand for everything, Brian was able to detach as best he could from his attachment to control and alcohol. "Today, I enjoy my wife and family, golf when I can, and I'm aware of my own needs, for my own benefit, not for everyone else's."

Brian's early scars with poor self-esteem led him to look for external validation for his internal holes. His people-pleasing skills were his way out. As he served others, he quickly lost a part of himself. He learned along the way how to control others, but these tenuous skills lacked staying power. Red wine was the medication that helped manage his sadness and anxiety. But that escape didn't work either. By trusting himself and being vulnerable, Brian was able to find joy and peace in his life.

THE ASPIRATION OF VULNERABILITY

Detaching from control can be an emotionally complex process. We all started from a different vantage point, learned different lessons from our past, and have distinct personalities. Yet there are some universal principles that apply to all types of control. Here's a look at each one.

Befriend Your Vulnerability

Being vulnerable is the lubricant for releasing your attachment to control. Whether you're controlling others, being controlled, being passive-aggressive, or pleasing people, if we learn to trust ourselves and let ourselves be vulnerable, we can detach from this attachment.

How does this work? Simply put, you are more likable, more trustworthy, and more authentic when you allow yourself to be vulnerable. Remember: Vulnerability is not weakness, but rather showing yourself to be human with the same flaws and imperfections as everyone else. People don't want others to be *weak*, but they do want them to be *real*. This reveals a vulnerability that demonstrates not only your humanity but also your capacity to manage and triumph over personal flaws.

In a counterintuitive way, the less control we have, the more we want to grasp. And the more we grasp, the less control we end up getting. A heavy-handed desire for control or an unwillingness to give your control away can come at a hefty price for yourself and others.

For the controllers, being vulnerable is not wearing your heart on your sleeve. Rather, it is recognizing that giving up some control begets more influence, and by empowering others, you share the control. Try to find love and forgiveness in your heart and identify what you can give up in the short term for long-term gain.

Not surprisingly, for those being controlled, you are already vulnerable with another person. Be open to new ways of thinking about vulnerability, like asking yourself what you want, standing up for yourself, being assertive, and publicly labeling the controller's behavior. Remember, no one can take away who you really are as a person.

For those who are passive-aggressive, vulnerability is getting in touch with your difficult emotions, your desire to avoid conflict, and the resentment you feel toward the other person. Try being more direct, ask a lot of questions, and discuss the emotional dance between yourself and others.

For the people pleasers, you are vulnerable when you choose to live in another person's shoes at the expense of yourself. You think that you are controlling others, but, in fact, they are controlling you. Hold on to your control and your self-esteem, and let others figure this out for themselves.

Translate Trust into the Tangible

Mistrust is the centerpiece for our attachment to control. When we mistrust ourselves, or other people, relationships are built on shaky ground. Controllers mistrust the capabilities of the controlled, while victims, people pleasers, and passive-aggressives lack confidence in themselves. Without trust, we are vulnerable to this attachment.

Detaching from control requires allowing yourself to develop a sense of trust, that intangible element that we all desire and need for mature relationships. We know when trust is present and lament its absence. Trust emerges when we grow out of our childish need to protect ourselves and learn how to build trust with others.

Trust can be elusive, having a dual nature through a door that swings both ways: Not only do we have to build trust with others, but we first need to learn to trust ourselves. To be trustworthy, we must maintain mutual respect for others *and* ourselves. But, trust is a very fragile quality, for, once earned, it can evaporate with a careless word or deed. Relationships built on trust are priceless, but they can break down if either of its dual components is absent.

Here are some actions to build trust from my first book, *The Healthy Company*:

- *Credibility*: Be truthful: your written and spoken words are always believable, and your actions are consistent with your words.
- *Dependability*: Make good on your promises and commitments. Your word is your bond, even in the most difficult or trying situations.
- *Predictability*: Be consistent in your values and temperament. You do not spring unpleasant or irresponsible surprises on people and do not engage in emotional outbursts.
- *Emotional safety*: Validate people's health, feelings, self-image, or principles. Take their concerns and interests to heart and provide enough safety to allow them to express themselves.
- *Valuing the common good*: Your words and deeds are driven not solely by self-interest but also by a desire for everyone to benefit. This requires wisdom and self-awareness to understand that the two are not mutually exclusive.

Mutual respect, trust, and open communication are the hallmarks of a great relationship. When two parties practice these principles, they connect as mature adults and are willing to be vulnerable with each other.

Practice Confident Humility

Confident humility, a seeming paradox, is a critical one that helps us build great relationships, and it especially helps people who struggle with the issue of control.

This paradox sits on a continuum: at one end is arrogance; at the other, self-doubt. Residing in the healthier middle is confidence and humility. The goal is to stay in the middle of the continuum. The four points on the scale are:

- *Arrogance*: You are self-serving, think you are better than others, and feel entitled to special treatment. You interact with fear, intimidation, and manipulation.
- *Confidence*: You possess positive self-esteem, have clear values, and act courageously. You defend yourself, share power, and act responsibly.
- *Humility*: You accept your shortcomings and limitations and listen and learn from others. You recognize people, empower others to succeed, and appreciate others' strengths.
- *Self-doubt*: You question your abilities, are insecure about your power, and fear failure. You give too much power away to others and accept their negative opinions of you.

You naturally lean to one side or the other of this paradox. Under stress, confidence can present as arrogance and humility can look like self-doubt. The best way to counteract this imbalance is lean to the opposite side of the paradox. You have great capacity to monitor and modulate in the middle ground.

To move from arrogant to confident:

- Take time to find out what others think and feel before you act.
- Ask someone you trust to help you understand your vulnerabilities.
- Learn to be a teacher *and* a learner.
- Ask questions more than you give answers.
- Let yourself be challenged, work through your discomfort, and be open to new ways of doing things.
- Show your appreciation and celebrate others' successes.
- Ask people what excites and motivates them.

To move from self-doubt to humble:

- Make a list of your strong qualities and repeat them regularly.
- Live your values every day and stand up for what you believe.
- Say what you mean and do what you say.
- Question and reject the showy signs of power.
- Remember that arrogant people are insecure.
- Trust yourself more than you trust others.
- Work with a coach to deepen your confidence skills.

From Peacemaking to Leadership

"Attention, affection, and acceptance. That's what's driven me in life. It's the source of my attachment to control, and the catalyst for my success."

To understand Molly, we must reach back to her childhood. She recalls that "I'm the youngest of three, and there are seven years between my next sibling and me. They were all fully baked by the time I came out. My brother was dominant and controlling, my sister was gifted and oppositional, and I was wired differently. My house was volatile and full of smart people. And as the baby in the family, I learned how to fight back, stand up for myself, and I got all the attention.

"I also became the peacemaker in the family, and a very strong part of me was the people pleaser. I would go into pleasing mode because I didn't want to see antagonism or conflict. I noticed I could control my world and shape my environment, just like an architect does, by becoming an expert at reading people. I figured out what people wanted and didn't want, and what I was good at. I was always aware of people's opinions of me, and people were drawn to me because of my value.

"My need for attention, affection, and acceptance led me to success. But success was not a driver for me. I didn't say 'I'm going to be the head of a company.' Nor did I have a plan. But I did end up getting attention for my people skills. I just wanted to have fun and be around people. I was lucky to be paired with people who saw the value of my personality." Eventually, Molly became the CEO of her consulting firm and built a fellowship who loves her.

Youngest children show common traits: charming, fun-loving, outgoing, and persistent. Molly fits the profile. Vulnerability from her early childhood became her strength in adulthood. By seeking acceptance and attention early on, she became intuitive and well versed in shaping her human environment. With trust, warmth, and confident humility, she became a good listener and negotiator, and people liked her leadership style. Molly ended up creating her own definition of success.

Let me leave you with one final thought when dealing with the attachment to control. Don't forget to practice the Serenity Prayer.

Grant me the serenity to accept the things I cannot change, the courage to change the things I can, and the wisdom to know the difference.

Reflections

- Are you a naturally trusting and trustworthy person, or are you cynical and mistrustful of others?
- What is your reaction to people who express vulnerability? Do you judge them, or is it safer being around them?
- If you find yourself being controlled by others, what can you do to take back your power?
- If you could become less controlling, what would your actions look like?
- What weaknesses can you accept and share with others? How would doing this make you feel?
- In what way will facing vulnerability bring you release, strength, truth, and peace of mind?

FIVE

THE ATTACHMENT TO PERFECTION

- Do you operate with unusually high standards?
- Would you consider yourself a workaholic?
- Are you a chronic worrier?
- Is it important for you to perform perfectly?
- Do you get embarrassed when you make a mistake?

You walk into a job interview, excited and prepared to show the interviewers that you would make a great addition to their company. Thirty minutes into the interview, they pop the question you knew was coming: "Can you tell me about one of your weaknesses?" You know enough not to say you're a micromanager. And you certainly wouldn't say that you like to get ahead at the expense of others. So you come up with a safe, endearing response: "I'm a perfectionist."

Little did you know that very response dashed your chances in the competition. Enlightened interviewers know better about the troubling effects of perfectionism.

Welcome to the "Attachment to Perfection," in which we will delve into its causes, beliefs, behaviors, and consequences, demonstrating how an alternative commitment to excellence would be a much better choice.

Believe it or not, the causes of being a perfectionist arise in our miraculous brain, which, according to Timothy Wilson, researcher at the University of Virginia, can absorb eleven million pieces of information a second, yet we can only process about forty.

Today's complex, race-car-speeding world demands a complex mind, capable of receiving, sorting, and digesting more new ideas in a week than an eighteenth-century citizen encountered in a lifetime! Additionally, social media and artificial intelligence are accelerating this deluge of information.

However, the human mind has its limitations. The staggering amount of news from the *New York Times* itself can send our brains into hyperventilation. Fortunately, we have a built-in generator that scans this onslaught, collects new information, and expands our minds every day.

WE ARE DEEPLY CURIOUS BEINGS

As it turns out, curiosity saves us by its very nature. As humans, we arrive in the world deeply curious. Children are intensely curious for much of their childhood, when their brains develop neurological pathways every day that reinforce their learning. That is why, for instance, when children learn a foreign language in their youth, they can tap into that data bank for the rest of their lives.

So, curiosity is the cornerstone for sifting through what is necessary and what is extraneous, settling on the best ways to fill in the blanks.

Having curiosity establishes an optimal avenue for your growth, personally and intellectually. Acquiring and assessing a body of knowledge builds a framework for you to see the world and your place in it. It fires your imagination, assists you in grappling with mentally complex problems, and allows you to set fresh goals repeatedly. And, it can prompt you to fashion a route for a better future.

The popular mantra "Use it or lose it" does not apply only to your body maintenance. Indeed, your brain's wonderful neuroplasticity allows you to create new, expanded networks if you continue to learn throughout your life. New weblike thought patterns help you link information in new ways. This expands your original ideas and mindsets, strengthening new and established networks through repetition and time. Stretching areas of your mind prevents it from atrophying. The opposite is true too. If you do not stretch your brain by being curious and seeking new vistas, certain regions begin to atrophy.

Surprisingly, you may find that your marvelous brain continues to "think" at night, when it gets busy storing the day's activities and creating new insights. It may also surprise you that our minds are most active at night, when it links the day's activities and learning with existing memories and habits and creating new insights, emerging the next morning smarter, more creative, and more conscious.

Several years ago, on a trip to India, I met Kumar Birla, the chairman of one of their largest companies, Aditya Birla Group, a large global conglomerate. I remember him saying his secret weapon to success was his learning. He said, "Every day is a new day for me. Every inflection point is a very powerful period of learning. It's like an exploding star that emits a lot of light within a short burst of time. So, I push myself and everyone around me to always be learning. Know what you enjoy doing and go after it. Aggressively seek out learning, know what you don't know, which skills you don't have, and what you need to understand better."

OUR JOURNEY TO SELF-IMPROVEMENT

Self-improvement is an innate, intrinsic motivation that drives us as individuals to determine the course of our lives. It's natural to want to improve. To many, the quest for self-improvement enhances our need to lead an autonomous life. To some, it could be an exercise of their free will. Regardless of its definition, it impels you to learn, conquer the unknown, take risks, and explore the world around you.

With self-improvement, life becomes a learning adventure that confirms for us that hard work matters more than intelligence, leveling the playing field. Pride and satisfaction result from being able to improve; it produces an inward smile and a hearty pat on the back with each step in the journey, rewarding you silently. And giving you something to look forward to: a purpose and a goal.

There are lots of reasons why we avoid the pursuit of self-improvement. Having to learn new patterns of behavior, exposing ourselves to new situations, and risking potential embarrassments can be tough initially—even humbling—exposing us to vulnerability, a place that few people enjoy. Yet true learning and growth through self-improvement require some diligence and willingness to feel those emotions honestly and courageously.

If you are reluctant to be around more experienced, "smarter" people, you might retreat from the open exchanges that could enlighten you. Or simply avoiding risk and edgy uncertainty could keep you from improvement. Sometimes, people might react to venturing out by building walls with a "know-it-all" attitude. Other deterrents could be fear of failure, lack of confidence, or the desire to avoid the discomfort of not knowing. Resolving to a plan of self-improvement demands a full commitment, for there is not a CliffsNotes version or a shortcut.

Perfectionism can be a big obstacle too. As we will soon learn, trying to be perfect is a form of obsessive self-improvement. Your perfectionism prompts you to be too critical of yourself and sabotages you and the people around you.

THE PURSUIT OF EXCELLENCE

It is a commonplace that "everyone wants to do a good job." With the right opportunities, if we work hard, commit to self-improvement, tap into our special talents, and pursue excellence, we can achieve personal satisfaction, material success, and professional recognition. As Wilma Koutstaal described in *Psychology Today*, "Excellence is a state of very high, yet attainable, standards in an effortful, engaged and determined, yet flexible manner."

People who strive for excellence are generally comfortable with themselves. They tend to be authentic and self-accepting; more open to diverse experiences; and they allow themselves to make mistakes, learn lessons, and bounce back with ease. They also create environments where others grow in capability and performance. This combination of skills regularly leads to superior performance.

What distinguishes people who commit to excellence versus perfection is their acceptance of their own imperfections. While we are by nature imperfect human beings, the healthiest among us accept and celebrate the imperfections in all of us.

As Stephen Hawking once said: "One of the basic rules of the universe is that nothing is perfect. Perfection does not exist. Without imperfection, neither you nor I would exist." We will delve into this later when we discuss the aspiration of excellence. Let me give you a quick example.

A Tale of Two Athletes

Our society admires those rare athletes who excel, towering over even the greatest who came before them. Michael Phelps, the Olympic superstar, is one of them. After wild success at the Athens and Beijing Olympics, Michael experienced a very public downward spiral that quickly tainted his athletic success. What led to Michael's downfall? How did he fall prey to the power of perfectionism? After he struggled with multiple DUIs, drugs, alcohol, and strained and broken relationships, he sensibly checked himself in to The Meadows, an inpatient treatment facility. There, Michael was able to be honest with himself and discover who he really was.

By his own admission, he drove himself to be perfect, fixated on being special and eminently successful. These goals torpedoed his ability to see himself as a whole person. Paradoxically, if Phelps hadn't been so committed to becoming the world's greatest swimmer, he almost certainly would not have achieved what he did.

However, what he did not consider was that "being perfect" in one skill or area of performance doesn't necessarily mean that it would make him perfect in all areas of life. Phelps's crisis forced him to realize that being the perfect swimmer didn't make him a whole human being. The difference between striving for excellence and pursuing perfection is that the first encourages ambition; the other leads to obsession.

Written into Michael Phelps's DNA and hardwired into his psyche were all of life's accelerators: drive, desire, practice, focus, resilience, and confidence—all desirable qualities. But these accelerators became his weaknesses too. Rehabilitation woke him up to the attachment to perfection and helped him see that even the "best in the world" need to work hard to be more conscious. Today, he is a global advocate for mental health.

Another sports giant, Tim Howard, the star goalie of the USA soccer team, presents a different kind of example. This World Cup holder of sixteen saves in a single match explains his successes to managing his emotions and pursuing excellence, claiming, "I don't really get too high or too low." By locking himself into the present moment, he takes each challenge one at a time, and he does not obsess over mistakes or errors, channeling his competitive spirit to the immediate play in front of him.

Howard learned that coping behavior from battling every day with Tourette syndrome, a neurological disorder that causes involuntary verbal or physical tics, which can be wildly distracting. Imagine trying to guard against the best soccer scorers with your head churning and your body ticking unpredictably. This disability from childhood taught Howard to turn a disadvantage into a competitive edge, making him a stronger person and better team leader.

ATTACHMENT TO PERFECTION

Perfectionism is way of thinking, feeling, and acting based on idealized, flawless, and excessively high standards. In reality, these high standards are unsustainable. Excellence and perfectionism both pursue high standards, but excellence is flexible; perfectionism is unforgiving. It's the difference between confidence and doubt, taking risks and fearing risks, being accepting or judgmental, and our willingness to be wrong versus having to be right.

In our performance-oriented society, striving for perfection is often central to our development. Some families initiate the process with inordinately high expectations for their children. Schools are increasingly competitive with demanding, rigorous standards. As people enter graduate schools, the competition intensifies. When we enter our careers, the expectations are clear that bigger salaries and promotions come from intense competition with our peers. Social media, like Facebook and LinkedIn, call for perfect presentations of our ideal lives. While the sports and entertainment industries reinforce the push for perfection, I wish politics would do the same.

One study that examined forty thousand American, British, and Canadian college students, ages eighteen through twenty-five, found that a majority showed signs of what the author called "multi-dimensional perfectionism—meaning perfectionism driven by unrealistically high expectations." So it shouldn't surprise us that the attachment to perfection is a worldwide epidemic.

Many of us develop in our careers inductively from generalist to specialist. As a graduate student, you learn to write code and eventually, you are hired as a cyber expert. Industry experts emerge from a person who trains as a cross-industry employee. After you graduate from medical school, you hang out your shingle for a few years as a general practitioner, but soon graduate again as a nephrologist. Getting stuck in an "expert" category allows you to believe that "I am what I know," and lets you languish in the discipline, becoming more and more inflexible every year because the mindset of being right and perfect is the most important metric.

The Perfect Word

Rae, a freelance writer, has worked with me for many years. By her own admission, she's a perfectionist. She says that "people pay me to be precise and to help them find the perfect word, the perfect organization, the perfect question, or the perfect tool. I've always been attached to perfection. Yet I'm more aware of it as I have gotten older.

"I remember from school days: A's were a good score; A+ was better; B's were totally unacceptable. I was always pushing myself to make things better, whether they improved the product or not.

"Being attached to perfection is exhausting. I'm always looking to raise the bar, to look for another option. And I feel hijacked by perfection. I need everything organized around me. If there's a lot of mess, I get distracted; I cannot think clearly unless my surroundings are neat and tidy. I also resist showing anybody an unfinished product unless I've had a chance to fix all the errors.

"Working on a team is hard for me where two minds are better than one, and many minds are best. But it helped me back away from having to be perfect the first time out of the gate." Rae shared a couple stories about working with me.

"I remember sitting in a meeting with you, and I wanted to make a point, but I got stuck on a word. I couldn't think of it, and I just said, 'I don't know the word.' And you put your hand on my arm and made a big deal out of it. You said, 'Oh my gosh, she's not perfect.' It's like the bottom fell out of my stomach at that moment. I felt that you had called me out on the carpet. It was not something I wanted to admit. But then you turned and looked at me and said, 'And we love you anyway.' It was a wonderful message that said, 'It's OK to work here. It's OK to be imperfect; we love you because you're imperfect.'

"On the flip side, I remember another time when you said to me, 'Rae, it's not your best work, since we had agreed this was only the first draft.'" As I recall, this comment wasn't very insightful on my part. Rae remembers, "I was upset all evening, and it took me 'til midnight to figure out exactly what bugged me. I felt unjustly reprimanded for being imperfect, my Achilles' heel. So I wrote you an email and stated clearly what my thoughts and position were, and how your response bothered me. And you called and apologized. I just needed some acknowledgment from you that it was unfair for you to expect the first draft to be perfect.

"Today, I'm working hard to acknowledge my perfectionism as part of being human. I try to identify my triggers, explore the underlying feelings, and embrace 'good enough.' I'm learning to treat myself with kindness and find that I'm more compassionate regarding the foibles of others."

Let's dig deeply into the psychology of perfection. How do perfectionists think? How do they feel? And how do they act toward others?

How Perfectionists Think

- *Excessive standards*: With their hyperactive minds, perfectionists see themselves as thorough. They think in extremes, always acquiring new information, and stay alert to anything that goes wrong. Preoccupied with making the right choice, they are always looking for imperfections and search for the exact right choice.

- *Inner rule book*: Rigid thinking and need for order creates a mental neatness in their minds. Their inner rule book guides their thinking, and their lists of lists keeps them on track. They also have an overgrown sense of responsibility and duty and hate making mistakes.

- *Procrastination*: Cautious and contemplative, they admittedly think too much, dwell on things that may not be relevant, always searching for right answers. Their need to find the perfect answer exacerbates procrastination, creates indecisiveness, and undermines their spontaneity.

- *Vulnerable self-image*: Perfectionists measure their self-worth on how smart they are and how they perform. Their unrelenting ability to analyze and judge, along with their self-criticism, envisions the worst possible outcomes, magnifies small gaffes out of proportion, and leads them to believe they are not as competent as they should be.

How Perfectionists Feel

- *Pressure to produce*: There is an inner pressure to produce all the time. Perfectionists are especially sensitive to being pressured by others and sensitive to their demands, real or imagined. Their angst about all-or-nothing thinking and their anxiety about performance often leads to burnout.

- *Chronic worrier*: Perfectionists rarely enjoy the moment, as they worry often about what people are thinking about them. These feelings of insecurity create high stress and anxiety and make it difficult for them to relax. They fear having people see their flaws and being found out.

- *Constantly critical*: Emotionally, their minds lean toward the negative and their critical attitude easily frustrates them. They rarely enjoy their excellent work, get angry with themselves when it's not perfect, and can get sad and demoralized. Their critical attitude can also be projected outward by being defensive and making it difficult to forgive others.

- *Fear of vulnerability*: Many fears sit underneath the surface of their ultracompetent demeanor. Guarded and unable to show feelings, they are often fearful of losing control, fearful of trusting self and others, and being dependent. Underlying these fears is a deep desire to be accepted and loved.

How Perfectionists Act

- *Workaholic*: Perfectionists are driven, often at the expense of their health and well-being. As they ruminate about work, they can miss deadlines and opportunities. They often devote every working hour to doing or thinking about work; consequently, they can shortchange their children, ignore their partners, or forget about friends. Excessive workaholism can ultimately lead to fatigue and diminished productivity.

- *Constant improvement*: A desire to be the best and an obsessive commitment to self-improvement demands perfect solutions. By measuring oneself constantly, perfectionists improve and polish every piece of work to avoid mistakes and receive the adulation for which they yearn and feel they deserve.

- *Stubborn and oppositional:* Perfectionists like to do things their way. It is not unusual for a perfectionist to act like a saint or to be a picky prima donna who imposes harsh judgments on spouses, friends, and work colleagues. Micromanagement is often their preferred style of leadership.
- *Intense pride*: Despite many of these challenging qualities, perfectionists take great pride in their work. They see themselves working the hardest, demanding the best, and delivering exemplary work. And this is all true, until it's not.

Clearly, not all perfectionists have all these qualities. There are some perfectionists who are outstanding workers and human beings. However, it's important to remember that a true attachment to perfection can be hazardous to your health.

Going Dark with Perfection

"Being perfect on the outside. That's what my childhood was like. It was unspoken. It was all about looking good, sounding good. It was projecting an image, and you couldn't show any crack in your armor. As you can imagine, I got easily frustrated as a child and I couldn't do anything about it."

Jonathan, a successful healthcare attorney and executive, shared an early story with me. "I'm probably seven years old. And I'm kneeling on my bed doing my spelling homework. I have one of those big Husky pencils in my hand, and I can't spell a word. I got so angry at myself that I whipped the damn pencil across the room. It made a big crack in the bookshelf. You can imagine how frustrated I was.

"Today, one of my patterns is to go dark, to shut down my feelings of resentment when I feel pressured to be perfect, yet I don't have any control over it. Little things can quickly turn into larger issues when the veneer of perfection is threatened. If I can't see an honest way out, I will manipulate the situation, so I still come out looking good, whether it's the right thing to do or not."

Jonathan admits he can't stand being controlled by others. "The less control I have, the more anxious I get. And I take things too personally. Then I start to run into trouble with my interpersonal relationships. I feel like I'm being taken advantage of, suddenly I'm angry, and my resentments get larger. Then the angry little kid with the pencil emerges. I kind of go dark to protect myself.

"I carry around attachments to control, perfection, and success. It can be so exhausting. There was a long period when having a few drinks and taking opioids and benzos was just magic for me. The combination helped me not care at all whether I was perfect, had control or not, and subdued the anxiety—until it didn't work anymore. Today, I just accept reality and deal with my difficult feelings."

Jonathan continues to work hard to accept his imperfections. He relinquishes control when he must. He manages his resentments as they appear. And he remains committed to his sobriety. You can't ask for much more than that.

Now, some people believe that perfectionists get a bad rap, and I can see their point. Nothing is wrong with dreaming, setting ideals, and working incredibly hard to reach a goal. But, when you are intensely attached to a certain outcome, like a perfect performance, you are at risk of disappointment and failure. By enjoying the pursuit while detaching from perfection, you loosen the chains and free yourself to fully enjoy the experience.

THE ASPIRATION OF EXCELLENCE

I have known Brian Cornell for many years. He has been leading companies ever since we met, taking him into the executive suites at Safeway,

Michaels stores, PepsiCo, and Sam's Club. Today, he is the chief executive officer of Target. He knows firsthand the benefits of dedicating himself to excellence. Part of his process is learning to be comfortable as a teacher and a student.

Brian shared this story with me: "Leaders who are mature recognize that they can't be perfect. I was criticized for wanting to be perfect at an early stage in my career. I wanted to make sure I was completely buttoned up. One day, my old boss sat me down and said, 'Brian, you do great work, you have an amazing work ethic, and you're always organized. Everything is perfect and every word's been thought out. But you should spend more time just being yourself, being genuine and staying approachable.'" Brian uses this lesson every day as he leads Target through the storm clouds in today's modern business world.

Here are some suggestions for achieving excellence and loosening your attachment to perfection.

Fall in Love with Your Imperfections

Stop trying to be perfect. You are an imperfect human being by nature. Acknowledge your perfectionism right out of the gate and view life as a journey of experimentation and continuous learning. Get comfortable with ambiguity and expect to make some mistakes. Practice mental toughness and mental tenderness. You deserve both.

Good enough is good enough. Work toward progress, not perfection. Expose yourself to situations that you fear, like your fear of embarrassment when you make a mistake in front of people. You might even practice being imperfect with others. Cultivate your confidence and humility—even if it hurts. And recognize your tendency to worry. When you feel anxiety, try meditation or take a walk in nature.

- Stop judging and putting yourself down for being imperfect and recognize the beauty of your imperfections.

- Seek out experiences that take you out of your comfort zone and don't be afraid to ask for feedback.
- Have confidence that you will perform excellent work.

Confront Your Inner Hijackers

Your perfectionistic mind plays tricks on you. Change your internal dialogue and self-talk. Throw cold water on your inner critic, and stop comparing yourself with others. Distinguish what you can and cannot control. The more honest you are about the difference, the less time you will waste and the less angst you will experience.

Reframe who you are, how you think, and how you act. Remember you *can* change. Acknowledge how your thoughts and feelings hijack you. Let go of your fears of being wrong. Be aware of how the external forces in your life—bosses and colleagues, teachers, and social pressures—can dictate your perfectionism. Are they pressuring you to be perfect? Are you influenced by the success of others? Remember: you control how these forces affect you.

- Tell yourself positive thoughts about your performance.
- Know your most vulnerable situations, like when you receive negative feedback from others.
- Catch yourself being rigid and overorganizing your world.

Rebalance Your Work

Perfectionistic work is not productive work. Loosen the pressure to produce all the time. Be flexible with your excessive standards and know your breaking point when you might burn out, or you stop being creative or productive. Get rid of your inner rule book that stifles you and imposes unnecessary restrictions. Schedule your time realistically and beware of getting sidetracked by details. Sometimes, it's best to tackle your most difficult work first and remember to take breaks throughout the day.

If you happen to live or work with a perfectionist, be aware of their negative effect on you. The key is to stay engaged with healthy boundaries between the two of you. When they show their perfectionistic side, don't take their behavior personally; don't deny your own feelings, foster your own self-esteem; and don't be afraid to embrace your own imperfections.

- For the perfectionist, be flexible with your excessive standards that can blind and shackle you.
- Set smart goals that are *s*pecific, *m*easurable, *a*chievable, *r*ealistic, and *t*imely. Being SMART will help you avoid procrastination.
- Separate your work time from family and personal time. When you do, try to be in the moment with your partner, kids, and friends.

Act with Constructive Impatience

Perfectionism influences how you interact with others at work too. To minimize its impact, practice constructive impatience. The constructive side aims to create a psychologically safe environment for those around you. It's where people feel good about themselves, feel empowered to take risks, and are open to new ways of doing things. You are understanding and patient and show people they are valued.

Another side of you is impatient, wanting visible, immediate results. So you push and make demands not only for yourself but those around you. You want everyone, including yourself, to stretch their abilities and eagerly pursue their goals. The combination of a constructive mindset and impatience avoids the effects of perfectionism and fosters excellent work.

- Create a healthy, safe environment for people while focusing on results.
- Involve people in decisions while nudging them out of their comfort zones.
- Set higher goals while helping people find meaning in their work.

FINDING YOUR CREATIVE SOLUTION

Jim has been my business partner for over thirty years, and I've experienced his attachment to perfection firsthand—both the benefits and the costs. Jim explains, "When I prepare for a business engagement, I will overprepare and stay up to 11 PM the night before. I should have closed the books at 7 PM, and I would have gotten to the same outcome. To me, efficiency is measured in perfection, and that's the problem. As a kid, in preparing for a piano recital, I would literally spend hours trying to get it perfect.

"Nothing in life is perfect, but 'perfect' *does* exist as a thought form in my mind and my behavior. Fortunately, I'm able to stand above myself and watch as I try to be perfect, yet I continue to see the negative consequences of that practice. I don't want to move off my standard; I just try to manage my work so it doesn't get out of hand.

"Ironically, my love of music helped me with my obsessive need for perfection. Grounded in my classical training, I started improvising with my music. Today, much of my music is emergent, created in the moment, and out of the box. It is the art of experimentation. I go there, knowing there are a lot of unknowns. That's the heart of jazz. Jazz gives you a set of principles. Within that, you have incredible freedom.

"There's a significant connection between my improvisational music and my attachment to perfection. The music creates flexibility in my mind and frees me to loosen my attachment to being perfect." His strategy must be going right, for Jim has created seven albums and enjoyed performing at Carnegie Hall.

Tara tells a different story of creativity, where her acting talents helped her shed her perfectionistic ways so she could fall in love with her imperfect self—unconditionally.

"If I could have been perfect, everything would have been OK. At least, that's how I felt as a kid," says Tara, an actress and marketing expert. "My parents separated, and I had to take care of my fraternal brother who had a spectrum disorder. I needed to be a certain way for people to like me, so when I was ten, I took up ballet. I was the perfect ballerina. I practiced four times a week and all day on Saturday. Perfection was bred into me.

"Two things were going on inside me. One was that I didn't feel good about myself, and two, I had to get better all the time. To cover up these feelings, I started drinking in high school. It was a cool way to be popular, and it gave me a sense of security.

"I was a binge drinker. I would show up at school wearing the right clothes, the right makeup, and my hair looked fine. And then, at night, I would come home in a blackout. I looked horrible. Blackouts were my way of not having to be perfect, not worrying about myself, not worrying about my brother or my parents. I also had bad self-esteem, and I drowned it out with alcohol to feel sexy and smart. Drinking would temporarily amplify my self-image, then ultimately tear me right back down.

"In May 2000, at age twenty-six, I stopped drinking. I've been sober now for twenty-three years. The alcohol kicked my ass, and as the desire to drink wore off, with the help of a therapist, I started doing work on myself. My first order of business was finishing college and getting a master's degree.

"With my BFA from the Tisch School of Arts at New York University and an MA in communications from Georgetown, I started pursuing acting. I had amazing training, but it's such a hard business, so I continued to take classes at Second City. Here I learned to let my feelings out: to cry, laugh, and be funny. At the time, my friends at Second City inspired me to create a one-act play.

"I was eight years into my sobriety and wanted to showcase the wonderful women in sobriety. Women are good at hiding their alcoholism. We drink at home where people have no idea who we are. Their image of recovering alcoholics is of miserable, shameful people, smoking cigarettes in church basements. But we're an incredible community of people, and I wanted to showcase that image. It was a huge motivator for me."

The play gave Tara an opportunity to bring together the distinctive voices and images of alcoholic women. Tara talks proudly: "I molded myself into a character named Hope, and created characters of others that I portrayed with different personas. It was an incredible way to tell parts of my story and bring all the disparate parts of other women onstage. Over the years, I've brought the play into a variety of venues, including treatment centers, to show what recovery looks like.

"That play has had an enormous impact on my life. Today, I work as a vice president of marketing and fundraising for a nonprofit organization. Yet tomorrow, I'm going to a singing lesson with a friend who is a Broadway actress!"

Tara is a stellar example of a woman who went from a childhood full of shame and perfectionism, through a painful bout of alcoholism, to a life full of pride and self-love.

When she put her whole life onstage, you could see a healthy, happy, and creative woman giving back to her community. "Why not," she says, "I'm living on my terms, and I'm happy."

Reflections

- Where do your perfectionistic tendencies come from?
- Do you worry about making the right choices in life? What's the impact this has on you?
- Do you question your self-worth when you make mistakes? How do you talk to yourself when this happens?
- Are you a procrastinator? What are the consequences of this behavior?
- Do you feel an inner pressure to produce? What effect does this pressure have on you and the people around you?

SIX

THE ATTACHMENT TO SUCCESS

- Do you need to be successful to be happy?
- Do you define yourself by your achievements?
- Are you envious of other people's successes?
- Do you sometimes feel like a failure?
- Do you feel that something is missing in your life?

I remember when I first learned about the attachment to success. It was twenty-five years ago, and I was so excited that I had finally gotten a breakfast appointment with the senior human resources executive inside one of the most respected companies in Washington, DC. I had been trying to get the meeting for quite a while. We had a great conversation talking about business, the market, golf, you know—the regular business topics.

As we were walking out of his office, he sprung the question on me: "So, are you married?" Taken completely by surprise, I said, "Yes." Well,

I really wasn't married. Jay and I had been partners for fifteen years, but gay marriage wasn't even a topic being discussed in the papers.

The second question came very quickly. "Do you have kids?" I responded, "Yep, five and two." Now, to this day, I don't remember whether I was referring to our dogs or simply wrapped up in the conversation and my dreams for future business. I consider myself an honest person. But there I was, in the moment, telling a big fat lie. Fortunately, we were close to the exit. He shook my hand and said, "I really enjoyed our breakfast. Let's get together. Why don't you come to the country club, and we can play golf and the kids can swim in the pool."

As you can imagine, I left excited about the business. When I got to the car, I grew anxious very quickly. I called my partner, Jay, immediately and said, "Honey, we've got a problem. We've got to find some kids." Well, the next twenty-four hours were miserable for me. I was completely out of alignment with whom I aspired to be. And it became very clear that my attachment to success had undermined my authenticity as a person. The next day, I wrote a letter to that executive and told him the truth. He never contacted me again. But it didn't matter. I had learned a great lesson. It's far more important to be yourself than it is to be successful.

When our desire for success turns into a preoccupation for achievement, we've got a real problem. Suddenly, we find our dreams dictating our lives. Sooner or later, we find ourselves attached to the very success to which we aspire.

WHAT IS SUCCESS?

Who doesn't want to be successful? Success is everyone's dream. Winning, getting ahead, achieving goals, making a positive difference—these objectives make us feel better about ourselves. They affirm our self-worth and humanity. And if there is one thing we know for certain about success, everyone's idea of it is different, forged by our own personal values, upbringing, education, and experiences. Whether you're a lawyer or nurse, an executive or government official, a nonprofit marketer or an athlete, artist, teacher, or craftsman, your definition is unique to you.

The word "success" originated in the 1530s from the Latin *succedere*, meaning "to create great results." I prefer a more personal definition. Success is "the ability to reach our goals in life, whatever they may be."

Thousands of books exist on the topic of success, along with as many lists of the best habits of successful people. Whether their source comes from longitudinal studies of children or interviews with high achievers, the same qualities seem to emerge every time.

THE QUALITIES OF SUCCESSFUL PEOPLE

- Hope and optimism
- Vision, purpose, and values
- Growth mindset
- Grit and willpower
- Resilience
- Confidence and courage
- Drive and practice
- Self-control and discipline
- Emotional intelligence
- Adaptability
- Anxiety management
- Health and well-being

Success resides also in the eyes of the beholder. Matt, my physical therapist and trainer, shared a personal example with me. When he participated in a CrossFit competition, he "set personal goals for myself, lifted 245 pounds, and exceeded my expectations. I felt proud, fulfilled, and excited about my accomplishment. Yet my partner and I took last place in the competition. Were we successful or not? Sure, we were." Whether subjective or objective, personal or public, success means something different to everybody.

The debate about what constitutes "success" is ongoing and enigmatic. All of us would like to have a clear path to success whether it comes through diligence, talent, intelligence, socioeconomic status, race, genetics, or tenacity or elbow grease. Parents all want success for their children and would love to find the formula!

This debate calls into mind the puzzle of a zebra that could be white with black stripes or black with white stripes. It depends on your perspective; neither solution for looking at the zebra brings resolution. And neither does the debate on the "right" path to having a successful life. Many believe in the "capabilities argument," which maintains that talent, skill, and intellect bestow success on the holder.

Just as compelling is the "circumstances argument," where luck or happenstance make the formula work. Neither, however, is correct. Success is not an either-or proposition. It is a mystifying combination of personal abilities and the environment around you.

THE WORK-SUCCESS CONNECTION

The average person spends 115,704 hours of their life at work, a yardstick that is often our primary measurement of success. That total is equivalent to more than thirteen years. For much of our lives, work provides social status, a feeling of belonging, and the rewards we need to live a healthy, successful life.

But Gallup's worldwide research reveals a different story. Workers generally fall into three categories: the thriving (20% engaged), the indifferent (62% not engaged), and the miserable (18% actively disengaged).

Being engaged or not is also the real issue for lots of people who search for meaning and success outside their workplaces. And what about college students, those who are not working, or folks in their retirement years? Where do they find success in their lives?

Fortunately, in today's world, success can be found in many different places as people reflect more and more on their success and the role it plays in their lives.

THE ATTACHMENT TO SUCCESS

Here's our dilemma. When we become preoccupied with success, something occurs inside us. We define ourselves solely by our achievements, becoming vulnerable when we strive too hard, underperform, or don't meet our own expectations. This outcome is inevitable, right? Not really. Truly healthy people strive to be the best, yet they don't need accolades to feel good about themselves.

This attachment to success is relentlessly pervasive in our society. From an early age, we are taught to achieve in life and compare ourselves to others. We each have our own dreams and perform at different levels, yet we all inherently know what it means to be successful. The problem starts to occur when our desire for success trumps our ability to be real and honest with ourselves.

We recognize this attachment when we see it. It's the people who feel the need to tell everyone about their accomplishments, or the neighbors who reach beyond their means in the cars they buy or the mortgages they take out on the houses they can't afford. Or it's the guy at work who can't wait to tell his colleagues about his bonus. Or the woman down the street who needs to tell everyone how many days she's been to church. Or the father who brags about staying late at work, skipping his kid's soccer game. In each case, the image of success reinforces the person's self-worth and who they present to the world.

OUR CULTURE OF SUCCESS

Let's face it. We live in a culture attached to success, a commercial culture where money and economics rule the world. It's everywhere you look around you. From designer clothes and fancy cars to multimillion-dollar athletes and movie stars, the business of America—and the world—is business. We idealize entrepreneurs like Steve Jobs and Jeff Bezos and put Warren Buffett and the Google boys up on a pedestal. We all collude in the problem. Over 50% of Americans own stock, yet we carry billions of dollars of debt on our credit cards to maintain our delusion of success.

In this free-market culture, wealth is now defined in a narrow way. We measure our worth by how much money we have and what possessions we own. Even if we fundamentally disagree with this narrow definition of wealth, it's amazing how easily we get seduced by these images and definitions of success.

Over time, these images become ingrained in the way we view ourselves and how we evaluate others. We chase after goals like titles, status, money, and power, but rarely do we ask ourselves what we are sacrificing in the process. How often do we compare ourselves with the neighbors down the street, or define our success by the quality and quantity of our possessions? When was the last time you raised the bar on yourself immediately after you achieved your goal, or asked someone what they do for a living?

Many of us grew up in families that intensified this attachment to success. For example, were your parents the hard-driving, successful types who were role models and set high standards? Did you feel accepted and valued only if you got good grades or performed well on the athletic field? Was there intense competition among your siblings that stayed with you into adulthood? Did you have to take care of yourself early in life, forcing you to become preoccupied with succeeding and getting ahead?

These family situations are all too common and keep us reaching for more and more. When this happens, we set off a vicious cycle of beliefs and behaviors that lead to more suffering and intensify our attachment to success. Driving this attachment is often our fear of failure.

OUR FEAR OF FAILURE

When we fear failure or success, we run from it in a variety of ways. Some of us simply avoid it by leading a risk-free life. Others take lots of risks and keep plenty of balls in the air, so when they do fall (as they always do from time to time), we can avoid failure at all costs. Many others simply choose to live in their own little bubbles, trying to convince themselves that they are special. So, whether it's feeling powerless, inadequate, or better than others, we stay stuck in our own worlds. In each case, we end up living a constrained life, attached to success, and disconnected from our real selves.

Our beliefs are the first to go. We think there is something missing in our lives. We see life's cup as half-empty, feeling that we don't measure up against others. Never satisfied with what we have or who we are, we have trouble accepting being "good enough." Our perpetual mental recording is that "I am worthy and lovable only when I am successful."

Our emotions kick in quickly. For some, the desire for success is insatiable. Obsessed with getting ahead, these people are always raising the bar on themselves and feel jealous toward others who are successful. Others personalize the inadequacy and turn the arrows against themselves. Both types of people never relax and worry all the time about their performance in the world.

WHAT CAUSES YOUR ATTACHMENT TO SUCCESS?

- Defining yourself only by your achievements in life
- Feeling like you are not enough, and something is missing in your life
- Needing acceptance and approval to feel good about yourself
- Aiming for stressful goals that undermine your health
- Feeling a skewed sense of insecurity, doubt, and lack of confidence
- Maintaining a feeling of overconfidence, entitlement, or arrogance
- Aiming too low and making achievement too easily obtainable
- Obsessing over winning and competing at all costs
- Exaggerating your successes and minimizing your losses
- Thinking that money is the only way to measure your success

A friend I knew really struggled with her attachment to success. Obsessed with her business, she rarely if ever took vacations, never relaxed, nor took good care of her health. Always trying to impress people, the conversation centered on how many customers she had and how much money she was making. Frankly, it got boring to be around her. I don't think she realized the impact she had on others and how her behavior pushed people away. In private, she told me how unhappy and stressed she felt. If only she could have loosened her attachment to success, I'm sure she would have been happier and more fun to be around. Unfortunately, she didn't have enough time to work on her obsession. Last year, she collapsed dead on her kitchen floor from a major cardiac event.

Lamentably, people like this are never fully comfortable with who they are. They constantly crave approval and attention, compare themselves to others, and find it hard to fully enjoy their lives. Career often takes precedence over family, health, and their relationships, and if they are lucky, they come to realize what they are missing in their lives.

OUR SENSE OF SCARCITY

In *The Tao of Abundance*, Laurence Boldt, a spiritual teacher and interpreter of Eastern philosophy in the West, talks about the inner experience of lack and scarcity in our lives. Many successful people, he says, feel their lives are incomplete, empty, or meaningless. Self-doubt and low self-esteem show their ugly heads. This sense of lack stems not from the lack of material things but rather from a sense of psychological lack inside themselves. No matter how much they possess or acquire, they have trouble being satisfied with their lives.

This psychological poverty comes from our fragile egos that are constantly comparing us to others. The trouble is we link our ego too much to what we own, what we have, and what we achieve, and not enough to who we are, what we believe, and how we feel. Consequently, we end up spending way too much time trying to protect and enlarge our egos and not nearly enough time on what really makes us happy.

As a personal example, I woke up one morning years ago and decided it was time to lease a Mercedes. I had been working for a couple years and was making a good living. I wanted to reward myself for my hard work and success. A Benz seemed like the ideal gift. When I told my partner about the decision, he immediately pushed back, "So why buy a Mercedes? Why not a Toyota, or a Ford, or an Acura." I really didn't have a good answer. So I made one up. "They've got a great safety record," I said. Now, you must know Jay. He's as frugal as they come (some would say "cheap"). He came right back at me: "I think you're buying it because of the status symbol." I denied the charge completely. So he challenged me: "Then why don't you drive the car for an entire year and take off the

Mercedes symbol from the hood." Well, as you can imagine, his point was already made. He was right.

THE DELUSION OF MONEY

For many of us, money is the measure of our success. But Deepak Chopra, in his book *Abundance,* warns us that "measuring wealth solely by money is spiritually empty. Money won't make a bad job bearable, won't make you better than others, and won't make others like you more." In fact, studies show that having enough money makes people feel better, but beyond a certain point, adding more may lower a person's sense of happiness.

For folks in the developed world, this is especially true, as we forget that one billion people worldwide live on less than one dollar a day, many without food or shelter. Some of these courageous people even find happiness in this devastating poverty. What does this fact say about us?

Deepak further warns us about our faulty thinking, too, like fantasizing about money and seeing it as the sole goal of life. Cheating and greediness—and betraying our core values—make matters worse, exacerbating our troubles when our external self is successful and our inner self becomes impoverished.

So, if you view the world as full of only winners and losers, and money is the sole scorecard for success, don't be surprised if you feel something lacking inside yourself. Fortunately, self-awareness can fill up the hole and put the importance of money into proper perspective.

The message is simple. Nothing is wrong with acquiring money and material things, but we should endeavor to stay psychologically detached from them, remembering that we are just fine without them. I ended up buying the Mercedes and was happy I did, but the question lingered inside me for as long as I owned it. And that probably was a good thing.

THE ASPIRATION OF ABUNDANCE

How do we recognize and rise above our attachment to success? How do we let go of wanting more, having more, being more, and liberate ourselves from the heavy chains that keep us locked onto the treadmill of success?

I believe the secret is to love ourselves unconditionally, fully accepting who we are, what we have, and feel that we have enough right now. Being authentic as a person and truly living a life of abundance is the key!

The word "abundance" derives from the Latin *"abundare,"* which means "to overflow" and to feel that your life is full right now, satisfied with both your possessions and the people around you. I'm reminded of a wise Unitarian Universalist expression that resonated with me immediately: "Do what you can, want what you have, and be who you are."

To live in abundance, we learn to free ourselves from our feelings of want and eliminate our need to prove our self-worth to ourselves and others. Just by being who we are, we free ourselves to reach our highest potential. When we live abundantly, we open our eyes to what is good in life. When we redefine what it means to be successful, we appreciate the simple things, have more time for our family and friends, worry less, and smile more. Studies show that becoming less materialistic leads to more joy and contentment in life.

WHO YOU ARE DRIVES WHAT YOU DO

An old paradigm that most of us learned and embraced heartily was the preoccupation with being successful. Amassing possessions, collecting accolades and titles—all the external, visible trappings of our post–World War II lives. The mindset that persisted for decades was "what you do defines who you are."

Imagine going to a social event now where you are asked "Who are you," instead of the polite conversation starter "What do you do?" Those mindful inquiries could initiate a welter of stories of your internal drivers of self-esteem and a validation of "self" instead of an innocuous description of your title or work activities and the mention of accomplishments.

Addressing what is important to you, who you are instead of what you do is, of course, quite personal. That is precisely the point, for it reminds you of who you really are. I would like to make the case that what is most personal to you is at the heart of your health and happiness. As one wise philosopher once said, "We admire people for their success, yet we love people for their brokenness."

Picture yourself as a large, sturdy oak tree with lush branches, a handsome trunk, and thick roots. Its exterior represents your public face, the part evident to society and the world. It projects your accomplishments, reputation, behavior, social standing. But the oak's real strength lives deep in the roots that sustain it and feed its life purpose, character, ethics, values, aspirations—the lifeblood of the true you.

As human beings, we all aspire to be healthy, grow strong roots, and belong to something bigger than ourselves. By tapping into those roots, we jettison the paradigm of being what we do and instead strengthen our aspirations and develop our desire to be who we are.

In 2014, I wrote a book about these healthy roots in *Grounded: How Leaders Stay Rooted in an Uncertain World*. I was elated and surprised when the book became a *New York Times* bestseller. But, like the message in this chapter, it ended up being a huge reminder to pay attention to my own feelings of abundance, independent of book sales.

As the diagram from the book shows, there are six dimensions of health and eighteen roots that define who you are, providing you with the inner strength needed to handle all that is coming your way. Think about where you stand on these roots.

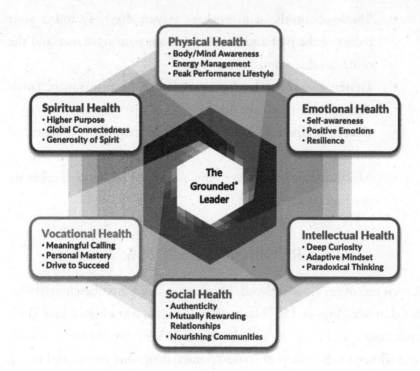

This root system builds a foundation for sustained well-being, like a whole body with a complex web of respiratory, cardiovascular, and skeletal systems working in synchronicity. While no one achieves a perfect six, these guidelines supply the groundwork for a way to know when to push the pause button on our striving and regain balance. I remember when I showed Alan Mulally, retired CEO of Ford Motor Company, this chart. He immediately jumped out of his chair, went to his computer, and produced a diagram of his own that simply proclaimed, "One Life / Life's Work!"

Here are some tips to consider:

- Your first job is to take care of yourself.
- Make a commitment to practice the six dimensions of well-being.
- Understand the case for taking care of yourself and reflect on what's meaningful for you.

- Think about the consequences if you don't. Examine your habits of the past and be honest about your resistance and the obstacles that stand in your way.
- Design a personal development plan that sets reasonable goals that you can raise over time.
- Don't be afraid to ask for help from friends, colleagues, or professionals.
- Measure your results over time. And don't be afraid to celebrate your successes.

RETHINKING SUCCESS

Sam is one of my closest friends. He grew up in a quaint Black neighborhood in Washington, DC. His mother, Lucretia, was a high school guidance counselor in the city's public schools. Every day, she went to work and witnessed the effects of broken homes, drugs and crime, and young kids dropping out of school. She was committed to doing everything in her power to protect her little Sam from the vagaries of city life. So, she saved up enough money, and after his sixth grade, against all odds, got him accepted into St. Albans, the prestigious white prep school for the rich and famous of Washington.

Sam was bright, hardworking, and a good athlete, but there were very few African American kids running around the fields of St. Albans. He learned quickly that life would be very different when you're sitting next to George Bush's son in math class. But he worked hard and charmed the right people, and after high school, was admitted to the University of Virginia. He did well in college and was accepted into Harvard Law School. To Sam, the thought of never going to college or graduate school was simply out of the question. He was on the fast track to success.

At Harvard, he did what most first- and second-year law students do: he interned at two big, white, corporate law firms. After graduation, he could have done anything with his life: clerk for a judge, work for a large corporation, practice in a corporate law firm, or run for political office. Each path would have led to making lots of money and moving up the socioeconomic ladder of success. But none would have made him happy.

Instead, Sam chose a different tack. He took a job teaching law at Howard University School of Business, located in the center of Washington, DC. Considered one of the best Black universities, prestigious in its own right, it clearly wasn't the fast track for a rising Harvard Law School graduate. Many of his friends thought he was running away from success, corporate America, and the white establishment. Back then, there might have been some truth to this conclusion, but, if you really examine Sam's path over fifty years, you come to realize that he wanted to create his own life and determine his own definition of success.

Today, Sam sits as one of the deans of the business school at Howard. He lives a simple, healthy life in the same apartment house he has lived in for many years, although he's moved up to a beautiful apartment on the third floor. He doesn't have a car; he rides his bike around the city. And from June to August, you can find Sam on vacation, traveling the world to one of the seventy-five countries he has visited since high school.

Sam could have allowed himself to define his success by some external standard, kidnapped by other people's expectations by what could be or should be in his life. But he chose a different path, a route mapped internally on his own terms and in his own way.

I have known Sam for fifty years now. He truly is happy with who he is and doesn't try to be somebody he is not. If you ask him whether he is contributing to the world, he is quick to respond: "Oh yes, I am challenging young Black students to think critically, to stand up for their beliefs, to challenge the status quo, and to be all they can be." To Sam, he is living a full life. He is happy and free. That is *his* definition of success. His story might not be yours, yet it shines light on what could happen if you put your attachment to success under the microscope.

SELF-TALK FOR ABUNDANCE

- Tell yourself: I am worthy/lovable/good just the way I am.
- Do what you can, want what you have, be who you are.
- Find happiness independent of your achievements.
- Be honest and celebrate your wins and losses.
- Remember your money is only one factor in abundant living.
- Congratulate others for their successes and accomplishments.
- Broaden the way you value yourself: personal, family, work, friends, hobbies.

When we define our success from the outside in, based on other people's judgments and expectations, we give up a part of ourselves, held hostage by the opinions of others and vulnerable to their evaluations and criticisms. But, when we define our success from the inside out, we become masters of our own destiny, creating our own dreams and determining our own path.

Wait a second. What about our desire for success, that spark inside that ignites us to achieve, driving us to work hard and move up in our careers? What about the yearning to learn a new language, or to lower our handicap, or win a tennis match? We certainly don't want to give up this "fire in the belly" that motivates us to reach our next level of performance.

For some of us, the attachment to success is deeply personal and central as an organizing driver in our lives. It defines who we are and provides the catalyst for our ambition and hunger to get ahead. In a strange sort of way, the attachment itself becomes our friend and confidant and the true positive motivator in our lives.

Yet we must always remember that there is a difference between our desire for success and our attachment to it. One inspires us to reach higher, to do great things; the other never allows us to fully enjoy these accomplishments when we achieve them.

MANAGING OUR WINS AND LOSSES

I first met Bert Brim in 1990 at a meeting sponsored by the MacArthur Foundation. At the time, he was chair of the Network on Mid-Life Development, a project where experts from diverse fields such as medicine, sociology, and psychology met regularly to conduct research on healthy adult development. I had the great fortune of being asked to participate because of my expertise on workplace issues.

What a treat to learn from these national experts. At thirty-two, I was the youngster of the group. Looking back, I probably spoke too much and listened too little, but I learned a great deal about multidisciplinary science and grew to be a humbler scientist.

Bert was the elder statesman of the group. I recall vividly an evening we spent together over wine and dinner when we talked about life and success—just the two of us. He was in the middle of writing a new book called *Ambition: How We Manage Success and Failure in Our Lives*. What an opportunity to learn from the master who had studied the topic for decades and was well into his late sixties.

I still remember his answer when I asked him about one lesson that he could share about life. "You know, Bob," he said, "when we go through life, we feel the need to reject the past to embrace the future. But when you look back on life, you realize that everything was connected. One stage of life simply builds on the next, and each one provides the foundation for the next phase of our lives."

I didn't realize how wise that statement was until years later. We all are the product of our experiences, successes, and failures, and all the people we meet and lessons we learn along the way. If we are too attached to success, we never fully appreciate the journey. We miss seeing our life as a story full of chapters and characters that lace together like a beautifully knitted quilt.

Bert's major idea was that we all share a basic drive for growth and achievement. It's not the mastery of those goals that determines our happiness. Rather, it's how we manage the wins and losses in our lives. Some of us are very content with who we are and what we accomplish. Others believe they never get a break or measure up to others. Still others fall apart with disappointment and rejection when they lose or take second place.

The happiest among us have a unique ability to modulate our successes and failures. We know exactly how to raise or lower the bar by changing our aspirations, resetting goals, or changing timetables in our life.

There is abundant research on the topic of happiness. You might be surprised to learn that age, gender, race, income, and education, when combined, only explain 10–15% of the variation in how happy people are. Most of the difference is explained by how we manage these wins and losses. Studies even show that people who are given a special prize like the lottery or who suffer a terrible loss return to their previous level of happiness within a short period of time.

The aspiration for abundance is clear: believe that "I am enough"—just the way you are. It's self-love in the very best sense, without feeling arrogant, grandiose, or too narcissistic. When we love ourselves, we embrace our imperfections and appreciate our accomplishments. We love others and allow others to love us. And we spread our love by giving and being of service.

Oscar Wilde said it best: "In this world, there are only two tragedies—one of not getting what you want, and the other of getting what you want."

THE PATH TO ABUNDANCE

To live a life of abundance and shed our attachment to success, we must design our personal path to health and happiness, which involves looking deeply at yourself and working through the four steps:

- *Step 1: Attachment*—Here you examine the attachment by experiencing the full range of your thoughts and emotions. You enter this phase when you realize your feelings of lack and scarcity are real, driven by your fear of failure. By being aware that you worry about your accomplishments and possessions, you deepen your insight and acknowledge the truth inside yourself. You are ready to exit this phase when you have identified the attachment to success as one of your vulnerabilities.

- *Step 2: Acceptance*—In this phase, you must investigate the success attachment that has hijacked you. By acknowledging it and digging deep into why it is causing you to grasp and suffer—for example, your early childhood experiences, the need to fill yourself up or impress others, or pressures from your friends and loved ones—you begin to gain deeper awareness and see yourself as separate from your ambitions and possessions. You are ready to exit this phase when you make sense of your attachment, realizing that who you are as a human being is NOT what you do or what you achieve.

- *Step 3: Aspiration*—Here, you decide to replace your attachment to success with your aspiration of abundance. You begin to believe that you are worthy and good without your possessions and stop comparing yourself to others. Clearly, you see the connection between your feelings of fear and your attachment to success. Imagine yourself without the attachment. By substituting envy and greed with contentment and abundance, you begin to retrain your mind.

- *Step 4: Action*—In this final phase, you practice your aspirations and rewrite your story. You enter this phase when you're
  ready to discard your attachment to success and substitute it
  with your commitment to live in abundance. You love yourself
  unconditionally and fully accept yourself for who you are and
  what you have. Practice the aspiration in a variety of situations.
  Make sure you forgive yourself for harboring this attachment.
  Enjoy the newfound wisdom, joy, and freedom in your life. This
  action stage will be a continuous process in your life.

HOW HARD TIMES SHED LIGHT

Life's hardships often produce our greatest lessons. Coping with these difficult onslaughts may bring even the most competent, self-actualized people
to their knees. I met Kathie thirty years ago. As an executive at Arbitron,
the radio ratings company, Kathie had everything she ever wanted—a
great job, a loving family, and lots of time to give back to her community.

Then, a cancer diagnosis, the downturn of the economy, and the
dwindling of her retirement income spun her world into a maelstrom.
The confluence of these events ended with her unexpected decision to
leave the company that she had loved for twenty years.

"I never thought in a million years that the situation at Arbitron
would have deteriorated as fast as it did. I was waking up in the middle
of the night, which never happens to me. I was raised to plan ahead. To
live in a way that secures tomorrow. But suddenly my world was changing overnight."

Like most aspirational people, Kathie started redesigning her next
step. "The first thing I realized was how much I struggle with my attachment to success. I am driven and didn't have a balanced perspective on
my life. I felt like I needed to get a job quickly. But I sat with my anxiety

as much as I could and let it instruct me about what to do next. I did some real soul searching and started asking myself: What was I supposed to be learning from all this?

"In the midst of all this turmoil, we were in the middle of a major home renovation that was costing a God-awful fortune. Every morning, I would wake up and see our contractors, Carlos and Julio, doing work around our house. If they didn't work, they were not going to be able to feed their kids.

"I got back in touch with my feelings of abundance. I realized that we live a life of luxury. We don't have to balance our checkbook. We are not hungry. And my husband and I have each other. So, we were finding odd jobs all over the house to keep them employed. We realized how lucky we were compared to so many people.

"That month was very instructive for me. My cancer and the economic meltdown told me that stability is largely an illusion and there's only so much you can do to prepare for the future. We live in a society that is so focused on success and the notion of letting go of that is hard. What I do know for sure is that my life is full, and my husband and daughter are everything to me."

This seeming crush of misfortune actually sent Kathie on to an even more amazing life: she became an executive for the next six years at the United States Institute of Peace, a federal institute, which gave her a front-row seat to the geopolitical realities of the world.

Recently, Kathie moved on to the next chapter of her life. "I don't consider myself retired; I just consider myself moving into the next chapter of engagement. I am not chained to my desk anymore. I sit on a couple boards, go to the gym more often, and get great pleasure from my gardening. And frankly, I spend more time on myself."

Kathie is more philosophical these days. "I recognize that I am small in the overall scheme of things; yet I continue to have impact on my circle of influence. I moved from my attachment to success to a new form of purposeful living that fits the rhythm of my life."

Let me leave you with some final thoughts by David Brooks, from his book *The Second Mountain*. He asserts that "Meritocracy reigns supreme in our society. Starting at a young age, we teach our children to follow an ethos that defines who we are by what we achieve. But underlying the meritocracy is a foundation of lies: the crux of these lies rests on the belief that life is an isolated journey—you are what you accomplish, that you alone can make yourself happy, and your worth derives from your skills." Brooks calls this challenge the "first mountain" of our lives to address.

Next, he sees another mountain in the distance: "Our individual salvation comes from community, not on the individualism that got us into the valley in the first place. The journey up the second mountain isn't a solitary one. At the top of that mountain, we let go of ourselves and seek a more fulfilled life."

It is there where we discover newfound freedom, one with greater meaning and purpose.

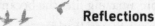

Reflections

Here are some questions to deepen your understanding of the attachment to success. My suggestion is to find some quiet time during the day or evening and reflect on these questions.

- Do I see myself as successful, and how do I measure success in my life?
- What is missing in my life, and how can I fill my life up with abundant living?
- What is my true motivation when I acquire possessions in my life?

- What and why am I trying to accomplish at work and life?
- Do I practice the adage that "who I am drives what I do?"
- How can I love myself unconditionally without all the trappings of success?
- How can I let go of wanting more, being more, having more?

SEVEN

THE ATTACHMENT TO PLEASURE

- Do you like to take risks and live on the edge of life?
- Do you have trouble expressing your most difficult feelings?
- Do you turn to pleasurable activities when you are stressed?
- Do you avoid painful and uncomfortable situations?
- Do you get hijacked by your desires and habits?

I t happened at the Italian Embassy, celebrating the work of Bernadette Peters at the Sondheim Award Gala in Washington, DC. Suddenly, while I was eating dinner with friends, my heart started beating so loudly that it felt like a fiery volcano was spewing hot lava in my chest. I excused myself quickly and escaped to the parking lot as fast as I could. At the time, I didn't know whether it was my atrial fibrillation, an impending heart attack, or intense anxiety. The sensation was all new to me.

Between my cardiologist and psychopharmacologist, we determined it was a panic attack. Because my father had them regularly, I just figured he had passed along his genetic gift. In the process, I learned about the eighteen inches of highway between my head and heart, and the intimate connection between them.

Years before, I had a couple surgeries. Like many patients, I was prescribed opiates, in my case, Demerol. Now, I was never a big drinker, nor did I take drugs in my adult life, yet when that needle went into my arm, boy, did I love the feeling. That fast, I had found opiates my "drug of choice." What I thought was true pleasure was actually my brain chemistry and dopamine receptors being activated. Then, off I went on the yellow brick road toward addiction. Vicodin and Percocet were my preferred opiates. They reduced my back pain and eliminated my anxiety. Plus, they were easy to get from doctors and clinics.

Slowly, I developed an addiction. I started using once or twice on the weekend, then all weekend, then for several weeks and months at a time during my "active" addiction that lasted for eight years. I tried many times to quit, but I always had trouble admitting I was powerless over the drugs, and I believed I could control my use. I consulted, gave speeches, educated leaders, and was convinced few people even noticed.

Eventually, I learned I was self-medicating my anxiety with opiates, trying to treat it with the wrong medicine. The opiates helped me celebrate the good life, camouflaged the underlying anxiety, and numbed my most difficult emotions. But the opiates were wreaking havoc on my mind and body, and it had to stop.

Fortunately, I have been free of opiates for four years. As with all people addicted to something, I live day to day, and my addiction is always with me. Indeed, pleasure can be a double-edged sword.

THE PLEASURE-PAIN PRINCIPLE

We live in a world of abundant stimulation. Our wired 24-7 lives give us access to an unlimited number of people, places, and things anywhere, anytime. This increasing variety and potency of highly rewarding stimuli positions us well for the pursuit of pleasure. Whether it's for food, alcohol, exercise, sex, shopping, or social media, our desire for pleasure and our pursuit of happiness drives and guides our thoughts and actions.

Who would be against a sensation that feels good and satisfies a deep, immediate desire that propels us through life? We feel pleasure when we enjoy a golden sunset, savor our favorite ice cream, beat an opponent in a golf match, or help out another person. Yet, when these needs are not met, the result is a state of frustration or anxiety. We can also get so focused on pleasurable experiences or substances that the addiction takes over.

Inside us as well is an equally powerful force that wants to avoid pain—at all costs. Sigmund Freud got it right years ago when he developed the pleasure-pain principle. He believed that "we are all wired to seek pleasure and avoid pain." What's pleasurable for one person may not be for another; not everyone starts at the same place; and each of us has our own "drug of choice."

The brain processes pleasure and pain in the same place, the two sensations working like opposite sides of a balance seeking equilibrium. When one goes up, the other goes down. But, in addiction, we lose our ability to manage our pleasures and tolerate our pains, both physical and psychological.

Unfortunately, as Anna Lembke, medical director of Stanford Addiction Medicine and author of *Dopamine Nation* warns, "Humans are great at pursuing pleasure and avoiding pain, but our brains are not prepared for a world of pleasure and abundance; and the net effect is that we now need more reward to feel pleasure and less injury to feel pain."

THE POWER OF DESIRE

Desire is one of our most potent feelings. When these desires combine with our attention, we are motivated to make choices so we can cherish and experience them. These actions entice our minds and bodies to want more.

Many of these desires are simple pleasures. Others are pleasurable forms of escape, like binge watching, reading novels, eating fast food, or watching internet porn. Still others put us on the razor edge of pleasure and pain, such as intense exercise, skydiving, mountain climbing, or motorcycle racing.

As we pursue these desires, our thoughts, feelings, and actions merge. Then, we develop habits. When these habits become entrenched, they give rise to deep learning in our brains. Because irrationality is an essential feature of being human, we become habit-making machines that are self-perpetuating and self-sustaining.

Over time, with the right body chemistry and the right pleasurable experience or substance, our habits can flood the reward pathways in our brains and crank up our engine of desire. As our sensations become more intense and need additional pleasure to satisfy ourselves, they can initiate serious attachment, or worse yet, an addiction.

DOPAMINE: THE PLEASURE NEUROTRANSMITTER

So how do our brains pull off this transition? The brain is comprised of eighty-six billion nerve cells, or neurons, that communicate across bridges, or synapses. These neurons carry chemical messages and electrical signals that keep our brain functioning. The chemicals, called neurotransmitters, may either excite or inhibit the passage of messages from one neuron to another.

Dopamine, one of the most important transmitters that occurs naturally in our bodies, functions in the pleasure and reward areas of our brain. Known as a pleasure chemical, it operates along with serotonin that enhances mood and sex, oxytocin that stimulates the love hormone, and endorphins that relieve pain and stress.

Having a healthy level of dopamine is necessary for our health and well-being. Fortunately, anything that feels good can release dopamine.

It tells our brains that "this feels good, I want more." When these pleasures go away, we want to re-create the good feelings. So, we are motivated to look for more pleasure that increases the dopamine in our brains. However, it's possible to get too much of a good thing.

Robert Lustig, emeritus professor of pediatrics at the University of California, San Francisco, and author of *The Hacking of the American Mind*, warns us to keep an eye out for this: "We've tolerated ever-available temptations (sugar, tobacco, alcohol, drugs, social media, and porn) combined with constant stress (work, money, home, school, cyber-bullying, internet) with the end result of an unprecedented epidemic of addiction, anxiety, depression and chronic disease."

THE PLEASURE ACTORS IN THE BRAIN

- *Amygdala*: Acquires and maintains emotional associations
- *Striatum*: Triggers automatic impulsive actions to pursue something
- *Orbitofrontal cortex*: Interprets highly motivating situations
- *Prefrontal cortex*: Provides self-awareness and self-regulation
- *Accumbens*: Pleasure center fueled by dopamine that drives action
- *Dopamine*: Acts as the pleasure chemical that drives desires
- *Serotonin*: Monitors mood, sleep, digestion, and sexual desire
- *Oxytocin*: Acts as the love hormone stimulated during intimacy
- *Endorphins*: Help relieve pain, improve well-being, and reduce stress

He further warns, "The more pleasure you seek, the more unhappy you get and the more likelihood you will slide into addiction or depression. Our ability to perceive happiness has been sabotaged by our modern incessant quest for pleasure, which our consumer culture has made it all too easy to satisfy. Those who abdicate happiness for pleasure will end up with neither."

THE ATTACHMENT TO PLEASURE

"I have a major attachment to pleasure," says Gary, a successful executive. "And it all started with my dad. His life was all about pleasure and reaping the benefits of what he earned.

"When I was younger, I spent a lot of time with him, on his boat and with his friends. He was a successful businessman and a pillar in the community, and I idolized him.

"Money came easy to him, and to me. It was his way of showing love. But there were always strings attached. I spent money I didn't have, and never learned to earn it, save it, or invest it. I never had to.

"When my father saw me struggling as a young adult, he threatened to cut me off, but he never did. There were never any consequences. When I was thirty, he gave me one million dollars, and said to invest it. As you can imagine, I squandered it away.

"Then came the partying and doing things I shouldn't have been doing. I loved gambling, and I remember my early days in junior high pitching pennies against the wall. I'd go to the pool hall and lost lots of money.

"In college, I lost thousands of dollars, a lot more than I could afford to lose. I never had enough money because I would gamble it all away, betting on sports.

"I never was a good poker player either, but we would go to Atlantic City, and I would lose all the money I brought with me. The pain of losing was much worse than the joy of winning, so I kept at it. When I got married, I brought my wealth, whatever I had left, into my current family, and then pissed it all away.

"When I was sixteen, I started smoking pot every day. And I smoked pot for fifty years. I often thought it wasn't addictive; everybody was doing it. Yet it took away some of the best years of my life.

"Another addiction of mine was prescription drugs. I loved taking pain medicine. It just relaxed me. My drinking was episodic. I never had withdrawal from drinking, but that's a distinction without a difference.

"My sex addiction was altogether different. I had free rein over my schedule, and I could meet up with women when I wanted. It was the thrill of the chase.

"When women did what I wanted, and made me believe they were enjoying it, then I felt good and wanted to do it again. But there were a lot of occasions where it didn't work out like that. Sometimes I felt sad and alone; other times I became obsessed with a woman. And I think they felt their boundaries weren't being respected. I guess I was seeking intimacy and control.

"I remember sitting in the parking lot of the CVS drugstore giving myself an AIDS test. It was a terrifying fifteen minutes while the test was percolating. Fortunately, I never got bad news.

"At the end, there was a woman who got ticked off at me and found my wife's phone number, called her, and basically said I was sleeping with her. Do you know I wanted to go back to see this woman again, even when I knew my marriage and family were in deep trouble?

"Eventually I drove myself to a hospital and checked myself into a psych floor. My life had gotten so out of control and unmanageable. I needed help.

"Today, I've been four years without my addictive behavior. I still see myself with many of these attachments, and I work on them every day. I try not to beat myself up, and to be honest as much as possible. I live within my means and have made a real commitment to therapy and support groups. My wife is a saint and has been so understanding. Yet I sometimes feel I'm not progressing fast enough."

Gary attributes many of his problems to his bad self-esteem. While that assessment may be partially true, if you look closely, Gary was set up from the beginning. His early family environment most likely helped to activate his attachments and addictions. Coupled with a genetic and chemical aberration, Gary was vulnerable throughout his life. The chasing of pleasurable stimuli at the expense of himself and others got in the way of his health and well-being, his career success, and his relationship with family. Driven by control, loneliness, and the need for intimacy, it took a crisis to help Gary see the better part of his human nature. Today, he works hard to become that man—on his own terms.

ATTACHMENT AND ADDICTION

As human beings, we have many desires that we pursue. Some pursuits develop into habits; others remain simple desires. When a habit develops, it may lead to a positive or negative outcome. If the habit is desirable enough, like walking for exercise, we yearn for it and repeat it often. If it's a negative habit, like smoking, it can turn into an attachment. When we start grasping or clinging to something we desire, we are vulnerable to developing an addiction.

As we move from desire to habit and then to attachment and on to addiction, we loosen our judgment and resistance, becoming a prisoner to the chains of our obsessions.

From my experience—and for the sake of simplicity—it's important to remember that addiction is a spectrum disorder, and it's possible to be a "little bit" addictive. For our purpose, I'm going to assume that many attachments to pleasure often lead to an addiction.

But, not for the reasons you might think. As I talk to people addicted to substances or activities, the attachment to pleasure is often a disguise for hiding the force of the addiction. Sure, liquor, marijuana, gambling, or unhealthy foods can be quite pleasurable, but it's the presence of difficult emotions, including pain, physical or emotional, underlying the attachment that often activates the addiction.

Remember, people will avoid pain at all costs. When there is a lot of pain lying under the surface, it's often much easier to anesthetize or medicate the pain with substances or activities so we don't feel it, rather than dealing directly with the source of the pain. For that reason, an attachment to pleasure is not only physiological, it also is an avoidance of pain.

ADDICTION IS A BRAIN DISEASE

Today, most scientists and healthcare professionals view addiction as a brain disease, an aberration of the reward system of the brain. The culprit is the reduction of dopamine in the synapses and the subsequent need for dopamine substitutes outside of the body.

Overcoming an addiction is not as simple as just stopping or exercising control over your impulses. It requires the rewiring of the brain and restoring the naturally occurring dopamine production inside the body.

Consider this example from the University of Pennsylvania. In a normal brain, when we experience a pleasurable event, like an orgasm, it results in a large spike in the dopamine levels in the brain, with a quick return to normal levels. Chocolate increases dopamine production by about 50%, sex about 100%, nicotine about 150%, and amphetamines about 1,000%.

In the addicted brain, when we drink heavily or abuse drugs, the dopamine levels rise much higher than the orgasm, the pleasure is often more intense and lasts longer, yet the dopamine levels never return to normal baseline. Rather, they plunge to zero. This depletion of dopamine causes pain and a withdrawal reaction where we feel restless, unhappy, and uncomfortable, which intensifies our desire for more dopamine, which means more alcohol, drugs, nicotine, caffeine, or whatever else.

Over time, the high you receive from these pleasurable substances transforms into a corresponding low with each successive event. The addicted person creates tolerance and must take in more and more to get less and less of an effect. When you try to withdraw from these substances, the effects can range from mild symptoms to a devastating experience.

THE PSYCHOLOGY OF ADDICTION

Addiction is a progressive, potentially fatal disease. Alcohol can destroy your liver. Opiates can poison your heart. Nicotine can infiltrate your lungs. And gambling can devastate your life. Yet some of the most painful effects are psychological, affecting your overall mental well-being. As someone once said to me, "Alcohol and opiates were my best friend. Unfortunately, I was a better friend than they were to me. They gave me strength, happiness, and connection. But it was all a delusion."

It's not unusual for addicted people to feel guilt and shame, believing they are responsible for their addiction, while completely ignoring the fact that their disease is caused by some combination of genetics, dopamine depletion, early development, difficult life events, and painful underlying emotions. Addicts and alcoholics are not bad people trying to be good; they are sick people trying to get healthy.

Addicted people also suffer from other psychological symptoms, such as anxiety, anger, pain, and sadness that can limit their recovery. They may deny their addiction, believe they can control their disease, or convince themselves that "this, too, shall pass." Nobody knows this better than the people who live with them. But sooner or later, addicted people must come to realize that they are powerless over their substance or activity and only as sick as their secrets.

Getting clean and sober can be difficult and painful. Most alcoholics and addicts don't ask for the disease. Yet they are given a choice to either isolate themselves with their drug of choice or commit to a renewed life of sobriety and recovery. A few of the most common addictions are:

- *Alcohol*: Alcohol-use disorder is a medical condition characterized by an impaired ability to stop or control alcohol use despite adverse social, occupational, or health consequences. According to the 2021 National Survey on Drug Use and Health, 28.6 million adults ages eighteen and older (11.3% in this age group) had alcoholism in 2021. The risk factors are drinking at an early age, genetics and family history of alcohol problems, and mental health conditions and trauma.

- *Drugs*: Drug addiction is a disease that affects a person's brain and behavior and leads to an inability to control the use of legal or illegal drugs or medicine. Types include cannabis substances, barbiturates, benzodiazepines, hypnotics, stimulants like meth and cocaine, MDMA (ecstasy), hallucinogens, inhalants, and opiates. Symptoms include problems at home or work, physical health issues, changes in behavior, neglected appearance, and money issues.

- *Nicotine*: Nicotine dependence occurs when you need nicotine and can't stop using it. The younger you start, the greater the chance you'll be addicted. Other risk factors are genetics, parents who smoke, peer pressure, and mental health problems. Tobacco smoke contains more than sixty known cancer-causing chemicals. Common consequences are lung disease, heart and circulatory problems, diabetes, gum disease, infertility and impotence, and respiratory infections.

- *Caffeine*: Caffeine is a stimulant to the central nervous system, and its regular use can cause physical dependence. It can be found in all coffees and many tea leaves, cocoa beans, energy drinks, various beverages, pain relievers, and cold medications. Withdrawal symptoms can include headaches, fatigue, anxiety, and irritability. Moderate daily use (three cups of coffee/day) causes no harm in healthy adults but can make other people more vulnerable to osteoporosis and cardiovascular disease.

- *Gambling*: Gambling disorder is the uncontrollable urge to keep on gambling despite the toll it takes on your life. Symptoms include needing to gamble with increasing amounts of money, trying to control gambling without success, and risks to work, school, or family relationships. Compulsive gambling is more common in younger and middle-aged people, more common in men than women, along with personality traits like impulsivity, workaholism, and competitiveness.

- *Sex*: Sex addiction is a lack of control over sexual thoughts, urges, and behaviors done in excess that significantly impact one's life in a negative way. Most experts believe that simply having "too much" sex or having sex with multiple partners are not signs of a problem. Problems do occur with unlawful voyeurism, risky behaviors, and committing criminal sex offenses, like rape.

- *Food*: Experts believe food addiction operates with the same reward and pleasure centers in the brain. Symptoms include overeating, purging, undereating, obesity, compulsive exercise and dieting, and too much highly processed food. About 14% of adults and 12% of children fit the criteria for food addiction. Over 40% of Americans are considered overweight.

- *Shopping*: About 6% of the US population is obsessed with shopping and cannot stop themselves. Materialistic and vulnerable to advertising, these folks get hijacked by the rush of euphoria, and they shop to escape boredom, anxiety, and depression. They spend more than they can afford, opening credit cards and lying about things they buy. Their temporary high leads to feelings of emptiness and poor self-esteem.

- *Social media*: We are trained to believe that busyness is good, so we get easily seduced by social media. Our phones, computers, and watches are linked to dopamine-inducing technology where algorithms are created to our specific choices and rushes. Harvard University did a study that showed that social networking sites light up the same part of the brain as does taking an addictive substance. Studies are clear. Too much social media causes stress, loneliness, and depression; isolation and fear of missing out; diminished social skills and family separation; poor concentration and sleep; and decreased performance. Five to ten percent of us are social media addicts. The recommended prescription is a good digital detox.

ALARMING STATISTICS

- Global deaths from addiction have risen in all age groups between 1990 and 2017 with more than half the deaths occurring in people younger than fifty.
- The World Happiness Report found that countries with higher wealth and life expectancy are showing decreasing reports of happiness.
- Richer countries have higher rates of anxiety than poorer ones. Rates of psychological and physical pain are increasing, and the USA reports more pain than any other country.
- Suicide rates in teenagers have reached an all-time high and continue to climb.
- In *Blind Spot*, the Gallup Organization cites significant data that shows the global rise of unhappiness and discusses how leaders have missed the trend.

THE ANXIETY-ALCOHOL CONNECTION

"I was not seeking pleasure. I was seeking relief from my pain and distress. That's why I chose alcohol to medicate my anxiety."

Scott, a writer, editor, and author of *My Age of Anxiety*, describes his relationship with both demons. "My anxiety and alcoholism are highly genetic. My mom was a worrier. The whole family tree is covered with anxiety; half of them are on some kind of medication. My dad, ironically, was, at least outwardly, the least anxious among us—and yet he developed trouble with alcohol in the family. By the time he reached his fifties, he would drink until he passed out on the floor every night.

"For me, it's my obsessive worry, wired inside me with highly reactive physiology, and overwhelming physical symptoms that became so bad I would use anything to reduce them.

"Since I was a kid, I've had a specific phobia, the fear of vomiting. My mom had it too. It's a common phobia, more common in women. I would sweat uncontrollably, my stomach would start to hurt, I would get anxious about my stomach pains, and it was all quite debilitating.

"Today, there are plenty of days when I don't feel the anxiety, or it's intermittent and not bad at all. During these times, I'm quite capable of experiencing joy, and I feel lucky and grateful about that. But at other times, my anxiety is truly debilitating. When it's bad, it can advance to agoraphobia, when it takes me completely out of my comfort zone, and I'm afraid to go out and travel.

"Because my anxiety is so florid—I shake and sweat and can't speak—I can get embarrassed when I'm with other people. Even though most of my friends know, I don't like to show them. It puts an invisible barrier between us that interferes with a true connection.

"Then I discovered alcohol. It became my drug of choice. It started out being magic, then it turned to medicine, only to end in complete misery. I liked everything associated with alcohol. I liked drinking in bars; I liked fancy Scotch; I liked how it disinhibited me and made it easier to get along with others.

"I didn't start intentionally self-medicating with alcohol until my late thirties. (I'm now fifty-four.) When my first book came out when I was thirty-four, I discovered alcohol could be a performance-enhancing drug for my public speaking. If I drank a little beforehand, I could take the edge off, and my anxiety gets even lower if I supplemented it with a benzodiazepine, like Xanax. It was like alcohol was my magic potion, my performance-enhancing drug, that would relax my body and all my troubles would fade away. The alcohol helped me fly around the country, give big talks, and perform on TV during book tours. At the time, I was pretty much a nightly drinker with occasional day drinking to deal with the stresses of the day.

"Then, my alcoholism progressed to where the substance was medicine: I needed it to function and deal with the daily misery I would feel. It wasn't just for public speaking anymore; I needed alcohol all day to maintain a baseline of functioning. It was no longer a performance enhancer; it became a performance enabler.

"Over time, I had to drink more and more to manage my anxiety. I had twelve years of progressively more problematic drinking, and two years of acutely advanced alcoholism, where my physical health was deteriorating. My workplace and wife repeatedly told me I needed to go for treatment. Once I descended into full-blown alcoholism, I was literally out of control. I wanted to go back to normal drinking, but it was impossible. It took me about a year of abstinence before I could stop wishing and fantasizing about a drink.

"Today, I'm sober and in recovery. I continue to try a variety of more appropriate medications to deal with my anxiety—from Paxil and Celexa to Zoloft, Lexapro, and Gabapentin with an occasional benzo for severely stressful situations. An anxiety disorder is somehow less shameful than alcoholism. But I'll do what it takes to get my life back."

Scott suffers from a serious anxiety disorder caused by generations of genetically linked family members. Motivated by his best intentions, alcohol became his drug of choice to alleviate what became debilitating mental and physical symptoms. His willingness to write about his disorder helped him and many others understand and manage their anxiety. Now he's speaking openly about his alcoholism, a process that will help even more.

GETTING COMFORTABLE BEING UNCOMFORTABLE

If brain research teaches us anything, it's that you are far more capable of handling discomfort than you probably believe. Indeed, humans have a real capacity to transform discomfort into positive energy and momentum for change.

For much of human history, great hardship was a given in daily existence. Today, we seek comfort, shortcuts, and an easy way to live. Our current world abounds in comfort and convenience and shuns adversity, hard work, and strife. In chasing comfort and pleasure, we turn on our autopilot and flee from negative feelings, subdue fear, and become complacent. We don't realize that adversity is our greatest teacher.

While being happy is a great goal, shouldn't our goal really be to experience life fully—the good and bad, the wins and losses, the celebrations and disappointments?

The truth is that discomfort is a catalyst for learning and change. Venturing outside your comfort zone may be painful—even scary—but when we stretch ourselves, we find discomfort a natural feeling. Without it, you'd have neither the motivation nor the desire to risk anything, and you miss out on opportunities to grow in ways you had not even imagined.

Developing skills to get back on your feet is, in fact, essential in life. Being trapped in shallow, narrow points of view won't help you find the world that exists just over the horizon.

Let's face it. We fall down all the time. The question is whether you get back up, and how fast you rebound. So don't run away from your discomfort. Look for the positive lessons it provides.

Here are some tips for getting comfortable being uncomfortable:

- Reframe the role of discomfort in your life.
- Lean into your pain and discomfort.
- Experience fully your most difficult emotions.
- Challenge your faulty assumptions and beliefs.
- View anxiety as a positive force for discovery.
- Allow yourself the freedom to be vulnerable.
- Be kind to yourself and forgive your mistakes.
- Tap into your natural courage, grit, and persistence.
- Build a repertoire of resilience skills.
- Challenge yourself to do uncomfortable activities.
- Focus on what went right, not on what went wrong.

STEPS TO IMPROVE YOUR RECOVERY

- Surrender to your addiction, then choose a new life.
- Put your sobriety first and keep showing up.
- Set clear goals and new life routines.
- Build a substance-free environment around yourself.
- Avoid triggers that make you vulnerable to relapse.
- Prioritize your health, well-being, and exercise.
- Attend support groups that nourish you spiritually.
- Don't be afraid to ask for help.
- Let go of selfish and self-defeating behavior.
- Take responsibility for your side of the street.
- Stop fighting and resisting the world.
- Do the next right thing.

Let me end this chapter with a story from a friend of mine who struggled hard with his attachment to pleasure yet found peace and freedom from his addiction to lead a positive, fulfilling life.

THE PERFECT DRINKER

Mark was born into a family of alcoholics and raised in a small town in Texas. "At sixteen, I took my first drink and loved it. Shy, introverted, and nerdy as a kid, alcohol changed my world and gave me an instant burst of social liberation. It was my way of making friends and coping with life.

"Now, I'm sixty-four and retired after a great career in airport management. I am a recovering alcoholic, and took my last drink on December 5, 1983, forty years ago.

"Underneath my alcoholism is an attachment to perfection. As far back as I remember, I was always raising the bar on myself. I remember bringing a report card home in tenth grade with straight As and a ninety-two in English. My mom looked at me and said, 'What happened in English?' I was hard enough on myself. I didn't need that comment on top of it.

"My standard of perfection never allowed me to be happy in the moment. It caused me to look outside for validation. But I was never allowed to be vulnerable. You couldn't ask anybody for help; otherwise, you would owe them something. If I had to be perfect and self-reliant all the time, my mindset put tremendous stress and pressure on me. Alcohol became a pressure valve.

"But alcohol made everything worse. When I hit my bottom, I was sick and tired of being sick and tired. I soon came to realize that having a drink was equivalent to drinking a glass of Drāno. It retarded my emotional life and destroyed my physical body. I was drinking myself to death.

"Fortunately, over time, I came to love myself, started living according to my real values, and lowered my impossible standards that reduced my anxiety and brought joy in my life."

Because Mark was born into a genetically vulnerable alcoholic family, his attachment to perfection exacerbated his alcoholism. With time, his keen intellect and painful experiences, along with the cognitive dissonance he felt between his alcoholic self and his healthier self, led him to get comfortable feeling uncomfortable. For forty years, Mark has been helping others find their way through these insidious attachments to pleasure and perfection.

 Reflections

- What are your true pleasures in life and how might you abuse them? What's the effect on your mind, your body? Your spirituality?
- Are you someone who runs away from pain and discomfort? If so, what causes you to do that? What are your greatest fears?
- What feelings drive you to abuse substances or activities? Do you notice what happens in your mind when these feelings get activated?
- Do you experience cravings of any kind? How does your thinking intensify these cravings? Do you know how to disrupt them?
- If you are addicted to something, how does this attachment affect your life and what are the consequences?
- What will it take to minimize your attachments to pleasure or eliminate your addictions altogether?

EIGHT

THE ATTACHMENT TO YOUTH

- Do you worry about getting older?
- Do you feel stress and angst at work?
- Are you constantly doing things to stay youthful?
- Do you think a lot about your health and illness?
- Do you feel you live an unhealthy lifestyle?

My recent fiftieth high school reunion was like a living lab for examining the effects of half a century of aging. Like many of you who have gone to reunions, I was excited to see who would show up, what people would look like, and how their lives had transpired. Fortunately, everyone had name tags!

The champion wrestler now walks with a cane. The women's field hockey star looked like a model in *Glamour* magazine. The skinny invisible geek from gym class stood six feet four and weighed 250 pounds. The quiet girl from homeroom wore huge diamonds on her fingers and had no wrinkles on her face. And who could forget the class heartthrob surrounded by women who were revisiting their high school fantasies. Sadly, many people had died.

Yet clearly, it was a reminder that the world is getting older and graying, people age in different ways, and it was a perfect setup for writing about the attachment to youth.

THE WORLD IS AGING, BUT NOT EVERYWHERE

The world's population is aging, and so are we. In 2022, the median age in the United States reached a record high of 38.9 years, a rapid rise from over 35 in 2000 and 30 in 1988. We are still younger than our European peers, whose median age is 44, and older than our Asian friends at 31.9 years.

Fewer kids are being born, and people are marrying older, as school and work dominate our lives. The only exceptions are the Middle Eastern countries, where 60% of the population is under 25 years old, with a median age of 22 years. African nations are even younger at 18.8 years.

In the developed countries, older folks dominate the world like never before—from politics to business, entertainment to government, and from medicine to farming. The workforce is also getting older, and baby boomers are leading our society. These elders bring a ton of practical knowledge and experience. Within this decade, the United States will have more people over sixty-five than under eighteen.

There are three happy truths about getting older. First, older people tend to be happier than younger folks. Surveys from all over the world show that adults are least happy in their twenties and midlife, with a low point at age fifty. At fifty-one, happiness levels increase and gradually rise through our sixties and seventies.

Older people also tend to be healthier people; most older people rate their health as good or excellent. In fact, according to the American Society on Aging, only 12% of adults sixty-five and older have some cognitive impairment. And mild impairment affects only 15% of people seventy-five through seventy-nine.

Our elders are emotionally healthy, too, with lower rates of mental health problems. In fact, older people over sixty-five exhibit the most stable and optimistic outlook on life. They report being happier with their relationships compared to their younger counterparts and show that certain psychological abilities—like gratitude, generosity, forgiveness, and conflict resolution—increase with age. Indeed, many people are living their best lives in their seventies.

So what do these statistics say about age?

AGING IS A LIFELONG PROCESS

Aging is a subtle, quiet, lifelong process. We age differently based on our genetics, family history, lifestyle choices, and access to medical care. One of the great differentiators, however, is the social determinants of health—the health disparities we find in socially disadvantaged groups. Economic stresses, violence, and impoverished neighborhoods all have a significant impact on health and disease.

As we age, we experience dynamic changes in our biology and physiology, our psychology and behavior, and our interactions with others. Our environment changes as well. Some age processes are benign, like graying hair. Other factors make us susceptible to disease or disability. We are at peak functioning at age thirty, so advancing age is probably the greatest risk for chronic disease.

The culprit is that our cells change with age. Becoming larger and less able to divide and multiply, they lose their ability to function properly. This loss accelerates the aging process. We live relatively robust lives until our fifth decade, at which point our cognitive and physical health begins a gradual and steady decline. We slowly lose our youthful strength and stamina, and our cognitive capabilities start to decline. But, we have much more control over this deterioration than you might think, as we will see later in this chapter.

In our lives, we go through seven periods of development: childhood, adolescence, twenties, midlife, retirement, elderly, and death. Each period presents its own life challenges and opportunities, psychological transitions, and a set of norms and culture—or "vibe," as our younger friends describe it.

Another way to look at aging is how we live our lives—from dependence in the early years, to self-sufficiency as young adults, to interdependence at work and with family, to dependence in older age. Research says we don't age at a constant rate but rather in bursts, with the biggest changes coming around ages fifteen, thirty-four, sixty, and seventy-eight on average. CNN's Sanjay Gupta asks: "How can we make those bursts smaller, and less pronounced, to slow our eventual decline?"

THE ART AND SCIENCE OF LONGEVITY

More than ten thousand people turn sixty-five every day in the United States. This demographic has spurred a global longevity marketplace that will reach $600 billion in 2025. The search for the fountain of youth is alive and well. Based on lifestyle research and bestselling books, our free time is spent on fitness; our workplaces are filled with well-being programs; lifestyle doctors and health coaches abound; and bedroom cabinets are filled with lotions, potions, and antiaging elixirs. The goal is to minimize illness, extend life, and push our diseases to the last year right before we die.

The irony is that the US longevity has declined in recent years compared with other high-income nations, primarily due to Covid, poor diet, lack of exercise, drug and alcohol abuse, suicide, homicide, and inadequate, unequal healthcare. Nevertheless, people are still emerging out of Covid with a keen interest in holistic health, aspiring to live longer, healthier lives where the new forty feels like twenty-five, and the new seventy feels like fifty.

In his bestselling book *Outlive*, Peter Attia, MD, explains that longevity has two components: how long you live, called "lifespan," and how well you live (free of disability and disease), called "health span." When you examine life from these perspectives, it's only natural to ask yourself how you can increase both simultaneously. To do that, we must examine how we age over time.

Dr. Attia, an oncologist, describes four major diseases that affect how we age: heart disease, cancer, neurodegenerative disease, and metabolic disease (type 2 diabetes). These diseases, products of multiple risk factors, intensify over time. Peter warns, "while the prevalence of each disease increases sharply with age, they typically begin much earlier than we recognize, and they take a very long time to kill you. To achieve longevity—to live longer and live better longer—we must understand and confront these causes of slow death."

The problem is that we treat these diseases at the wrong end of our lives, allowing them to incubate in our bodies for a long time, intervening too late after the disease has taken shape. But, we can slow the rate of aging because, today, we can identify the genetic, lifestyle, behavioral, social, and environmental factors that influence these age-related diseases.

This attitude demands a paradigm shift in our thinking about health and medicine. Rather than react to illness at the back end of the time-table, when serious symptoms appear, we need to be more proactive and place much greater emphasis on prevention by monitoring the biomarkers that predict disability and disease. And each of us must take more responsibility for our own health.

DATA BANK

- Current maximum life expectancy for people in developed nations is about 93 years—less for men and a little longer for women. But in the United States, life expectancy is only 77.

- According to the Centers for Disease Control (CDC), more than 40% of the US population is obese (defined as having a BMI greater than 30), while roughly another third is overweight (BMI of 25–30).

- Cardiovascular (CV) disease represents the leading cause of death: 2,300 deaths every day in the United States. Not only affecting men, women are ten times more likely to die from CV disease than breast cancer. Fully half of all major adverse CV events in men and a third in women occur before 65; in men one quarter occur before 54.

- A 2022 CDC study indicated 11% of the US adult population has clinical type 2 diabetes, including 29% of adults over 65. Another 38% of US adults—more than one in three— meet at least one of the criteria for prediabetes. Patients with diabetes have a much greater risk of cardiovascular disease, cancer, and Alzheimer's disease.

- Globally, 12–13% of all cancer cases are thought to be attributable to obesity. And extreme obesity is associated with a 54% greater risk of death from all cancers in men, 62% in women.

- In the United States, about six million people are diagnosed with Alzheimer's; 1.4 million with Lewy body dementia, and one million are diagnosed with Parkinson's disease. Alzheimer's is almost twice as common in women than men.

- The CDC estimates that more than 100,000 Americans died from drug overdoses in 2020–2021.

ATTACHMENT TO YOUTH (AND AGING)

People can be attached to youth in five ways. I include aging here because it's not always clear whether people are trying to stay young or whether they are avoiding getting older. The five subtypes are yearning for youth, suffering midcareer angst, fear of aging, obsession with illness, and sabotaging one's life.

Yearning for Youth

Twenty years ago, I got a hair transplant—one thousand new follicles implanted on the top of my head. As you can imagine, I was distressed with my receding hairline and wanted to look younger. After the procedure, I was a little self-conscious about going back to work. My first appearance was facilitating an executive team meeting in a Midwest company. I figured that, coming to the heartland, people would be nice and accommodating. So I walked up to the front of the room, feeling both timid and courageous. With my little brown Scottish cap covering my new hair, I introduced myself by referring directly to the transplant.

"Now you might be wondering why I'm wearing this cap today," I said. "Well, to be honest, it's because I'm phallically challenged." Everyone in the room broke into hysterical laughter. My follicle humor had worked. Then, I realized what I had said. How embarrassing! I suspect I got the attachment to youth from my mom with her two facelifts and breast implants. The things we go through to stay young.

Why do we yearn for youth? Some of us choose to stay stuck in adolescence, not wanting to grow up. Either we feel that we grew up too quickly, or we want to be taken care of and don't want to leave the nest and take responsibility for ourselves.

Others enter adulthood with a job and family, yet they never want to leave the feeling and freedom that youth provides. Often, we idealize our youth and spend whatever it takes to stay that way. Still others notice their aging minds and bodies and don't want to get older.

We do everything possible to stay healthy and youthful in attitude and appearance, although when asked if we wished we were young again, most people say no. In each case, those too attached to youth remain stuck, often obsessed, ignoring the fact that we are aging constantly. It's great to aspire to being youthful, but not at the expense of our peace of mind.

Research shows that our late twenties and early thirties can be the worst times in our lives. Many young adults feel what's been deemed a "quarter-life crisis." Confused and lonely, many seek their first "real" jobs without prerequisite skills and talents, rent their own apartments, and feel the stresses of dating and the pressures of finances. A growing number are still living at home and experience mixed messages about being an older child or a younger adult.

One such study was conducted by the Harvard Graduate School of Education. They found that young adults suffer from anxiety and depression twice as often as teenagers (36% vs. 18%). Their worries included: finances (56%), pressure to achieve (51%), lack of direction (50%), and things falling apart (45%).

Happify, a positive psychology app, also looked at various psychological indicators of 88,000 people. It found that people experience sharp increases in stress levels in the late twenties and early thirties, but the level moderates during our thirties and forties, with a sharp decline during retirement. These changes occur as we learn to regulate our emotions, put things in perspective, and believe in ourselves.

Fitness Will Set You Free

"When I was younger, I was skinny and not very good at sports. At eighteen, one of my friends introduced me to working out, and off I went into the world of fitness. I immediately liked it and started to develop a bit of a body."

These are the words of Joe, a fifty-year-old finance guy from England. "Initially, it was primarily about my looks, yet my reasoning today is definitely my well-being and stress relief." No doubt, improving his abs and making muscles are still strong motivators. In contrast, I have one ab, and the poor thing is still searching for some visibility.

Joe continues, "I work out every morning at 6 AM and in the evening with a combination of weights and cardio, either on the treadmill or in the pool. Even when I'm tired or achy, I'm off to the gym. I don't have a car, so biking around London is my preferred mode of transportation. And it's great for fitness."

Like so many others, Joe spends his day at home on his laptop, analyzing graphs and counting numbers. "I'm not afraid of growing old; however staying fit helps me feel better. I surround myself with people who are young. Yet I had a grandmother who died at 105 and was an inspiration to me. Young at heart, she lived on her own, loved sudoku on her computer, and did her exercises every day.

"I live a very active life. I do fear slowing down, and worry a lot about how I look, minus the wrinkles, but I can't do anything about that."

Committed to his fitness and health, Joe openly discusses his fear of aging. Nothing is wrong with his commitment to health, but his attachment to youth and the anxiety he feels about getting older sometimes interferes with his peace of mind. Inevitably, his aging mind and body will be either his liberator or his slayer.

HOW OUR BODY AGES

According to the Mayo Clinic, as you get older, your body changes. Sometimes it's subtle; other times it happens overnight. Here are some common changes as you age:

- *Cardiovascular system*: Stiffening arteries, thicker heart muscle, slowed heart rate or high blood pressure cause your heart to work harder, leading to heart attacks or strokes.
- *Lungs*: Your respiratory system loses elasticity as oxygen intake declines. As the lungs weaken, they are less able to fight off diseases.
- *Immune system*: Immunity weakens over time, slowing healing and increasing sickness. Vaccines can be less effective, and cancers can grow.
- *Bones, joints, muscles*: Bones shrink in size and density. Muscle loss reduces strength, endurance, and flexibility. Cartilage thins. Calcium and vitamin D decrease. All affect weight, stability, and balance.
- *Digestive system*: Structural changes to the stomach and intestines occur. Constipation intensifies without enough exercise and fluids. The incidence of colon cancer increases with age.
- *Bladder and urinary tract*: Less elastic system leads to more urination, inflammation, kidney stones and disease, and gout.
- *Memory and thinking*: Slow or fast deterioration of brain cells reduces memory, clarity of thought, and emotional regulation.
- *Eyes and ears*: With age, we experience more difficulty focusing on objects, night driving, and too much light and glare. Hearing loss is common, too, especially high-pitched sounds.
- *Teeth*: More decay, dry mouth, and gum disease can cause more cavities, extractions, and root canal work.

- *Skin*: Epidermal skin thins and becomes less elastic and fragile, and it bruises more easily. Skin cancers increase in number.
- *Weight*: Metabolism and exercise slow down, leading to weight gain. Poor nutrition exacerbates lifestyle diseases.
- *Sexuality*: With age, sexual needs and performance change. Menopause and erectile dysfunction can affect sexuality.

You can't stop the aging process, and everyone ages differently. But, you can make choices that improve your ability to maintain an active, healthy life.

Mid-Career Angst

As we enter midlife, another attachment to youth raises its ugly head. This time, it involves our intelligence, careers, and overall happiness.

According to Arthur Brooks, professor at Harvard Business School, and author of *From Strength to Strength*, many people experience anguish in the middle to late part of their careers. Decline sets in between our thirties and early fifties, when our prefrontal cortex starts to degrade. Victories come less frequently, and we feel more isolated from friends and family. Research shows that we are most creative in the earlier parts of our careers. This *fluid intelligence* allows us to be more innovative, think flexibly, and solve abstract problems. But those raw smarts begin to decline in midcareer. In the latter parts of our career, we develop *crystallized intelligence* that is more focused on wisdom and a desire for service, teaching, and advising others.

Here's the problem: As we move through our careers, many of us suffer three addictions in midcareer: obsession with work and success, attachment to worldly rewards, and a fear of decline. Some of us are bored and lonely, others self-medicate and have sleep problems or feel burned out. Still others experience workaholism, hooked to the successes from their past. We desire "being special" over "being happy," killing ourselves working for more money, approval, power, and prestige. Not until we acknowledge this inside us and allow ourselves to be vulnerable can we move successfully from fluid to crystallized intelligence. Healthier people make this transition and have a fulfilling second half of their careers.

The problem for midlifers is that they get too attached to their earlier selves. They obsess over success without reflecting enough on its impact on their lives and families. They get stuck on the ambition train and don't appreciate what brings true fulfillment to their aging selves. Sadly, they rarely give themselves permission to reinvent their lives and choose a new path.

Fear of Aging

You wake up one morning, look in the mirror, and it hits you. You are now an "older adult." It might be a surprise, or you may have known it was coming. You start to notice facial wrinkles, graying hair, and senior moments. You see body changes like bruises and age spots and feel less stamina and muscle strength. You might begin to dress differently without noticing and find yourself wearing glasses or hearing aids. Others of us try our best to ignore the inevitable. Yet, inside your body, the four major lifestyle illnesses are ticking away without you even knowing. Welcome to the end of midlife.

Many of us are fearful about getting older. In fact, one survey found that 87% of Americans are scared of aging and death. We fear not living up to expectations, stop taking risks, and become fearful of the future. Some of us fear we are over the hill; others fear pain and disability; and still others are concerned about becoming dependent on others. For many, financial insecurity is on the top of the list.

Most of this angst comes from our internalized ageism. Negative voices in our heads say that aging is not for the faint of heart. Over 80% of people between fifty and eighty subscribe to ageist stereotypes. It starts in childhood with fairy tales and evil witches. As we get older, we tell jokes about aging, buy ageist birthday cards, celebrate young bodies in advertising, and may even feel age discrimination at work in hiring, promotions, and terminations. Despite our best intentions to shut down these thoughts, the antiaging industry takes hold and can undermine our self-esteem. Some of the most intense internalized ageism comes from older people themselves.

However, there is a major discrepancy between what people expect and what older people experience. Research by Becca Levy, professor of psychology and epidemiology at Yale School of Public Health, has confirmed a link between our beliefs about age and our health consequences—how positive and negative beliefs about getting older have profound effects on our physical and mental health.

Levy says, "Self-stereotypes influence memory and cognitive ability, our will to live, and cardiac survival rates. Negative stereotypes even predicted Alzheimer's disease markers."

In another study, people who had internalized more positive age beliefs, on average, lived 7.5 years longer. Levy reasons that people with internalized ageism are less motivated to take their medicine, eat well, and exercise. It can also lower self-confidence, raise people's stress levels, and put them at risk for heart disease and stroke.

These results should not come as a surprise when a 2016 World Health Organization survey of more than 83,000 people in fifty-seven countries found 60% of respondents said that older people are not respected. The lowest levels of respect were reported in high-income countries.

But there is good news, claims Levy. "People can shift their negative feelings to improve their well-being. When people are reminded of the many positive things about aging, they can experience immediate benefits such as becoming stronger and having more will to live. Age beliefs are not set in stone; they're malleable."

Obsessed with Illness

Some of us are too attached to our bodies. We monitor every sign and symptom of our bodily sensations. We talk constantly about our health with friends. We are hypervigilant about our medications and make frequent visits to our doctors and urgent clinics without any real apparent illness. It's normal to worry about your health, but it's not healthy to be obsessed by it.

This syndrome is a type of attachment known as "illness anxiety." Some call it "hypochondriasis." Folks with this attachment often feel real headaches, shakes, stomach distress, or heart palpitations, yet they are often unaware that anxiety and depression may be causing their symptoms. For many, this disturbance of perception where normal sensations are magnified into catastrophic thinking can be debilitating. Some of those afflicted even learn the apparent benefits of being sick—like getting attention. However, telling someone that their symptoms are "all in their head" won't go over well.

Often, there's a trigger that activates our "fight-or flight" system and stimulates our fears that translate into symptoms. These worries can preoccupy us, and suddenly our minds confuse minor symptoms with major illness. In fact, Swedish researchers found that people with hypochondriasis were 84% more likely than people without the disorder to die of dozens of conditions.

I had an up-front look at this attachment. My father had this illness anxiety. Many nights, he would call me to complain about his daily symptoms. He truly was in distress, and I had to talk him down from the ledge. He managed this condition with anxiety meds and became close friends with all his doctors. Clearly, you don't want to miss a symptom or sensation that is the first sign of serious illness, but this attachment can worry you to death—literally.

Sabotage Your Life

Many of us travel through life ignoring our health, placing ourselves at serious risk for the four major diseases. By engaging in unhealthy lifestyle risk factors like smoking, substance abuse, bad nutrition, inadequate sleep, and lack of exercise, we develop the diseases we fear most. Ignoring biomarkers like hypertension, physical exams, and other new preventative metrics only exacerbates the problem. This should not be a surprise, given how little we spend on preventative health and how much we spend on illness medicine.

Some of us live in denial, pretending our lifestyles have no effect on our health. Others simply don't care that they are poisoning their bodies with nicotine, sugars, alcohol, and drugs. I was one of those people for a time. Since exercise is most critical for staying healthy, it's amazing how many people complain they don't have enough time nor the interest to stay fit and prevent these diseases.

It's easy to undermine our health. The stresses of daily living, the tensions and trade-offs of work and family, and the challenges managing our finances are enough to preoccupy anyone. Add to that fatigue, anxiety, depression, and resentments, and you can easily reach a crisis point. This attachment hijacks us as we build plaque in our arteries, allow polyps to grow in our colons, ignore our diabetic meds, and allow our minds to languish. By wearing these blinders, we sabotage our lives.

Hiding From Age

Peg is eighty-six years old. She grew up in a small town in Upstate New York in an Irish Catholic family. "My family was flawed with illness," says Peg. "My mother had polio and lived in a wheelchair from the time I was six years old. My father had diabetes, as did his two brothers. And my sister had encephalitis at two and became dependent on me.

WHY ARE WE KILLING OURSELVES?

- US life expectancy is falling behind peer countries: US 76.8; Scotland 78.3; Taiwan 80.6; and Norway 83 years.
- The United States has the greatest number of excess deaths between ages 35–64 compared to peer nations.
- Lifespans in the United States's richest communities have been inching upward but lag far behind comparable areas in Japan, Canada, and France.
- Chronic illnesses erase more than twice as many years of life among people younger than 65 than all overdoses, homicides, car accidents, and suicides combined.
- According to the CDC, 80% of all strokes are preventable.
- Cancer has grown among people younger than 50, with the highest increase in breast, thyroid, and colorectal cancer.
- One in seven US citizens still smoke, according to the CDC.
- Younger Americans have the most extreme death rates compared to peer countries due to opiates and guns.
- Adults 35–64 in the most rural areas of the United States were 45% more likely to die each year than people in the largest urban centers.

"For those reasons, I spent many years of my life ignoring my health—and aging. I didn't want to think about it. That time was difficult, and it still affects me.

"I wanted to live my life differently. Despite smoking for twenty-five years, I was able to live a healthier life—to feel good, do things, and be free. When I did feel pain, I figured it would just go away."

It's 5:30 in the afternoon, and Peg has a glass of wine in her hand. She reflects: "At eighty-six, I know that life can be difficult, and I've got that coming, no doubt sometime, but not right now. I still see myself as physically and emotionally healthy."

The next day, the world changed for Peg. One of her best friends died, and over the next twelve months, Peg attended six funerals of her dear friends.

Later, she told me, "This year has been difficult for me. I miss my friends a lot, and I miss my lifestyle with them. We had wonderful friendships and traveled the world together.

"But reality set in and forced me to think about illness and my eventual death for the first time. This year I really got to sit with my feelings. Now, I do fear illness, but I don't fear death. I've lived a full life, longer than either of my parents, and I'm grateful. But I don't feel regret much at all."

Denial can be a powerful blinder. It helps to protect us from our feelings of pain, especially fear. In Peg's case, she put thinking about disease and aging in a tiny crevice in the back of her mind. Her personal fears about being like her infirmed parents lay dormant inside that crack for years.

Like many of us, a life event, like divorce, being laid off, or illness, or a death can open the crevice and release our fears into conscious awareness. Peg's attachment to youth—in her case, her fear of illness and deterioration—emerged at the back of her life.

LEARNING TO AGE GRACEFULLY

The key to aging gracefully is to confront your attachment to youth head-on. Whether you are yearning for youthfulness, suffering from mid-career angst, fearing the aging process, obsessing about illness, or living an unhealthy lifestyle, you must look inward and then change your behavior. Here are some recommendations:

Live Longer and Live Longer Better

- How can you maintain your health, strength, and energy to stay vital throughout your life?
- How can you lengthen your lifespan and extend your health span?
- How can you evolve naturally and be the best version of yourself at any age?
- How do you prioritize your overall well-being while you accept the aging process?

From my review of the research, we can now answer these questions with considerable certainty. By adopting eight lifestyle habits, we can add decades to our lives—by not smoking, staying physically active, managing stress, eating a healthy diet, having good sleep hygiene, avoiding binge drinking, rejecting addictive opiates, and maintaining positive social relationships.

Men who adopt all eight health habits by middle age live twenty-four years longer on average than men whose lifestyle included few or none of the habits. Women increased their lives by twenty-three years. Mortality rates declined as the number of healthy habits they followed increased.

No doubt, as we age, the risk of the four major diseases grows exponentially. We can delay these illnesses for a long time by committing to these essential health habits. This decision demands more of you—to stay well informed, set clear goals, change habits, confront problems early, and put skin in the game. It will be the best decision that you make for your entire life.

Here's the surprise: Exercise is by far the most important health habit. According to Peter Attia, MD, "Exercise contributes the most to our lifespan and health span. Through aerobic efficiency, maximum aerobic output, strength and stability, regular exercisers live as much as a decade longer than sedentary people."

The US government's physical activity guidelines suggest that "active adults should engage in at least 30 minutes of moderate-intensity aerobic activity, five times per week (or 150 minutes in total). This exercise is to be supplemented with two days of strength training, targeting 'all the major muscle groups.'"

Exercise targets all four of the major diseases—it strengthens the heart, maintains metabolic health, fortifies our immune system, fights off cancer, stimulates new muscles and stronger bones, and helps to keep the brain healthy. Not a bad investment!

At age forty-two, I was diagnosed with atrial fibrillation. Who knows where it came from? For years I never thought about my heart. Now suddenly, in early midlife, I started to experience my ticker every moment of every day. It's weird how that happens, and I suspect my fellow heart patients know exactly what I'm talking about.

Over time, with medication and a baby aspirin, I made peace with my periodic palpitations. Three years ago, my sinus rhythm in my right atrium started to slow down, and I got a pacemaker. After some adjustment, I accelerated my exercise routine and feel more vital than ever.

Vitality is a popular way of describing everything that affects our ability to pursue life with health, strength, and energy. It's a driver and an outcome of health and work/life engagement, and essential for individuals, organizations, and communities. It includes our physical, emotional, spiritual, social, intellectual, occupational, financial, and environmental health.

A 2022 Cigna/Evernorth Vitality Index surveyed ten thousand adults across the United States. Higher vitality people experience better mental and physical health and higher levels of job satisfaction and performance. Fewer than one in five US adults have high levels of vitality, a combined 82% fall in the low and medium vitality categories.

One group in the top category offers the role models for all of us—the super agers. According to AARP, "a super ager is someone over eighty with an exceptional memory—one at least as good as a person 20 or 30 years younger.

"So, what are their secrets? They control their blood sugar and blood pressure, talk to friends—a lot—avoid stress and prioritize mental health, and get a good night's sleep. They also protect their vision and hearing, push themselves physically, and do more hobbies and activities."

STATS ON FITNESS

- For 77% of the US population, exercise is not part of their life.
- Only about a fifth of all adults in the United States get the minimum recommended amount of vigorous activity (about eleven minutes a day).
- According to the JAMA, cardiovascular fitness is inversely associated with long-term mortality with no observed upper limit of benefit.
- A ten-year observation study of 4,500 people, ages fifty and older, found that those with low muscle mass were at a 40–50% greater risk of mortality than controls.
- Having more muscle mass is highly correlated with a lower risk of falls, a leading cause of death and disability among the elderly.
- According to the CDC, more than 27% of Americans over age forty-five suffer from chronic pain, and about 10–12% say pain limits activities on most days. Back pain is the leading cause of disability around the world.
- Short sleep (less than six hours a night) is associated with about a 6–26% increase in cardiovascular disease and a 20% increase in heart attacks. Sleeping six to nine hours a night was associated with a reduction in heart attack risk.

For many of us, "memory peaks between the ages of 30 and 40. Overall brain volume begins to atrophy in our 50s, particularly in the areas linked to complex thought processes and learning. But the brains of the super agers don't behave this way. Their brains are shrink-resistant; have memory cells that are supersized; and have more social intelligence cells."

Super agers overcome the wear and tear that cognitively average people succumb to and live a physically and intellectually active lifestyle. By constantly challenging themselves and moderating their indulgences, the super agers conquer the threats of dementia.

Practice Conscious Aging

The secret to growing older is to practice conscious aging. Knowledge is power, so educate yourself about what to expect as you age. Make sure you separate fact from fiction. Remember you have the freedom to live the way you want at any age. Don't compare your life to others. Love and accept yourself at every stage. And make a commitment to health your entire life. Here are some specific suggestions:

- *Talk about aging with your friends and family.* Everyone experiences their own version of aging. Learn from the best of them. Don't exclude people of any age. We have much to learn from children, teenagers, midlifers, and our elders. Talk about your fears and resentments with someone you trust. When you keep these fears to yourself, they can grow larger and more daunting.
- *Focus on the present.* The more you live in the here and now, the less attached you will be to the past or the future. Don't dwell on what may or may not happen today or tomorrow. Make every minute count. Notice what is good in your life, savor your joyful moments, and ponder the lessons you are learning. Research shows that meditation serves as an excellent buffer against aging anxiety.

- *Discover your higher purpose.* The sooner you realize your higher purpose, the more meaningful life will be for you. Is it raising children, making money, giving back, etc? It took me forty years to discover that my higher purpose was "helping people become a little bigger and better than I found them." I wish I had figured that out earlier in my life. Nonetheless, it has guided me ever since.

- *Practice gratitude.* Research shows that focusing on what you feel grateful for significantly lessens your aging anxiety. Keep a gratitude journal and write down what you are learning at each stage along the way. The more you express gratitude to yourself and others, the more you will appreciate what you have in your life and the less compelled you will be to rush through it.

- *See the beauty and benefits of aging.* In today's youth-obsessed culture, more and more people associate aging with losing beauty, athletic prowess, and even love and respect. Instead, reframe your traits as positives. You've lived a good life and earned it. Savor your memories, enjoy your deepening friendships, and take comfort in your sense of self. Don't forget to strengthen your commitment to health: exercise daily, eat a full meal, get plenty of sleep, learn new things, and stay socially connected.

Marian, a retired high school teacher, provides a good example of this commitment. "I'm very conscious of aging, yet I'm not worried about it; it's just my path of self-realization.

"My husband is my best friend. I'm involved in local politics, women's rights, Black Lives Matter, animal welfare, and social justice. And I still go to bed at 10 PM and wake up at 5 AM to start my day.

"I was wild in high school and college. Yet I have lived a healthy lifestyle ever since. When I was in my twenties and thirties, I thought

I was going to live forever, and didn't worry about my health. Now the most important aspect of my life is good health—physically, emotionally, and mentally. If you don't have your health, you have nothing. I'm clear about what I can and cannot control. I wake up and say to myself, I'm going to do the best I can today.

"I don't have the same energy I had when I was thirty. When I find myself getting stressed, I try my best to go to a place that soothes me to safeguard myself against the toxicity in the world.

"Today, I look at my life as a journey, not a destination. I truly feel blessed."

Maintain a Youthful Personality

Maintaining a youthful spirit is one of the great gifts we can give to ourselves. Regardless of our age, we can always look at life with positive energy and adventure. Scientists are now investigating the effects of this personality type on well-being and longevity. Youthful personality traits include:

- Optimistic attitude and carefree outlook that leads to joyful living and youthful energy, enabling us to live life to the fullest.
- An open and creative mind that loves to learn. A youthful personality stays curious, takes risks, thinks quickly, and enjoys new experiences.
- A desire to challenge and believe in themselves. With self-awareness, these people recover quickly from failure or disappointment.
- Youthful personalities enjoy being around people. They are more approachable, more forgiving, and don't take themselves too seriously.
- They make self-care a priority by reducing stress, adhering to core beliefs, and optimizing physical and mental energy.

People with these personality types are likely to live longer. In fact, this way of living predicts greater longevity five decades later.

Develop a Blue Zone Around You

Dan Buettner, author of *The Blue Zones: Secrets for Living Longer*, set out on a worldwide search for places where people are living longer. Called "blue zones," these pockets of longevity were hot spots where health and longevity stemmed from their surroundings. He wanted to focus on the environments in which they lived; their communities, workplaces, homes, and businesses.

In his search, Buettner discovered six blue zones around the world: Sardinia, Italy; Nicoya Peninsula, Costa Rica; Ikaria, Greece; Okinawa, Japan; Loma Linda, California; and Singapore. He profiled each blue zone and distilled their common characteristics:

- *Food:* They live on a whole-food, plant-based diet, avoid meat, and snack on nuts. The residents buy healthy foods in grocery stores and restaurants, grow healthy foods in their gardens, and drink plenty of water. They drink wine at 5 PM, eat a light dinner until they are 80% full, and even fast occasionally.

- *Movement*: People in the blue zones live full and meaningful lives. They enjoy their work and slow down as needed, take regular naps, and move naturally every twenty minutes. They improve their walkability and bike-ability that helps them travel around their communities.

- *Family*: Their immediate families are paramount in their lives and their aging parents live nearby. They have unrushed family dinners, and their goal is to get closer to family, beauty, and nature.

- *Friends*: Finding their tribe and laughing with friends they trust is a high priority. They enjoy volunteering and belong to nourishing social support groups.

- *Values*: The blue zone residents are committed to living their values. They care about their higher purpose, always giving something back, and work hard to be interested and interesting. They choose safe neighborhoods and cities, buy good health-care, and live a good life.

Why don't you try creating a blue zone around you?

 **Reflections**

- In what ways are your body and mind showing signs of aging?
- How do you sabotage your own health and well-being?
- What are your personal lifestyle risk factors, and how can you reduce them?
- How does your internalized ageism affect how you think and act?
- How does your work stress affect your health?
- What is your level of energy in the morning? Afternoon? Evening? How can you improve it?
- How will you embrace each stage in your life and remain healthy throughout?

NINE

THE ATTACHMENT TO SELF

- Are you sometimes uncomfortable in your own skin?
- Do you avoid showing your real self to others?
- Do you ever feel lonely or isolated from others?
- Do you have difficulties with your romantic relationships?
- Do you have trouble reading people's thoughts and feelings?

n Greek mythology, Narcissus, the handsome mortal son of gods, falls in love with his own beautiful image reflected in a pool of water. Obsessed with himself, he is punished for his vanity, self-absorption, and lack of empathy. As he takes his dying breath before drowning in the lake, his last words to his *own* reflection were, "Goodbye, my love."

Narcissus's attachment to himself died at that very moment. In modern times, this narcissism is marked by grandiosity, selfishness, and the need for attention. Yet when the nymphs turned his body over after his death, they found underneath a beautiful narcissus flower blooming in all its glory. What was left behind was his healthier self: his awareness, inspiration, creativity, and vitality that never went away. This chapter is about both sides of ourselves.

LIVING WITH YOURSELF

As far as we know, no other animal can think about itself because self-reflection requires a prefrontal cortex that is distinctly human. Your ability to be self-aware helps you look in the mirror and explore your inner thoughts and feelings. Only a few animals, like chimpanzees and dolphins, can see their mirror image as their own.

As humans, we have a rich internal life, one full of pleasures, habits, and elaborate stories we tell ourselves. We search for a higher purpose, consciously manage our lives, and intentionally bounce back from adversity. We have language capability that enables us to think about our goals, make decisions, and evaluate other people's perspectives. We can motivate ourselves, exhibit self-control, and develop confidence and courage.

Our internal lives enable us to observe ourselves as unique individuals, distinct from other people and our surroundings. However, as Narcissus's tale illustrates, we also have a dark side. We can get self-absorbed and preoccupied with our own needs and desires. When we become too attached to ourselves and too disconnected from others, problems occur. Arrogance, depression, anger, and anxiety can take hold, and if we're lucky, we come to realize we are living on an island, all alone in the world.

Fortunately, we also have an innate wisdom and humanity resting dormant inside us—complete with empathy, generosity, and love—that connects us to ourselves, other people, and the world.

CONNECTING WITH OTHERS

All life is connected and interdependent, from the micro level of cells, the interpersonal nature of relationships, and the macro space of the environment. Let's start with our cells.

Scientists say that our bodies—down to the cellular level—are in constant communication with our environment. One distinctive quality of any cell is its dependence on both its internal properties and its connections with other cells. Although it can exist as a single entity, it is better equipped for survival when it interacts with other cells.

A healthy cell allows only essential nutrients to enter it, shutting out toxins and other harmful substances. According to cellular biology researcher Bruce Lipton, a cell's genes can also be turned on and off by chemical and electrical signals stimulated by our thoughts and feelings. Although we can survive on our own, we also grow and learn to adapt by joining other organisms and interacting with our external environment.

At the interpersonal level, we are much closer to each other than you might think. Human beings are biologically and psychologically programmed not only to form social bonds but also to connect in deep, personal ways. We are born to belong, and our brains are wired to seek out these connections even at the micro level.

As it turns out, we, as humans, are equipped with two warrior brain neurons that can help us share empathy with others and influence others' moods and behaviors. One of these helpers is the "mirror" neuron, aptly named because of its function. Smiling, laughing, or scowling at someone can affect their attitude as well as our own. For example, our senses these days are bombarded by grisly scenes of disasters, crime, and war. Our mirror warriors react with empathy for those we see with real sadness. On the other hand, there is a reason that NBC chooses to end its *Nightly News* broadcast with "There's good tonight in the world," followed with a report of random acts of kindness and feel-good events that leave us feeling connected and happy.

The second warrior neuron, the "spindle" cell, signals positive vibes and affects our interconnectedness with others. A study involving how people react to a performance evaluation shows how this works. One group of people received a negative evaluation, but it was delivered with positive emotions, like smiles and nods. A second group got positive evaluations with negative emotional signals, like frowns and stern expressions. In interviews afterward, those who received positive signals and negative evaluations felt better about themselves and presumably performed better after the review. The tenor of the emotions made all the difference.

As I write this, I'm reminded of Ken Samet, CEO of MedStar Health, who runs a $4.1 billion regional health system with thirty thousand associates, and Linda Rabbitt, CEO of rand* construction, a global leader of women-owned businesses. Both colleagues of mine for over twenty years have that special spark of authenticity and humanity that inspires everyone they touch.

Ken says, "You must be real; you cannot fake it. It's important for people to believe that I'm very sincere and real in what I've been telling them." Linda agrees: "I have a philosophy that everything counts. You're the same person everywhere you go—at home, at work, at church, and at school—in your personal and public life." Together, in their own way, by connecting to themselves, they successfully connect with others.

At the macro level, it's not rocket science that our global environment is interconnected. At home, the bees pollinate flowers in our gardens. Tree roots communicate and send nutrients to each other. We share the air with animals, plants, and people.

On the world stage, global travel, social media, and transportation connect us like never before. As the world gets smaller, cultural connections spur more diverse communities. Global trade accelerates all these connections as customers, talent, money, and materials are shared around the globe in record time.

But there is bad news. Pollution and rising CO_2 levels are warming the planet. We are experiencing flooding and rising oceans, incessant migration and food shortages, more pests and evolving diseases, and extreme weather events. To make matters worse, global political instability and our angst about the future fester inside the souls of our global citizens.

The best analogy I've heard comes from Thomas Friedman, author of *Hot, Flat, and Crowded*, who links the body's health to the health of the planet. When our body temperature is 98.6, we feel well; when it reaches 100.6, we feel under the weather; and when it reaches 102.6, we are very ill and stay in bed. Sometimes we go to the hospital. The same is true for Mother Nature and our global planet. With a two-to-three-degree increase in global warming, our ecosystem is very sick and needs medicine as soon as possible.

HUMAN BEINGS AND DIGITAL MACHINES

You can't talk about relationships anymore without discussing our connection with digital machines. I've been fascinated by this evolving relationship for years and how it is changing our lives and the new world of work. Social platforms have expanded exponentially. From LinkedIn, Facebook, WhatsApp, and YouTube to Google, TikTok, X, and Pinterest, we brand ourselves and connect with others worldwide. Manufacturers, retailers, restaurants, and hospitality sites link suppliers, investors, employees, and customers, and are capitalizing on greater speed and agility that these technologies offer.

Now artificial intelligence and ChatGPT are revolutionizing our lives. Virtually every job will eventually be affected by AI. This new way of living and doing business will require new mindsets and behaviors. Digital brainpower is quickly becoming our new core capability. The digital-savvy people will think critically, experiment with new ideas, make faster decisions, and develop more advanced social skills.

Machines are not human minds—yet—but they are assuming more of the attributes we used to believe were uniquely human: reason, action, language, logic, and learning. The future is now.

Paradoxically, we are alone in the world *and* connected to it at the same time—linking family, friends, and technology to organizations, communities, countries, and our planet. How we live our lives, build relationships, support our organizations, and protect the planet will make all the difference moving forward.

DEVELOPING YOURSELF AND BEING WITH OTHERS

Father Berard Tierney has lived a good life. At eighty-two, he has lived in two separate worlds at different times in his life: one in the Catholic monastery for twenty-two years surrounded by fellow Carmelite priests; the other for forty-two years with his husband and their friends. In both worlds, Berard is a deep thinker, committed to his own spiritual and psychological development, frequently asking the hard questions of life: Who am I? What's my purpose? What's next in my life?

The other part of Berard is clearly connected to people—his family, his friends, his fellow priests, and his community. Affable, engaging, and inquisitive by nature, Berard invests much time and energy in his relationships and prides himself on his lifelong friendships. To me, he represents someone who balances knowing and loving oneself while staying closely connected to others.

"At sixteen I had an image that one day I would become a priest," recalls Berard. "My dream came true soon after, and I entered the Catholic monastery. There, I received my high school, college, and graduate degrees. It was a good education."

The monastery is a place for individual reflection, community living, daily prayers, church worship, and deep relationships with fellow priests. "I enjoyed my studies and quiet time," says Berard, "and the community provided great companionship. I never experienced loneliness, and I got along with everyone. I was the haircut guy, and you can imagine that everyone had a story to tell. The expectation was that everyone kept their celibacy vows, and dating was not allowed."

At the age of thirty-nine, after a decade of living in the monastery, Berard found himself often in deep discernment as he started to question his commitment to celibacy and the church. "I knew I was gay, but up to now I was unwilling to act on it.

"One day on my travels to another seminary, I met a wonderful fellow seminarian. Although I was still deeply embedded in the church, I quickly fell for him. Over the next year, we talked and saw each other often.

"Eventually, we left religious life together, but the decision to leave was not easy, primarily because I had to tell my siblings. Back at the monastery, some friends were upset, and the provincials who led the order were clearly not happy with me. But my deep relationship with myself won out.

"At the monastery, we never had to make money because, early on, we took a vow of poverty. Our greatest fear upon leaving was supporting ourselves and our lack of commercial skills. I started out as a bank teller, then moved up to head of employee relations, and became vice president of human resources at a nearby hospital. At the back end of my career, I worked as an executive coach, primarily with the World Bank." Through it all, Berard always sees people as bigger than themselves and enjoys helping to unleash their potential.

"I have been married for forty-two years. And like our church community, I have lots of friends and enjoy entertaining others. This is my community outside the monastery.

"Recently, I had a stroke and a bout of melanoma. Aging is inevitable and I accept it. If you have a good relationship with yourself, and good friends, it certainly makes aging a lot easier.

"I still have a deep spirituality, although I would say my relationship with God has changed. I have different questions for God these days."

HOW WELL ARE YOU BALANCING YOUR LIFE?

Being with Yourself
- Do you naturally observe and reflect on yourself?
- Are you comfortable in your own skin?
- Do you stand up and protect yourself when needed?
- Do you have ideals and values and live by them?
- Do you take responsibility for your actions?
- Are you confident and humble?
- Is your goal to be happy and fulfilled?
- Do you pride yourself in being real and authentic?

Connecting with Others
- Do you have good relationships with family and friends?
- Do you talk about your "inner self" with others?
- Are you aware of other people's thoughts and feelings?
- Are you the same person in all situations?
- Are you open-minded and listen and learn from others?
- Do you prioritize telling the truth to others?
- Are you an empathetic and caring person?
- What is your relationship to digital machines?

ATTACHMENT TO SELF

Let's take a closer look at how we can get locked up inside our own heads. When this happens, we isolate ourselves, act as if we are the center of the universe, or believe we are better than other people. In each case, we disconnect from ourselves and the world and truly believe we can thrive without authentic, meaningful relationships.

The Isolated Self

The data tells the story:

- According to US Census data, there are 31 million adults living alone in the US, reaching a record high. Nearly 16 million people aged 65 and older live alone in 2022, three times as many as those who lived alone in the 1960s.

- A 2021 US Census Bureau report found a quarter of 40-year-olds in the United States have never been married, compared with 1980, when 6% of 40-year-olds had never married.

- A 2022 report from the University of Virginia National Marriage Project found the median age of a first marriage has increased over the last 50 years, from 23 in 1970 to 30 for men, and from 21 to 28 years for women.

- Over one-third of people getting divorced are now over the age of fifty. That number has doubled since 1990, and 50% of them are living alone. Projections predict that the number of single-person households, ages seventy-five and over, will soar in the coming years. Many will be women.

- A 2021 survey by the Survey Center on American Life found that men are more alone than ever. Only 48% are satisfied with their friendships. One in five said they have gotten emotional support from a friend in the last week, compared to four in ten for women.

- A recent Meta/Gallup survey found nearly one in four adults across the world in 142 countries reported feeling lonely. The rates of loneliness were highest in young adults.

- Among older adults, social isolation and loneliness have been linked to increased risk of dementia, infections, heart disease, and cancer. People who are socially isolated have a 32% chance of dying early compared with those who don't experience social isolation.

- The US Centers for Disease Control and Prevention reports that more people (49,449) died in 2022 from suicide than any other year on record, dating back to at least 1941. Men were four times more likely than women to die from suicide, and rates were highest among senior men. But the suicide rate increased twice as much for women in 2022.

Nothing is "wrong" with living alone. In fact, many people, of all ages, savor their independence and enjoy the comforts of single living. They may be single or coupled, create wonderful partnerships living in two different households, or they manage a reconstituted family with children from a previous marriage. Others need alone time to transition from the loss of a loved one or the birth of a new relationship. Many of us simply live alone and create a new family with a diverse network of great friends.

Yet there's a difference between living alone, social isolation, and loneliness. Living alone describes your social lifestyle; social isolation refers to your lack of social connections; and loneliness is your feeling of being alone.

A growing body of research indicates that loneliness is a biological and psychological phenomenon with significant negative health consequences. People feel lonely for lots of different reasons; they lose a friend or loved one, relocate to a new community, or don't like people at work. Poor coping skills and difficulty in relationships can also exacerbate these feelings.

When these circumstances occur, the brain's neurotransmitters, important for bonding and connection, go awry. The fight-or-flight response goes into overdrive; we feel threatened with greater anxiety, and we can get hijacked by self-defeating thoughts or feelings of fear and shame when we are alone. Sometimes, we can even be surrounded by others and still feel lonely as hell.

The Selfish Self

Some people choose to live on islands of self-interest where they focus inward, stay attached to self, and distance themselves from others. Whether their intentions are conscious or unconscious, they often wear blinders and tarnish the quality of their relationships.

Selfish people are generally preoccupied with themselves and lack consideration for others, like bosses who are obsessed with their own career progression and ignore the stresses and work concerns of their teammates.

Self-centered people put themselves at the center of everything in their life, while ignoring others around them. Some call this egocentricity. When conversing with others, they often change the subject back to them and their experiences, with "I," "me," or "myself," and never really listen when the other person is speaking to them.

Self-absorbed people are preoccupied with themselves and their own affairs, deeply entranced by their own needs, interests, and activities. I must admit that when I'm writing a book, I can get self-absorbed and ignore the dog's barking, forget to wash the dishes and clean my office or answer the phone. The Tibetan proverb says it all: "Don't notice the tiny flea in the other person's hair and overlook the lumbering yak on your own nose."

The Narcissistic Self

"Narcissism" is a popular word in our modern lexicon. The diagnosis is thrown around a lot, but people forget that it operates on a spectrum, from healthy narcissism with confidence, self-esteem, and pride to unhealthy narcissism, complete with a variety of dysfunctional thoughts, feelings, and behaviors.

Along with selfishness, self-centeredness, and self-absorption, fully baked narcissists feel special and entitled, lack empathy and compassion, and manipulate others. They can ignore rules and standards of behavior and exploit people as pawns in their lives. Underneath their feelings of superiority lie deeply embedded, unconscious feelings of inadequacy and fears of insignificance. Scared of feeling threatened and vulnerable, they often blame others and never take responsibility for their own actions.

Each of these types—the isolated, selfish, and narcissistic types— sabotage their health, happiness, and success. Only through deep self-reflection and self-awareness, and often professional help, can they overcome their negative habits and feelings and unlock their attachment to self. Over time, feelings of unconditional love, compassion, and empathy can surface and help them detach from their overly invested selves.

Lost and Found

Chris, a construction general manager, shared a story with me. At eighteen, "I was partying hard one night and a friend asked me to give him a ride home. 'Sure,' I said, but I left the party early to spend time with my girlfriend, instead of doing the right thing and giving him what I promised. My friend died that night, and I spiraled out of control, went down a hole of partying and drinking. Over a couple years, I had three DUIs, suspended licenses, and was arrested seven times and off to jail. I thought I would end up in jail and never get out.

"When I was in my younger days, I blamed everyone else for my problems. I blamed my friends, my family, everybody, everywhere. At some point you've just got to look at the bigger picture and ask what's really the problem. The problem wasn't everyone else. The problem was me. I was immature and only thought about myself, and it was easier to blame somebody else than it was to look in the mirror.

"At twenty-four, I met Sarah. She was different, already working on her career, probably the most stable person I knew, more mature, more responsible. I looked up to her. We have just hit sixteen years of marriage.

"It took some time to change. I set short-term goals for myself that were reachable. But first, I had to get a job. I worked as a day laborer and a waiter in a restaurant, but my work wasn't going anywhere. Then I landed a construction service manager job. Eventually I got promoted to senior project manager overseeing carpenters, painters, roofers, and stone guys—about thirty people at any one time. That position felt much better, and I set five-year goals for myself.

"I had my daughter during the partying days. Today she's sixteen and a beautiful young teenager. We have joint custody, and I want to be the father she looks up to, to direct her in the right direction, to be loving, set boundaries, and help her believe in herself. I don't want her to make the same mistakes that I made in my life.

"Today, I'm a better person, husband, father, manager, and friend. Nobody's perfect, but I try to practice what I preach."

Chris grew from a self-absorbed, selfish teenager who isolated himself in his own little world, blaming others for his problems, to a mature, loving, responsible adult. And he did it himself, with the help of Sarah.

When we fixate on self-focused thoughts and feelings, like Chris did, it's not unusual to experience a variety of psychological symptoms such as depression and anxiety. Yet as we loosen our attachment to ourselves, it leads to greater self-compassion and well-being.

A 2018 study proved just that. Researchers created a seven-item test measuring non-attachment to self, examined people across age, gender, and religious demographics, and measured the impact on their well-being. On the assessment, people were asked to what extent they agreed or disagreed with these types of statements: "I can let go of unhelpful thoughts about myself," "As time goes on, I feel less and less of a need to be a certain way," and "I can experience my personal ups and downs without getting caught up in them." The people not attached to self were healthier compared to others who were self-absorbed.

DIFFICULT RELATIONSHIPS

In our disconnected, polarized world, it's not surprising that many of us struggle with difficult relationships. Deepak Chopra talks about how we pass along our negative feelings about ourselves to our relationships with others by "attacking, blaming, clinging, dominating, manipulating and controlling others."

So how does this transference happen? Early childhood relationships set the stage for how you build relationships as an adult. Much like our attachments in early life, there are four types of adult attachments: secure, anxious, avoidant, and disorganized.

The "securely attached" people express their emotions freely in an atmosphere of intimacy, honesty, and tolerance. They trust others, communicate easily, and manage conflict well.

"Anxiously attached" people worry about their partner's commitment, need approval from others, and often cling to their relationships. They are highly sensitive to criticism, feel unworthy of love, and have difficulty being alone.

The "avoidant" types are generally strong and self-sufficient, withdraw from emotional intimacy, and often push their partners away. They like their independence and enjoy spending time alone or with friends.

The "disorganized" partners want intimacy and closeness but have trouble trusting and depending on others. They have difficulty regulating their emotions and often are fearful of rejection.

As you think about what type you are, do you ever wonder why you gravitate toward one type of person or relationship and avoid others? One reason might be that we are attracted to people who speak to the inner child within us and all the unmet needs and feelings that we felt early in our lives. Some of us unconsciously choose partners in a senseless repetitive pattern that tries to relive these relationships but never leaves us fulfilled.

All these chronic patterns of dysfunctional romantic relationships are doomed to frustrate or fail us. I like to call them "neurotic locks," mainly because we chase after these relationships, get imprisoned by them, and repeat them over time. You know the patterns: the chaser and distancer, the controller and dependent, the rejector and depressed, the caretaker and sufferer, and the sadist and masochist. If we want to get rid of these psychic chains, we must look inward to examine the deep childhood dynamics that dictate our adult relationships.

We need deep connections now more than ever, but some of us don't know how to have healthy relationships. There's certainly a plethora of books outlining what *not* to do. They seem to fall in common categories:

- *Poor communication*: Many of us don't know how to communicate. We are blinded by our scars and fears about money, sex, jealousy, and commitment. We also lack empathy skills and run away from direct, respectful conversations.
- *Destructive conflicts*: Suspicious of others' intentions, we feel threatened, resentful, and vulnerable. We isolate ourselves or blame them while playing winners and losers.
- *Misunderstandings*: Many of us feel unheard and misunderstood as our partners talk over us and negate our opinions or experience. These disconnects intensify and leave both parties unfulfilled.

- *Lack of intimacy*: Emotional distance is one of the loneliest feelings in any relationship. Living in our heads, lacking physical intimacy, or never laughing sets the stage for triggering our partners with hurt, fear, and anger.

Many of these problems are triggered by our own attachments—especially ones focusing on the past, the future, control, and perfection.

John Gottman, one of the world's experts on relationships, has studied more than forty thousand couples over his career. He believes he can predict divorce with 93.6% accuracy by measuring the amount of criticism, contempt, defensiveness, and stonewalling in a relationship.

Fortunately, we are getting smarter about our relationships. Helen Fisher, a senior researcher at the Kinsey Institute and chief science adviser for Match.com, studies the behavior and attitudes of single people in the US every year. In 2022, she asked people what they were looking for in a prospective partner. She got the usual answers—trustworthiness, common interests, and sexual attractiveness, but this year another characteristic made it to the top. People wanted emotional maturity from their friends and partners, the ability to deal with their feelings.

Learning the Art of Relationships

Don Sloane, one of the most well respected recovery leaders in the US, didn't start that way. His story is about his attachment to himself and how he courageously learned to reach beyond his own little world to help hundreds of people with their life challenges.

"My parents divorced when I was eight months old," says Don. "My father was absent, and I lived with my mother and older brother. All I remember is that we lived in a broken home; it was deeply ensconced in my DNA. And I grew up feeling like a broken person. Over time, I built a life of faulty beliefs and behaviors that reinforced who I was.

"When I was fourteen, I was told I had a very high IQ, but believed I would never come close to reaching my full potential." Don's sense of brokenness continued through adolescence. He married at age twenty-one and swore he would never get a divorce. But the arguments blossomed, and divorce was inevitable.

Don then went looking for job stability. "With the help of my mother, I started a home improvement business, and with little skill, I realized halfway through my first job that I had no idea what the hell I was doing. It was a time when I disappeared out of the blue, detached from my mother and others.

"My drinking and drugging took over in my early twenties. I remember a doctor gave me a prescription for Valium and told me to take one when I didn't feel good—which was often. From benzos to pot, pot to alcohol, and alcohol to cocaine. I felt broken as a person, lost in my own little world, as the alcohol and drugs numbed me from the pain. I wondered how I would ever get from being broken to being unbroken.

"At thirty, with the help of therapy, meditation, and prayer, I turned the corner and kicked my addiction." Then, dormant feelings of confidence, courage, and capacity started to emerge. Don recalls, "I had fantasies and worries about my future, but the brokenness still clouded my self-image."

With patience and persistence, Don left his destructive cocoon and began to loosen his attachment to himself, his problems, and his limited worldview. "At that point, I started to open the door to the people around me."

Slowly, the new Don emerged. "I was lucky that I was surrounded by men in my life who gave me permission to explore being a new person. I didn't have to hold on to the chains from my past and didn't have to hide the empathy, loving kindness, and generosity hidden deep inside myself. I was able to experiment with letting these gentler core feelings out, and to experiment with them." This is not an uncommon feeling among men today.

Eventually, Don became the man he always wanted to be. From corporate leader, to entrepreneur, to sponsor and thought leader. Today, he is happily married and reconnected with his children. With his deep background in addiction, he runs his own successful recovery business, seeking out people to nurture and protect, and helping them with their own journeys.

LEARNING TO LOVE GENEROUSLY

The first step in detaching from "self" is that you must learn to love generously. A true survival emotion, loving yourself acts as a catalyst for loving others and building healthy relationships by practicing generosity, kindness, and forgiveness. This mindset establishes a feeling of belonging to a larger whole and connections—even across cultures and religions.

The twentysomething musicians Yaron Kohlberg from Israel and Bishara Haroni from Palestine together present piano concerto performances as "Duo Amal," ("amal" meaning "hope" in Arabic) to much critical acclaim in Europe, Asia, the United States, and the Middle East. As such, theirs is a success story of "We." Transcending political, cultural, and religious boundaries, their dynamic concerts serve as a role model for people and countries to correct long-standing tensions and animosities. Their alliance through music inspires us all with hope for a brighter future.

We all can take our cue from them and create a better balance between the "I" and "we." People who use the word "I" more than "we" are more self-absorbed, self-centered, and struggle to put themselves in other people's shoes. They also are at a higher risk of heart attack! Research on human connections shows that people who love generously and maintain diversified networks of friends and communities are happier, healthier, and higher performing.

Brené Brown, in her book *Braving the Wilderness*, reports that we cut ourselves off from others because of fear of vulnerability, hurt, pain, criticism, and conflict. Yet, deep inside, "We want to be a part of something bigger . . ."

The pride that comes from "I," with the belonging that comes from "we," starts with practicing self-love first and then extending that love generously to others to create healthy relationships.

THE FOUR INGREDIENTS TO HEALTHY RELATIONSHIPS

In my travels talking to people around the world, I've observed that there are four powerful social ingredients that help foster great relationships with others—empathy, fairness, communication, and appreciation. Let's look at each one.

Empathy: Don't Leave Home Without It

Empathy is deep understanding on an emotional and cognitive level about the aspirations, fears, and concerns of people. Being empathic is not always easy. You may need to understand someone who is fundamentally different from you, confront negative feelings you have about the person, or address your fear that being too nice will send false signals. The secret is to understand what is influencing your reactions, work hard to put yourself in the other's shoes, and interact with them as a whole person. Don't forget to share something personal about yourself. It's amazing how good you and others will feel.

Fairness: It's Genetic and Fundamental

Most human beings are intrinsically fair. Consciously or unconsciously, we monitor situations and do all we can—actively and passively—to remedy any unfairness we may witness. Healthy people fundamentally understand this unspoken principle. If you take advantage of people, they will feel it and retaliate, generally up to the level of the original transgression. Fair play is built on trust and cooperation. It enables us to form great relationships, at work and home.

Communication: Conscious, Clear, and Courageous

Good communication is *conscious*: You are aware of your intentions, the situation, your psychology, and others. Deep listening to other people, without interruption and preparing a comeback, is a great gift. Honest communication is *clear*: you know exactly what you want to communicate, and you speak with clear intent. Effective communication is *courageous*: you are direct, straightforward, and courageous to speak your truth and to let the other person own their view of the truth. Their truth may be fundamentally different from your own and fundamentally flawed. But they have a right to their truth, and it's your responsibility to listen—even if you disagree.

Appreciation: Recognition Inspires People

In many relationships, the absence of true appreciation is more noticeable than its presence. Studies confirm that appreciation taps into our positive emotions and often is more important than money. We all want respect for our thoughts, feelings, values, and fears; respect for our unique strengths and differences; respect for our desire to learn and develop; respect to be heard and recognized for our opinions and accomplishments; and respect for our personal and family life, as we define it.

When you embody these four attributes, you shine a light on yourself and others, rather than casting shadows. David Brooks shares in his book *How to Know a Person* that "there is one skill that lies at the heart of any healthy person, family, school, community organization, or society: the ability to see someone else deeply and make them feel seen—to accurately know another person, to let them feel valued, heard and understood."

John Gottman, in his work with couples, agrees. His secret for successful couples: disarm verbal conflicts; increase intimacy; show respect and affection; practice empathy; nurture fondness and admiration; let your partner influence you; and turn inward, not away from the relationship.

The hormone in the brain that stirs these feelings of kindness is oxytocin, produced when a person acts generously toward others. In turn, this feeling of well-being makes us feel more trusting and closer to the other person.

Oxytocin may also explain the idea of "reciprocal altruism." Many acts of generosity are returned with equal or greater kindness. By doing for others, you do for yourself. That is why kindness makes us feel better. By being kind to others, we stir compassion in ourselves, increasing our own feelings of generosity and gratitude.

Gary Chapman, author of *The Five Love Languages*, reminds us that we are different in how we love. We all speak different love languages and have different needs. In our primary relationships, some of us want words of affirmation; others need quality time with our partners. Some people enjoy receiving gifts or acts of service, while others measure love in physical touch. To feel loved, it's important that you are aware of your primary love language and that of your partner.

Loving generously must be inclusive too. As we learn to respect our differences in age, ethnicity, and gender as well as education, religion, sexual orientation, and politics, we broaden our capacity to see the world. We become more mentally and socially agile, gain access to more ideas and choices, and expand our potential and performance.

Here are some tips for loving generously:

- *Assess yourself*: Take a moment to simply stop and reflect on whether you are loving generously today. Does your behavior make you feel better or worse? Keep a generosity journal and write down how you exhibited love today.

- *Practice the Golden Rule*: Do unto others as you would wish they would do unto you. Ask people what excites and motivates them. Give without expecting in return. Honor people with your full attention. Tell someone today that you love them.

- *Consciously relate to others*: Be aware of how you interact with others. What impact are you having? Tell people how grateful you are to have them in your life. Not only will you feel better, but you will also brighten their day.

- *Commit to being civil every day*: Be kind and loving. Write a note of personal appreciation. Look someone in the eye and smile. Catch people in the act of doing something right. Words and actions matter; they turn ill will to goodwill.

- *Create psychological safety*: Create caring relationships built on a foundation of deep trust and respect. People will feel supported, affirmed, and nurtured without fear of blame, retribution, and ridicule.

- *Inspire positive emotions*: The more we focus on our positive emotions—hope, compassion, forgiveness, joy, generosity, and love—the more these emotions will be reciprocated by others. Remember that 99.9% of people are good-natured, each with their own imperfections, biases, prejudices, and blind spots.

- *Build a flourishing network*: People who consciously invest in and grow their networks stand out in a crowd. As higher performers, they are considered better leaders. Expand your network of family, friends, and colleagues.

THE PLANNER AND THE WANDERER

Amanda and Curtis have been married for ten years. At age thirty-nine, they have two lovely kids, eight and six, and enjoy a partnership built on love and generosity. They also have complementary attachments ("defaults," as they call them) that lead to deep, playful conversations, and ultimately help them become better people.

Amanda is a high performer. She sees herself as "super-methodical and focused. I'm always planning to fill up this limited time on earth with special moments. But I overthink everything and fear making a mistake or the wrong decision. I guess I suffer from FOMO—a fear of missing out—and this can become crippling." You might say Amanda has an attachment to the future.

Curtis is more spontaneous and even-keeled. "I like to live in the moment, always ready for a surprise, and don't like to limit myself by an overly thought-out plan. I don't like change all that much and pride myself in being a "flaneur," like a wanderer, who likes to look around, enjoying the experiences of the moment. Some might say I have an attachment to stability."

Years ago, they went on a honeymoon to Europe. Talking together with me, they said, "There were days when we had tension, debating about the silliest things about what and how to schedule our time. We had different perspectives and distinct default buttons. Yet we've worked on this over the years, to our mutual benefit."

"Today, I help Amanda to be more flexible and imperfect," says Curtis, "to let go of her obsessiveness, and live in the moment." Amanda jumps in: "And I help Curtis focus on what he wants to get out of life and vacations, and plan from time to time.

"Recently, we went on holiday to Costa Rica with the family. There were many possibilities. We could enjoy a sunset, play in the waves, ride ATVs, hang on a zip line, go on a boat ride, among others." Initially, Curtis was quick to say, "We'll get to that tomorrow." Amanda started schedul-ing. But this time was different. Amanda loved the spontaneous walks in nature, and Curtis loved the planned fishing trip with his son. I guess family attachments can be great learning moments if you love generously.

Reflections

- To what extent do you enjoy self-reflection and introspection? Can you get too preoccupied with your internal life, and how can you give yourself some slack?
- Do you consider yourself securely attached, anxiously attached, or avoidantly attached to others?
- How would you describe your life? Are you more isolated or socially connected? Where do those tendencies come from?
- Are your relationships generally authentic and meaningful or shallow and disconnected?
- How comfortable are you with digital machines and artificial intelligence?
- Would you say that you are someone who loves generously?

TEN

THE ATTACHMENT TO LIFE

- Do you have difficulty stopping things that don't work anymore?
- Do you find it hard to be grateful for what you have in life?
- Do you fear death and the dying process?
- Do you feel attached to being attached?
- Are you having difficulty retiring from work?

Alice in Wonderland may really have been onto something! Step "through the looking glass" and—poof!—instant transformation! New identity, new curiosity, new vistas, new behavior. Suddenly, our attachments fall magically away.

One of life's greatest mysteries is that we are transforming constantly. Strangely, every minute, your body changes; your cells die and replace themselves. Brain cells regenerate regularly, particularly when you sleep; your skin cells give you a renewed surface every two months. Biologically, you become a new you all the time, so why should transformation of yourself be such a daunting challenge? Humans are built for change.

Several years ago, I took a business trip to Japan. There, I discovered the concept of wabi-sabi, an Eastern philosophy and approach to life. Wabi-sabi sees beauty in all living things. In nature, people, pets, or art, we are all considered imperfect, impermanent, and incomplete, growing and decaying, developing over our lifetimes. Based on the principles of Taoism and Buddhism, this concept opened my eyes to the beauty of life and death.

Life is full of beginnings and endings. Like our bodies, people and relationships live and die. Our pets, plants, and nature go through the same process. Ideologies flourish and become obsolete. We go through different stages of life and then we put them to bed so we can move on to the next phase. Projects, teams, and companies give birth to entrepreneurial ideas, expand to profitable products, then dwindle out. People win and they lose, vacations start and end, possessions are thrown out, and attachments come and go. The more comfortable we are with these births and deaths, the easier it is to live a full and conscious life.

Here's the dilemma. Many of us are too attached to life and fearful of death. And I don't just mean death at the end of our lives, I mean death throughout our lives, to surrender and let go of people, ideas, and practices that don't serve us anymore. As Tara Brach, psychologist and Buddhist, shares in *Radical Acceptance*, "we should welcome the experiences that we fear, such as dying, and fully accept our own death as an empowering part of your life."

THE STAGES OF CONSCIOUSNESS

One of the great challenges in life is to make sense of our experiences. Many scholars have tried to explain this complex process. My favorite is Harvard University's Robert Kegan, who focuses on the five stages of adult development, outlining different ways of perceiving and engaging with the world across our lifespan. These include:

- Stage 1: *The impulsive mind.* This thinking occurs when individuals are primarily concerned with their own needs and desires. Egocentric, and often struggling with impulse control and limited empathy, this stage is often seen in early childhood and adolescence.

- Stage 2: *The imperial mind.* As we build on our impulsive mind, we begin to identify with our family and social groups, conform to group norms, and seek approval from authority figures. Often adopted in adolescence and early adulthood, this ethnocentric perspective views others with suspicion.

- Stage 3: *The socialized mind.* When we begin to develop mutually rewarding interpersonal relationships, we develop a greater capacity for empathy. Building on the imperial mind, we can consider multiple viewpoints, and our major developmental tasks are to take more initiative and exhibit more self-management. This stage usually develops in early adulthood to midlife.

- Stage 4: *The self-authorizing mind.* People in this phase of growth learn to appreciate their own identity and take a more self-guided, responsible approach to life. Independent and agenda-driven, we work toward owning our belief systems, ideologies, and personal codes of conduct.

- Stage 5: *The self-transforming mind.* Here, finally, we learn to appreciate multiple ideologies, embrace complexity, and think systemically. With this broader sense of humanity, and by embracing a high degree of agility and adaptability, we adopt a holistic mindset, appreciate the interconnectedness of all living things, and give back to the world.

These stages delineate the development of our cognitive and emotional development. We move through these stages in chronological order, yet we each travel through them at differing speeds. In the best of all worlds, as we expand our awareness, we include and integrate each stage of life. Admittedly, though, some people get stuck along the way—temporarily or permanently. The real adult work happens during the last three stages of development.

Self-authoring and self-transforming people have the greatest chance of success. The less developed, socialized-minded people must work harder to understand and manage themselves, especially in a climate of mistrust, worry, and resentment. Those stuck in the impulsive and instrumental stages have plenty of work to do before they can even enter adulthood.

Each of us moves through these stages with our own lens, depending on our genetics, personal development, life experiences, and personality. We each have a story, rooted in history and culture, that evolves over time, with lifelong questions like: Who am I? What are my values? What do I believe? What matters to me? And, what's next in my life? No one really teaches us how to understand our lives or how to distill the lessons from it. We are left roaming through the wilderness, asking questions and searching for answers.

If we stay open, positive, and aware, we can experience the fullness of life. We can deepen our self-knowledge, stay present in our relationships, and learn from our diverse experiences. By letting go of our attachments and embracing gratitude and love, we can stay vital with a sense of peace and well-being.

OUR ATTACHMENTS STAND IN THE WAY

Along the way, many of us deepen those attachments that can sabotage our development, keep us locked on land mines ready to explode at any moment, or hide them in dark caves chained to our outdated stories. The only way to banish these attachments is to examine the fear that accompanies each of the attachments underneath the surface. Like a submarine in enemy waters, our fears help us see the adversary above, and by examining our attachments, we can see a glimmer of sunlight so we can surface from the murky waters.

Our fear of change resides below the attachment to stability. Haunting memories keep us stuck in our attachment to the past. Constant worry fuels our attachment to the future, while the fear of losing command of our lives drives our attachment to control. Fears of mistakes and inadequacy lock us into our attachment to perfection.

Feelings of insignificance and failure fuel our attachment to success. Experiencing discomfort is the fear behind our attachment to pleasure. Aging drives our attachment to youth. Fear of intimacy and loneliness sit below our attachment to self. And death itself keeps us stuck on the attachment to life.

How are your attachments working for you? If you are someone who carries these heavy bags around with you, it's not surprising that you are not getting what you want or getting what you don't want out of life. Your inner critic may be keeping you weak, worried, or wallowing in sadness. Emotionally unfinished business may be sabotaging your relationships. Or your fears may be hijacking you as you try to build a healthy, successful life.

Some of us are even attached to being attached, so we wrap our attachments around us and tie a knot. Over time, they engulf our entire identity. In some strange way, they serve us by blaming others for our problems or seeing ourselves as the source of our unhappiness. Some even become the identified patient in our family or with friends, making it even harder to get rid of them.

The only remedy is to detach—to surrender—to let go of our attachments, and most importantly, understand their origins, experience the full range of our emotions, and expose them into conscious awareness. By shedding light on the darkness, we free ourselves from these burdens so we can gain full acceptance of our full selves.

BEGINNINGS AND ENDINGS

At ninety, Jean Barton has traveled through the stages of life. Born in Portsmouth, Virginia, she reflects, "We were very poor and had no money. My mama was a country girl and Daddy swore she never had shoes until he married her. He had no skills either, except auto mechanics. We lived in an old shack where the downstairs was his garage. There was no running water, no heat, and only a potbelly stove.

"We were the only white family in a Black neighborhood. The Black principal of our school lived with his wife in the elegant house across the street. I wanted to grow up Black because they were the elegant people."

Some people have a past and want to run away from it. Others feel inferior and never recover from it. Still others feel good about where they come from and celebrate their past. "I was always so afraid that people would find out about my humble beginnings," says Jean, "but I got over it.

"When I was fifteen, Johnny, who was nineteen, lived a block away and asked my mama if he could have my hand in marriage. She said to me, 'You marry Johnny, and you'll be taken care of for life. His daddy owns a plumbing company.' I chose education instead. It was my way out.

"It took me seven years to go to college. I finished and became a drama teacher, then a guidance counselor, for thirty-two years at a middle school. Early on, I got married and had full responsibility for working and raising three amazing children. But I was unhappy in our marriage and went into a depression. Stress ruled my life without a lot of joy. My husband was never self-sufficient, and I made a courageous decision to get out of the marriage and put this phase of my life to bed.

"Then I found Richard. A light switch went on, and suddenly, my world became truly joyful. We married, and for the next forty years shared everything—from our friends, opera, and theater to travel, our big family, and a deep commitment to politics and the community. Today, I've got all the creaks and cranks of old age. But I have absolutely no regrets."

Jean is a great example of living three different lives: the first, her humble beginnings; followed by her education, children, and a failed marriage; ending with her wonderful forty years with Richard. Birth and death. Beginnings and endings. A light switch truly shines in the second half of her life.

THE THIRD TRIMESTER

As we age, we have an opportunity to accelerate our adult development. Let's start with retirement. For each of us, this milestone happens at different times and for various reasons. Some of us are committed to working our entire lives and get true pleasure doing something meaningful, with or without a paycheck. Others work part-time and fill in their days with hobbies, exercise, grandkids, or charity. And then there are those who can't wait to turn in their keys to go off into the sunset to play golf, read, paint, or take nature walks. It's the beginning of the go-go years, the slow-go years, the no-go years, and eventually death. This rite of passage can also be a time of deep personal transformation.

Underneath the surface, we often harbor complex feelings about leaving our work identities and moving on to this next phase of our life. We ask BIG questions: Do I feel valued without my work? Am I fearful of giving up a regular income? Will I get bored with nothing to do? Will people still love and respect me? Do we have enough money to live?

I remember having breakfast with a CEO of a large company in Sydney, Australia. He had retired the day before, and it was his first morning without work. He had plenty of resources to rely on, but he turned to me and said, "I'm not getting any emails. I feel invisible. Is this what retirement is all about?"

As we enter the third phase of our life, we begin a time of self-reflection, accompanied by a newfound sense of freedom and the burdensome weight of internalized ageism. Clearly, we encounter Medicare, senior moments, and changes to our bodies. Yet we also begin to think about choices made and unmade and opportunities lived and missed over our lifetimes. Questions about mortality begin to emerge.

As a gay man, I lost many friends too early in their lives, including two of my best friends. The AIDS epidemic, people dying two weeks after diagnosis, and premature funerals happened regularly. The crisis touched millions of unsuspecting families and accelerated thoughts of mortality for many young people.

The lessons were profound: the fragility of life, the poison of prejudice, the importance of friendship, and the limitations of medicine. Today, AIDS is a chronic disease treated with life-sustaining drugs. The scars still exist, but now, there is a silver lining. The crisis created the greatest catalyst for coming out and changing attitudes about LGBTQ+ people around the world.

THE TWO PATHS

As we travel on the journey toward older age, we hit a crossroads and a choice where there are two different paths in front of us. One path is lined with introspection. It's an opportunity to open your mind with deeper awareness, become less self-centered, and get more in touch with your empathy, compassion, and gratitude. Although time seems like it's moving faster, we can feel less anxious and cynical, and we don't have to be right all the time. On this path, you can also begin to let go of many of your attachments—material things, wardrobes, sexual potency, and the resentments you acquired along the way. It's a time to clean up toxic relationships and complete unfinished business.

The other path is lined with fear: fear of loneliness, fear of pain, and fear of death. You can also feel isolated from friends or disconnected from family. Questioning your life's purpose becomes common, and resentments and regret may preoccupy your psyche.

Along the way, some of us will meet up with a life-changing illness, likely one of the four degenerative illnesses we discussed in the attachment to youth. When medical situations intervene, many of us choose to look inward to explore our feelings of pain, disease, and death. We might even need caregivers to support us during this time, tapping into our childhood fears and feelings of dependency.

Yet as Connie Zweig, psychotherapist and author of *The Inner Work of Age*, recommends, "Step onto the path of late life with your gains and losses, gifts and limitations all gathered within you now as the wisdom of a lifetime. It can be a summons to trade the image of youth for the depth of age, to trade distraction for self-knowledge, to trade reaction to reflection, to trade information for wisdom, and to trade a tight grip for an open hand."

OUR HEARTS ARE RESILIENT

Jon retired after a successful career as a futurist. "Now, at seventy-five," he says, "I'm at a different stage in my life. When I was younger, my identity was tied to my ego and accomplishments. I went to work with all good intentions, and the work was meaningful, yet I had illusions about myself, thinking I was more important than I was. Retirement gave me a more detached view of myself and my life.

"One of the first things I changed was how I spent my time. When I was younger, I could walk by another person without seeing them or be in a conversation without hearing them. Rather than listening deeply, I was focused more on what I was going to say next.

"Today, I'm much more aware and appreciative of my surroundings. On one of my walks with my dog, I saw a man on a bench. I would have walked right by him in the past. He was homeless and seemed to have a mental illness. Yet we talked for a good half hour, and it seemed important to him that I take his email address. So, I sent him an email. I would never have done that in my past life.

"Several years ago, I was diagnosed with cardiomyopathy. Erik Erikson, the well-known psychologist, wrote that 'wisdom is the detached concern with life itself in the face of death itself.' For many months, I faced death. The medical waiting rooms, the side effects of drugs, fear of infections, and the prospect of a heart transplant led me to walk my heart back to health. I got up to eight to ten miles per day until one of my knees blew out. Go figure?

"I'm at peace these days. My heart is doing well. My knee's replaced. And I'm living a full, happy, and loving life. I grasp less, detach more, and pay attention to the quiet parts of my life. I think the denial of aging is a terrible lost opportunity.

"If I ever lose perspective, I just wake up and go downstairs to see my wonderful granddaughter, Libby. Her face lights up with a big smile, as does mine, and I realize it's the most wonderful part of being old."

Jean and Jon are advanced in their adult development. They have a strong sense of self with distinct personal values, a high degree of agility and adaptability, and a commitment to their own growth and transformation. Grounded in self-awareness, they are connected to a broader humanity.

DEATH IS PART OF LIFE

All living things die. It's plain and simple. Yet why do we have so much difficulty accepting the natural process of death? And why is it so painful to think about death and dying? Are we simply scared of death, the pain and suffering that might come with it, and our not knowing where we might go afterward? Or are we afraid of leaving our past behind, or departing the world not having made any lasting contribution? By fearing death, we risk becoming too attached to life. But, if we feel gratitude and appreciation for a life well lived, we can see life and death as inevitable and just part of life's evolution.

Peg and Bill, ages ninety-three and ninety-two, were great teachers of mine. Occasionally, they would enjoy a night out for dinner with the younger whippersnappers. Our conversations covered health and religion, politics and world affairs, and they were always candid about aging and death. They had stopped reading newspapers to reduce the stress in their lives and said they would decline all extraordinary health-sustaining measures to reduce the exorbitant costs of end-of-life care.

Rather than deny, run away, or be overwhelmed by death, they talked openly, accepted the inevitable, and let go of their attachment to life, which helped them reframe death without any leftover baggage. If we don't prepare ourselves for death, like Peg and Bill did, we can experience intense feelings of fear, grief, anger, and regret.

Ram Dass, psychologist, writer, and spiritual teacher captures it best: "If you know how to live and to love, you know how to die . . . at the moment of death, you are neither grabbing at life nor pushing it away. You are neither pushing nor pulling. It's the attraction to life and the aversion to death that keeps you holding on when it's time to go."

DEATH CHANGES US

Amy is a progressive, eco-friendly funeral director who has a lot to say about life and death. Part of a $22 billion industry, she specializes in personalized green burials, home funerals, and witnessed cremations. The urns are biodegradable, and the caskets are built with sensitivity to the plight of the planet. Although she suffers from her own attachments to control and perfection, she recognizes that all living things birth, die, and rebirth, sometimes just as memories. Amy says, "Loss is beyond the person. It's the life you had with them, who you were when they were alive. It's the relationship you had, and how you are different since they've gone.

Some people want everything to go back to normal. That's not how it works. Our lives can't be refolded back into an envelope. Life and death happen, and your world changes. The secret is to talk about it. But it's hard for some people. I've worked with a couple men who have died surrounded by their teenage children, and these men were not able to talk about their deaths. It's so sad, leaving the kids behind without any sense of closure."

Grief is a natural emotion that accompanies loss and death. On average, normal grief, after the loss of a loved one, can last up to two years, yet many people find that grief starts to improve after six months. Folks who have an underlying depression or depressive personality can struggle for longer periods of time.

Amy sees it differently. "I tell people not to hope or aim for closure at all. Closure is a mirage. Grief, even for healthy people, sometimes has no end, truly. I encourage people to learn to see grief as a doorway to maturity, and that it will be with you for the rest of your life."

THE ASPIRATION OF GRATITUDE

Some of the simplest words that children learn very early in their lives are "please" and "thank you." They are muscle-memory words that acknowledge appreciation for a kind act, gesture, gift, or compliment. They are, in themselves, gifts to the other person. In fact, they combat cynicism and mistrust, opening ourselves up to civility and compassion.

Being grateful is the lifeblood of spiritual health. Showing it creates an aura around those near you and radiates outward. It is an act of humility that reveals your humanity. Just like the flutter of birds across the sky, showing gratitude can prompt others to respond in kind and uplift whole communities and cultures.

We have so much for which to be grateful. By changing all the time, we experience life's beginnings and endings as we develop and mature. Our full range of emotions—from hope, love, and generosity to worry, sadness, and anger—enlivens us so we can feel fully human. Our minds are agile and adaptive, expanding our vista with each passing moment. We are proud of our accomplishments and resilient in the face of adversity. Self-aware, we are also connected to everything around us and capable of giving back to the world. At the end of our lives, we can look back with pride, contentment, and completion.

Sonja Lyubomirsky, professor of psychology at the University of California, Riverside, has studied the well-documented connection between gratitude and happiness that together improve our self-esteem, reduce stress, neutralize negative emotions, and help us cope with adversity. They also strengthen our immune system and cardiovascular health and improve our sleep.

Here are a few suggestions for improving your sense of gratitude:

- *Live a higher purpose*: Ponder these questions: What do you love doing? When do you feel most alive? What are your special talents and gifts? What would you change in the world if you could? We all have special talents and hidden gifts that can improve our own journey in life or can pave the way for someone else. Imagine how you could move from mere survival day to day to finding ways to unearth your talents and using them to improve yourself and others.

- *Drive with values and principles*: Recognize what you value, what ethics guide your behavior, and what fundamental principles help you solve problems. What is the true north on your compass? By facing challenges and staying grounded in your principles, you will stand firm when others try to knock you off your moral foundation. Know what tenets guide your actions and what values undergird your guiding light.

- *Translate intentions into right actions*: Every action starts with your intent—your internal drive to act. Act deliberately for the right reason. Intentions can be slippery, loaded with kindness, service, and excellence, or they can be fueled by greed, jealousy, envy, and fear. By examining your intentions, you can confidently speak your truth, keep commitments, practice integrity, and bring real value to the lives of others.

- *Build civil relationships*: The foundation of all relationships is to practice being courteous and considerate. It's the Golden Rule: "Do unto others as you would have them do unto you." You get what you give. In our world today, it is too easy to demean, belittle, insult, bully, or dismiss other people. Understanding other cultures and communities is at the heart of simple civility. Being kind, loving, and understanding can revolutionize an interaction and start a meaningful exchange. Start with a smile.

- *Give back to the world*: The mantra that "it's better to give than receive" is a truism. Giving back to others is the direct result of being grateful for what you have been given. Research at Harvard Business School showed that what made people happy was spending money on others rather than on themselves. Sharing what you have—your time, energy, ideas, muscle, and money—enhances the well-being of others. Volunteering brings a special feeling that you experience when you do it; your mind smiles inwardly and it feels good. So, give to the charity of your choice. Help your neighbors. Protect our planet. Volunteer!

LIVING GRATITUDE EVERY DAY

Mark personifies the spirit of gratitude. As a family man and president of an institutional management firm, "I believe in the fundamental goodness of everyone," says Mark. "I am deeply grateful that God has given me gifts throughout my life, my positive outlook, relative intelligence, good health, some athleticism, and a desire to excel. I enjoy the simple miracles in life, have a natural interest in getting to know people, and feel responsible to serve others. You just need to peel back the onion a little bit before you see all the goodness. I am truly blessed."

Today, "Gensh," as his friends fondly call him, is surrounded by wonderful women in his life: his wife of forty years, and four great daughters. "We also have eight grandchildren who are growing up to be wonderful little human beings."

Confident and humble, positive and playful, Mark enjoys his big network of family, friends, and colleagues. "I try to help people feel comfortable in their own skin."

I asked Mark what suggestions he might share with others for living a good life. He said, "Life is difficult, so you first must have hope, a kind of faith, that guides you. My faith is in God, yet everyone finds their own faith. You also need to be part of a community. You can't do it alone. None of us has the answers, and we need help along the path. Finally, we need to love each other. It's so easy to love people, but we hide behind our computers and phones, and end up hating each other."

Mark is a special man. He sheds light, not darkness; lives with gratitude, not regret; and guides his life with love, not fear.

 **Reflections**

- Which stage of consciousness are you in (impulsive, imperial, socialized, self-authoring, self-transforming)? How can you accelerate your progress?
- How does your attachment to life stand in the way of your ongoing development?

- How would you describe your ability to detach from your attachments?
- How comfortable are you accepting the inevitable losses in your life?
- If you are retired, which path are you taking in your third trimester?
- What is your relationship to death, and how are you feeling about it?
- To what extent do you live with a sense of gratitude?

LIVING A MORE
FULFILLING LIFE

Finland is rated the happiest country in the world. This Nordic nation has been at or near the top of international rankings for years. The Finns' secret to success: live simply, build community, connect with nature, and most of all, practice gratitude. This country supports this mindset with a robust safety net, excellent healthcare, free education, and a healthy work-life balance.

Underpinning these rankings, the science of happiness is compelling. People who spend time outdoors, create a community feeling, and reject materialism have greater physical and mental health. However, it's the feeling of gratitude that has the greatest effect on one's overall happiness. Finnish sociology professor Jukka Savolainen explains that the gap between people's expectations for life compared to their actual day-to-day experiences matters. The smaller the gap, the happier people are. Learning to be grateful for the life you have colors everything.

Clearly, our genes play a role. Each of us has a different happiness set point that contributes to our feelings of well-being. In fact, some scientists believe that 30–40% of feeling good is genetically derived. No doubt, our early development, life experiences, and personality play a role too. By now, you've also come to understand that our unhealthy attachments can have a significant negative effect on our happiness.

Many ask whether success creates happiness or if it's the other way around. Studies now show that it's the feeling of happiness and its attendant optimistic effect that leads to work and life success. Who doesn't want to be around positive people?

YOUR INNATE WISDOM

So, happiness emanates from within. Part of being human is having this innate wisdom. We each have a natural intelligence, a genuine sense and sensibility, and a fundamental sanity. Our minds are naturally curious; our hearts are naturally compassionate. What stands between you and your innate wisdom are your unhealthy attachments and the tough, cruel world we live and work in.

There is a wellspring in each of us, and it's up to us to find and awaken it. How do you do this? You open your heart and open your mind. An open heart fuels the fire, enabling you to be emotionally honest, compassionate, and joyful. An open mind shines a light: it enables you to be self-aware, curious, and practical. An open mind and open heart are both expressions of the better angels of our nature— principally love.

Dilip Jeste, neuropsychiatrist and author of *Wiser*, believes wisdom is a complex personality trait. The executive brain's reasoning and judgment and the emotional brain's positive feelings play a major role in wisdom. What emerges is the capacity for self-reflection, emotional stability, and prosocial behavior like empathy and compassion. Balancing decisiveness with the acceptance of uncertainty, along with a belief in something bigger than yourself, is important too.

THE TEN ASPIRATIONS

Living a good life depends on aspirational thinking. In this book, Eastern philosophy has helped us understand the concept of attachments, while Western thought has taught us about the power of aspirations. Throughout, I've tried to help you turn your unhealthy attachments into healthy aspirations. By living according to these higher principles, you will learn to know yourself, be yourself, and love yourself, the secret ingredients to a fulfilling life.

Here are the ten aspirations to follow:

Master Agility

Moving from an attachment to stability requires agility. By accepting uncertainty as reality, you can stay agile and adapt easily to change. *Go deep* to harness the power of introspection. *Think big* to imagine a world of possibilities. *Get real* by being intentional about change in your life. *Step up* and act boldly and responsibly.

Let Go of Your Past

Here, we release our attachment to the past by accepting and forgiving our old demons and facing the truth with honesty and compassion. Try practicing the five steps for letting go: Get comfortable being uncomfortable. Discover your deepest emotions. Learn to surrender and let go. Forgive others and yourself. And rewrite your story. Whether it's pain, fear, worry, loss, or anger, look at each emotion head-on, and be tough and gentle with yourself.

Live in the Present

The attachment to the future is banished by living in the present moment. The practice of mindfulness and mindful actions will prevent you from being hijacked by your intruding thoughts or emotions. Learn how to reduce your worry about the future and teach yourself how to close the gap between your current reality and your desired outcome.

Embrace Vulnerability

By practicing trust and distinguishing what you can and cannot control, you can make friends with your vulnerability, the antidote for the attachment to control. Whether you are compelled to control others, be controlled by others, act passive-aggressively, or feel the need to overplease, here are some universal guideposts: view vulnerability as a strength, not a weakness; translate trust into tangible actions; and practice confident humility.

Pursue Excellence

By accepting your shortcomings, you can befriend your imperfections and loosen your attachment to perfection. Learning how perfectionists think, feel, and act will go a long way. Here are some suggestions for loosening your attachment to perfection: fall in love with your imperfections; confront your inner critic; rebalance your work; and act with constructive impatience.

Live Abundantly

The aspiration of abundance rejects the attachment to success. By practicing abundance, you can celebrate your achievements and live a healthy, productive life. Who you are drives what you do. Consider these principles: confront your fears of failure; practice the six dimensions of well-being; love yourself unconditionally; and turn your feeling of scarcity into abundance.

Learn to Surrender

By experiencing pain, you can help eliminate your attachment to pleasure and find peace and comfort in life's ups and downs. Unfortunately, many of us run from pain and anesthetize it with pleasure. Understand the difference between desires, habits, attachments, and addictions. Surrender to pain and view anxiety as a positive force for discovery. And remember, addiction is a brain disease.

Age Gracefully

By practicing acceptance, you can reduce your attachment to age and allow yourself to age gracefully. Unfortunately, people associate aging with diminishing beauty and health. Hence, we yearn for youth, stay fearful of aging, obsess over illness, or live unhealthy lifestyles. Choose to live longer and better; practice conscious aging; maintain a youthful personality; and develop a "blue zone" around you.

Love Generously

By loving generously, you can avoid the attachment to self and feel true intimacy and connection with others. We cannot live selfish, cynical lives and thrive. It's not good for our health, organizations, or communities. What we need is generosity and a deep sense of belonging. This mindset requires greater emotional maturity; deeper, caring relationships; and a much stronger commitment to the health of our global society and the sustainability of the planet.

Live with Gratitude

Our attachment to life is complex. There are three ways we get tripped up: we get too attached to life, too attached to death, or too attached to our own attachments. By feeling grateful, you can lessen your attachment to life and move through it with grace, flexibility, and conviction. Here are some recommendations: see life with beginnings, losses, and deaths; practice letting go of unhealthy thoughts, feelings, and people; master the practice of gratitude; and conduct periodic life reviews and complete your unfinished business.

I am hopeful about the future. As human beings, we are a work in progress as we mature over our lifetime and across generations. Our negative, selfish drives have not evolved very much since their inception, but our positive emotions have strengthened and accelerated over time. Our culture has changed, too, as we evolve toward a healthier society.

Nonetheless, I do have real concerns about the state of the world and its growing selfishness, mistrust, and lack of awareness. Today, many people still struggle with their attachments that skew their perceptions, shrink their minds, incite negative emotions, and spur unhealthy behavior. Underneath all of these attachments is fear.

Detach does not mean being uninvolved or disconnected. Quite the opposite. By ridding ourselves of our attachments, we free ourselves to pursue our dreams and embrace life fully, staying engaged in what matters—our health and well-being, our families and communities, and our democracy and the environment.

We have a choice. We can choose to live our lives in fear or love—or somewhere in between. Love is the guiding light. I hope *Detach* will help you make the right choice and become your personal guide for living a more fulfilling life.

ACKNOWLEDGMENTS

Detach is truly a life's work. From study and reflection, chats with family and friends, lessons from great teachers and students, and wisdom from clients and colleagues, these experiences crystallize into a rich kaleidoscope of learning.

To Jay and Tessa, who bring love into my life every day.

To my friends, family, and colleagues who have shared their life stories with me. You know who you are. Your vulnerability and courage inspire me and shed light on the world.

To Tom Miller, my agent; Matt Holt, my editor-in-chief; Glenn Yeffeth, my publisher; Katie Dickman and Mallory Hyde Hickok, and their incredible teams; Tom Eslinger, our master creative genius; Mark Fortier and Margaret Rogalski, our talented publicists; and Simon & Schuster, our worldwide distribution partner, along with Marty Calderwood and Liza Gookin Hodskins—none of this happens without their commitment and hard work.

To my colleagues at Healthy Companies who, over many years, have challenged and encouraged me to cultivate my mind and heart. Special thanks to my dear friend and business partner, Jim Mathews.

Finally, to you the reader. Thank you for picking up this book, shining a light on yourself, and stretching to be a little bigger and better tomorrow than you are today.

REFERENCES

The Baggage We Carry

Aswani, Romina. "The Law of Detachment: What Does Buddhism Teach Us? Hard Times Build Determination and Inner Strength." *The Apeiron Blog. Medium,* January 29, 2021. https://theapeiron.co.uk/the-law-of-detachment-what-does-buddhism-teach-us-395f090f6a40.

Rosen, Bob. *Calm in Chaos: How to Thrive in the New World of Work.* Healthy Companies, 2023.

Chapter 1: The Attachment to Stability

Asher, Claire. "Chameleon Has One of the Fastest Tongues in the Animal Kingdom." *Science,* January 4, 2016. doi: 10.1126/science.aae0171.

Chödrön, Pema. *Comfortable with Uncertainty: 108 Teachings on Cultivating Fearlessness and Compassion.* Shambhala, 2003.

David, Susan. *Emotional Agility: Get Unstuck, Embrace Change, and Thrive in Work and Life.* Avery, 2016.

Eurich, Tasha. "What Self-Awareness Really Is (And How to Cultivate It)." *Harvard Business Review,* January 4, 2018. https://hbr.org/2018/01/what-self-awareness-really-is-and-how-to-cultivate-it.

Kahneman, Daniel. *Thinking, Fast and Slow.* Farrar, Straus and Giroux, 2011.

Kitchener, Peter D., and Colin G. Hales. "What Neuroscientists Think, and Don't Think, About Consciousness." *Frontiers in Human Neuroscience* 16 (2022). doi:10.3389/fnhum.2022.767612.

Martin, Kristen. "'The Body Keeps the Score' Offers Uncertain Science in the Name of Self-Help. It's Not Alone." Review of *The Grieving Brain* by Mary-Frances O'Connor. *Washington Post,* August 2, 2023. https://www.washingtonpost.com/books/2023/08/02/body-keeps -score-grieving-brain-bessel-van-der-kolk-neuroscience-self-help.

Rosen, Bob. *Grounded: How Leaders Stay Rooted in an Uncertain World.* Jossey-Bass, 2014.

Rosen, Bob, and Emma-Kate Swann. *Conscious: The Power of Awareness in Business and Life.* John Wiley & Sons, Inc., 2018.

Rosen, Robert H. *The Healthy Company: Eight Strategies to Develop People, Productivity, and Profits.* Jeremy P. Tarcher, 1991.

Sloman, Steven A., and Philip Fernbach. *The Knowledge Illusion: Why We Never Think Alone.* Riverhead Books, 2017.

Steffen, Patrick R., Dawson Hedges, and Rebekka Matheson. "The Brain Is Adaptive Not Triune: How the Brain Responds To Threat, Challenge, and Change." *Frontiers in Psychiatry* 13 (2022). doi:10.3389/ fpsyt.2022.802606.

Chapter 2: The Attachment to the Past

Bates, Jordan. "'Letting Go' by David Hawkins: The Book That Shifted My Entire Reality." Review of *Letting Go: A Pathway to Surrender* by David R. Hawkins. Substack, June 30, 2019. https://jordanbates.life /letting-go-david-hawkins.

Boksic, Bruno. "*The Body Keeps the Score* Book Summary, Review, Notes." Review of *The Body Keeps the Score: Brain, Mind, and Body in the Healing of Trauma* by Bessel van der Kolk. Growthabit, accessed August 19, 2024. https://growthabit.com/psychology-books/the-body-keeps-the-score-book-summary-review-notes.

Brown, Brené. *Daring Greatly: How the Courage to be Vulnerable Transforms the Way We Live, Love, Parent, and Lead.* Gotham Books, 2012.

Chödrön, Pema. *The Places That Scare You: A Guide to Fearlessness in Difficult Times.* Shambhala, 2002.

David, Susan. *Emotional Agility: Get Unstuck, Embrace Change, and Thrive in Work and Life.* Avery, 2016.

Davis, Tchiki. "Letting Go: How to Put the Past, Anger, & Fear Behind You." Berkley Well-Being Institute, accessed August 19, 2024. https://www.berkeleywellbeing.com/letting-go.html.

Haidt, Jonathan. *The Happiness Hypothesis: Finding Modern Truth in Ancient Wisdom.* Basic Books, 2006.

Harvard Business Review. *Mindfulness.* Harvard Business Review Press, 2017.

Johns Hopkins Medicine. "Forgiveness: Your Health Depends On It." Accessed August 19, 2024. https://www.hopkinsmedicine.org/health/wellness-and-prevention/forgiveness-your-health-depends-on-it.

Lindberg, Sara. "How to Let Go of Things from the Past." *Healthline*, March 21, 2023. https://www.healthline.com/health/how-to-let-go.

Luna, Aletheia. "Letting Go: 42 Ways to Release Fear, Grief, and Anger." LonerWolf, March 18, 2023. https://lonerwolf.com/letting-go.

Pohl, Mel. *A Day Without Pain.* Central Recovery Press, 2011.

Portka, Katarzyna. "Learning How to Let Go: A Technique for a More Fulfilling Life." *Medium*, June 29, 2021. https://medium.com/curious/learning-how-to-let-go-a-technique-for-a-more-fulfilling-life-f659005c72c7.

Psychology Today. "Forgiveness." Accessed August 21, 2024. https://www.psychologytoday.com/us/basics/forgiveness.

Robbins Research International. "Change Your Story." *Relationships* (blog). Accessed August 22, 2024. https://tonyrobbins.com/blog/change-your-story.

Robinson, Lawrence, Melinda Smith, and Jeanne Segal. "How to Stop Worrying and End Anxious Thoughts." Helpguide, July 12, 2023. https://www.helpguide.org/articles/anxiety/how-to-stop-worrying.htm.

Rosen, Bob. *Calm in Chaos: How to Thrive in the New World of Work.* Healthy Companies, 2023.

Rosen, Robert H. *The Healthy Company: Eight Strategies to Develop People, Productivity, and Profits.* Jeremy P. Tarcher, 1991.

Sakyong Mipham. *Turning the Mind into an Ally.* Riverhead Books, 2003.

Sasson, Remez. "What Is the Meaning of Letting Go?" *Letting Go* (blog). *SuccessConsciousness.* Accessed August 19, 2024. https://www.successconsciousness.com/blog/letting-go/what-is-the-meaning-of-letting-go.

Smidt, Mirna. "Rewrite Your Story, Change Your Life." Happiness Academy, October 3, 2019. https://happiness-academy.eu/rewrite-your-story-change-your-life/.

Surya Das. *Awakening the Buddha Within: Eight Steps to Enlightenment.* Broadway Books, 1997.

Surya Das. *Awakening the Buddhist Heart: Integrating Love, Meaning, and Connection into Every Part of Your Life.* Broadway Books, 2000.

Surya Das. *Letting Go of the Person You Used to Be: Lessons on Change, Loss, and Spiritual Transformation.* Broadway Books, 2003.

Thich Nhat Hanh. *You Are Here: Discovering the Magic of the Present Moment.* Translated by Sheran Chödzin Kohn. Shambhala Publications, 2009.

Thorp, Tris. "How to Rewrite Your Life Story." Chopra, July 21, 2016. https://chopra.com/articles/how-to-rewrite-your-life-story.

van der Kolk, Bessel. *The Body Keeps the Score: Brain, Mind, and Body in the Healing of Trauma*. Viking, 2014.

Viorst, Judith. *Necessary Losses: The Loves, Illusions, Dependencies, and Impossible Expectations That All of Us Have to Give Up in Order to Grow*. The Free Press, 1986.

Watson, Stephanie. "Signs of Resentment." WebMD, August 2, 2024. https://www.webmd.com/mental-health/signs-resentment.

Zimmerman, Rachel. "How Does Trauma Spill from One Generation to the Next?" *Washington Post*, June 12, 2023. https://www.washingtonpost.com/wellness/2023/06/12/generational-trauma-passed-healing.

Chapter 3: The Attachment to the Future

Abraham, Micah. "How to Stop Anxiety and Unwanted Thoughts." Calm Clinic, February 12, 2021. https://www.calmclinic.com/anxiety/symptoms/unwanted-thoughts.

Ackerman, Courtney E. "How to Live in the Moment: 35+ Tools to Be More Present." *Mindfulness* (blog). *Positive Psychology*, October 22, 2018. https://positivepsychology.com/present-moment.

Allen, Summer. "How Thinking About the Future Makes Life More Meaningful." *Greater Good*, May 1, 2019. https://greatergood.berkeley.edu/article/item/how_thinking_about_the_future_makes_life_more_meaningful.

Bailey, Sarah-Louise. "How to Stop Obsessing Over the Future and Live in the Present." Life in a Break Down, April 18, 2022. https://www.lifeinabreakdown.com/how-to-stop-obsessing-over-the-future-and-live-in-the-present.

Barksdale, Nate. "What is Future-Mindedness?" John Templeton Foundation, April 3, 2023. https://www.templeton.org/news/what-is-future-mindedness.

Camerer, Colin. F., George Loewenstein, and Matthew Rabin, eds. *Advances in Behavioral Economics*. Princeton University Press, 2004.

Cantor, Caitlin. "3 Ways to Keep from Getting Attached Too Soon." *Modern Sex* (blog). *Psychology Today*, June 1, 2021. https://www.psychologytoday.com/us/blog/modern-sex/202106/3-ways-to-keep-from-getting-attached-too-soon.

Cuncic, Arlin. "How to Live in the Moment: Ways to Be More Present in Your Everyday Life." Verywell Mind, March 24, 2023. https://www.verywellmind.com/how-do-you-live-in-the-present-5204439.

Dixit, Jay. "The Art of Now: Six Steps to Living in the Moment." *Psychology Today*, November 1, 2008. https://www.psychologytoday.com/us/articles/200811/the-art-now-six-steps-living-in-the-moment.

Ferguson, Sian. "How to Live in the Moment and Be More Present." *PsychCentral* (blog), September 12, 2022. https://psychcentral.com/blog/what-it-really-means-to-be-in-the-present-moment.

Gilbert, Daniel. *Stumbling on Happiness*. Alfred A. Knopf, 2006.

Gorbis, Marina. "Five Principles for Thinking Like a Futurist." Educause, March 11, 2019. https://er.educause.edu/articles/2019/3/five-principles-for-thinking-like-a-futurist.

Johansen, Bob. *The New Leadership Literacies: Thriving in a Future of Extreme Disruption and Distributed Everything*. Brett-Koehler Publishers, Inc., 2017.

Kress, Anna. "3 Steps to Releasing Your Attachment to an Outcome." *Dr. Anna Kress* (blog), February 5, 2019. https://drannakress.com/3-steps-to-releasing-your-attachment-to-an-outcome.

Langer, Ellen J. *The Mindful Body: Thinking Our Way to Chronic Health*. Ballantine Books, 2023.

The Plane Truth. "About Jim Hardy." Accessed August 20, 2024. https://www.planetruthgolf.com/about-jim-hardy.

Psychology Today. "Behavioral Economics." Accessed August 19, 2024. https://www.psychologytoday.com/us/basics/behavioral-economics.

Rosen, Robert H. *Just Enough Anxiety: The Hidden Driver of Business Success*. Portfolio, 2008.

Ruiz, Don Miguel, and Janet Mills. *The Four Agreements: A Practical Guide to Personal Freedom*. Amber-Allen Publishing, 1997.

Tolle, Eckhart. *The Power of Now: A Guide to Spiritual Enlightenment*. New World Library and Namaste Publishing, 2004.

Chapter 4: The Attachment to Control

Carey, Michael P., and Andrew D. Forsyth. "Teaching Tip Sheet: Self-Efficacy." *American Psychological Association*, 2009. https://www.apa.org/pi/aids/resources/education/self-efficacy.

Cherry, Kendra. "How to Recognize Passive-Aggressive Behavior: And How to Respond . . ." Verywell Mind, December 16, 2022. https://www.verywellmind.com/what-is-passive-aggressive-behavior-2795481.

Davis, Tchiki, and Eser Yilmaz. "5 Ways to Boost Self-Efficacy: Discover the Theory Behind Self-Efficacy and Find Out How You Can Boost It." *Click Here for Happiness* (blog). *Psychology Today*, February 13, 2023. https://www.psychologytoday.com/us/blog/click-here-for-happiness/202209/5-ways-to-boost-self-efficacy.

Dibdin, Emma. "Need to Control Everything? This May Be Why." *PsychCentral* (blog), March 29, 2022. https://psychcentral.com/blog/why-you-need-to-control-everything.

Epstein, Sarah. "18 Signs That You're Dealing with a Passive Aggressive Person." *Between the Generations* (blog). *Psychology Today*, September 28, 2021. https://psychologytoday.com/us/blog/between-the-generations/202109/18-signs-youre-dealing-passive-aggressive-person.

Evans, Patricia. *Controlling People: How to Recognize, Understand, and Deal with People Who Try to Control You*. Adams Media, 2002.

Formica, Michael J. "The Neurotic Complement in Relationships: Fitting Together Like a Lock and Key." *Enlightened Living* (blog). *Psychology Today*, January 12, 2019. https://psychologytoday.com/us/blog/enlightened-living/201901/the-neurotic-complement-in-relationships.

Gabriel, Roger. "4 Steps to Self-Mastery." *Meditation* (blog). Chopra, August 14, 2017. https://presence.app/blogs/meditation/4-steps-to-self-mastery?_pos=1&_sid=486f47017&_ss=r.

Hill, Tamara. "9 Signs You Are Being Emotionally Controlled & How to Stop It." *PsychCentral* (blog), September 20, 2017. https://psychcentral.com/blog/caregivers/2017/09/5385.

Rao, Anthony, and Paul Napper. "Seven Ways to Feel More in Control of Your Life. Developing Greater Agency Can Help You Make Important Life Decisions and Feel Less Overwhelmed, Stuck, and Lost." *Greater Good*, April 15, 2019. https://greatergood.berkeley.edu/article/item/seven_ways_to_feel_more_in_control_of_your_life.

Rao, Anthony, and Paul Napper. *The Power of Agency: The 7 Principles to Conquer Obstacles, Make Effective Decisions, & Create a Life on Your Own Terms*. St. Martin's Press, 2019.

Rosen, Bob. *Calm in Chaos: How to Thrive in the New World of Work*. Healthy Companies, 2023.

Rosen, Bob. *Grounded: How Leaders Stay Rooted in an Uncertain World*. Jossey-Bass, 2014.

Rosen, Robert H. *Just Enough Anxiety: The Hidden Driver of Business Success*. Portfolio, 2008.

Rosen, Bob, and Emma-Kate Swann. *Conscious: The Power of Awareness in Business and Life*. John Wiley & Sons, Inc., 2018.

Rosen, Robert H. *The Healthy Company: Eight Strategies to Develop People, Productivity, and Profits*. Jeremy P. Tarcher, 1991.

Chapter 5: The Attachment to Perfection

C., Becca. "10 Reasons Why You Shouldn't Be Striving For Perfection." *Basics by Becca* (blog), June 30, 2021. https://basicsbybecca.com/blog/strive-for-perfection.

Chopra, Deepak. *Abundance: The Inner Path to Wealth.* Harmony Books, 2022.

Gaudreau, Patrick. "On the Distinction Between Personal Standards Perfectionism and Excellencism: A Theory Elaboration and Research Agenda." *Perspectives on Psychological Science*, 14 (2), 197–215. doi:10.1177/1745691618797940.

Gilbert, Daniel. *Stumbling on Happiness.* Alfred A. Knopf, 2006.

Harburg, Fred. "I'm a Little Bit of a Perfectionist"—The Dark Side of the Drive for Flawlessness. *Musing* (blog). PathNorth, July 18, 2019. https://www.pathnorth.com/blog-hidden/im-a-little-bit-of-a-perfectionist.

Hawking, Stephen. *A Brief History of Time.* Bantam Books, 1998.

James, Stefan. "Perfection Doesn't Exist. Give It Up. 3 Steps to Conquer Perfectionism." *Medium*, March 20, 2018. https://medium.com/@stefanjames/perfection-doesnt-exist-give-it-up-f2b77c768cb1.

Koutstaal, Wilma. "Getting Creative by Striving For Excellence vs. Perfection." *Our Innovating Minds* (blog). *Psychology Today*, October 26, 2021. https://www.psychologytoday.com/us/blog/our-innovating-minds/202110/getting-creative-striving-excellence-vs-perfection.

Mallinger, Allan, and Jeannette Dewyze. *Too Perfect: When Being in Control Gets Out of Control.* Fawcett Books, 1992.

Rosen, Bob. *Grounded: How Leaders Stay Rooted in an Uncertain World.* Jossey-Bass, 2014.

Rosen, Robert H. *Just Enough Anxiety: The Hidden Driver of Business Success.* Portfolio, 2008.

Rosen, Bob, and Emma-Kate Swann. *Conscious: The Power of Awareness in Business and Life.* John Wiley & Sons, Inc., 2018.

Chapter 6: The Attachment to Success

Boldt, Laurence G. *The Tao of Abundance: Eight Ancient Principles for Abundant Living.* Penguin Compass, 1999.

Brim, Gilbert. *Ambition: How We Manage Success and Failure Throughout Our Lives.* Basic Books, 1992.

Brooks, David. *The Road to Character.* Random House, 2015.

Brooks, David. *The Second Mountain: The Quest for a Moral Life.* Random House, 2019.

Cherry, Kendra. "9 Tips for How to Find Success in Life." Verywell Mind, July 20, 2022. https://www.verywellmind.com/how-to-be-successful-in-life-4165743.

Chopra, Deepak. *Abundance: The Inner Path to Wealth.* Harmony Books, 2022.

Clifton, Jon. *Blind Spot: The Global Rise of Unhappiness and How Leaders Missed It.* Gallup Press, 2022.

Goldsmith, Marshall, and Mark Reiter. *What Got You Here Won't Get You There: How Successful People Become Even More Successful!* Hyperion, 2007.

McGee, Michael A. "This Is to Have Succeeded." Sermon, Unitarian Universalist Church of Arlington, Virginia. May 31, 2009.

Peterson, Britt. "What Gen Z Wants in the Workplace." *Washington Post,* June 16, 2023. https://www.washingtonpost.com/business/2023/06/16/gen-z-employment.

Rosen, Bob. *Grounded: How Leaders Stay Rooted in an Uncertain World.* Jossey-Bass, 2014.

Rosen, Bob, and Emma-Kate Swann. *Conscious: The Power of Awareness in Business and Life.* John Wiley & Sons, Inc., 2018.

Tracy, Brian. "7 Habits of Successful People That Will Make You Feel Unstoppable in 2020." *Personal Success* (blog). Brian Tracy International, accessed August 19, 2024. https://www.briantracy.com/blog/personal-success/seven-good-habits-of-highly-successful-people-goal-oriented.

Chapter 7: The Attachment to Pleasure

Attia, Peter, and Bill Gifford. *Outlive: The Science and Art of Longevity.* Harmony Books, 2023.

Berger, Allen. *12 Stupid Things That Mess Up Recovery: Avoiding Relapse Through Self-Awareness and Right Action.* Hazelden Publishing, 2008.

Buettner, Dan. *The Blue Zones Secrets for Living Longer: Lessons from the Healthiest Places on Earth.* National Geographic, 2023.

Caron, Christina. "When Does Anxiety Become a Problem?" *New York Times*, June 23, 2023. https://www.nytimes.com/2023/06/23/well/mind/anxiety-screening-symptoms-treatment.html.

Carr, Tara. "Motivating by the Pain Pleasure Principle." University of Wisconsin-Green Bay, July, 2017. https://www.uwgb.edu/sbdc/assets/multi/news/201611-Motivating-by-the-Pain-Pleasure-Principle.pdf.

Cherry, Kendra. "How Freud's Pleasure Principle Works." Verywell Mind, September 6, 2023. https://www.verywellmind.com/what-is-the-pleasure-principle-2795472.

Clifton, Jon. *Blind Spot: The Global Rise of Unhappiness and How Leaders Missed It.* Gallup Press, 2022.

Cook, Jodie. "Expanding Your Comfort Zone: Lessons from a Year of Adversity." *Forbes*, July 21, 2021. https://www.forbes.com/sites/jodiecook/2021/07/21/expanding-your-comfort-zone-lessons-from-a-year-of-adversity/?sh=68066762f401.

Crowley, Chris, and Henry S. Lodge. *Younger Next Year: Live Strong, Fit, and Sexy—Until You're 80 and Beyond.* Workman Publishing, 2005.

Cuncic, Arlin. "How to Get Comfortable Being Uncomfortable." Verywell Mind, February 21, 2023. https://www.verywellmind.com/how-to-get-comfortable-being-uncomfortable-5204440.

Galeffi, Gabo. "Be Comfortable Being Uncomfortable (My 5 Takes)." LinkedIn, January 31, 2019. https://www.linkedin.com/pulse/comfortable-being-uncomfortable-my-5-takes-santiago-gabriel-galeffi/.

Gleeson, Brent. "8 Ways to Get Comfortable Being Uncomfortable." *Forbes*, Aug 8, 2023. https://www.forbes.com/sites/brentgleeson /2023/08/08/8-ways-to-get-comfortable-being-uncomfortable.

Goodman, Brenda. "Food Addiction." WebMD, March 15, 2023. https://www.webmd.com/mental-health/eating-disorders/binge -eating-disorder/mental-health-food-addiction.

Hartney, Elizabeth. "What is a Shopping Addiction? What to Do If You Think You're a Shopaholic." Verywell Mind, December 15, 2022. https://www.verywellmind.com/shopping-addiction-4157288.

Hazelden Betty Ford Foundation. "The Four Paradoxes of Addiction Recovery." *Recovery* (blog), January 31, 2022. https://www.hazelden bettyford.org/articles/recovery-paradoxes.

Hilliard, Jena. "Social Media Addiction." Addiction Center, December 7, 2023. https://www.addictioncenter.com/drugs/social-media -addiction.

Koren, Leonard. *Wabi-Sabi for Artists, Designers, Poets & Philosophers.* Stone Bridge Press, 1994.

Lembke, Anna. *Dopamine Nation: Finding Balance in the Age of Indulgence.* Dutton, 2021.

Lustig, Robert H. "The Pursuit of Pleasure Is a Modern-Day Addiction." *Guardian,* September 9, 2017. https://www.theguardian.com/comment isfree/2017/sep/09/pursuit-of-pleasure-modern-day-addiction.

Mayo Clinic. "Nicotine Dependence." April 19, 2022. https://www .mayoclinic.org/diseases-conditions/nicotine-dependence/symptoms -causes/syc-20351584.

Mayo Clinic. "Compulsive Gambling." June 18, 2022. https://www .mayoclinic.org/diseases-conditions/compulsive-gambling/symptoms -causes/syc-20355178.

Mayo Clinic. "Drug Addiction (Substance Use Disorder)." October 4, 2022. https://www.mayoclinic.org/diseases-conditions/drug -addiction/symptoms-causes/syc-20365112.

National Institute on Alcohol Abuse and Alcoholism. "Understanding Alcohol Use Disorder." National Institutes of Health, 2020. https://www.niaaa.nih.gov/publications/brochures-and-fact-sheets /understanding-alcohol-use-disorder.

National Institute on Drug Abuse. "Understanding Drug Use and Addiction." National Institutes of Health, June, 2018. https://nida .nih.gov/publications/drugfacts/understanding-drug-use-addiction.

Newport Institute. "The Mental Health Effects of Social Media Addiction and Overuse in Young Adults." Accessed August 21, 2024. https:// www.newportinstitute.com/resources/co-occurring-disorders/social -media-addiction.

Psychology Today. "Sex Addiction." Accessed August 21, 2024. https:// www.psychologytoday.com/us/basics/sex-addiction.

Resnick, Ariane. "Can You Be Addicted to Dopamine?" Verywell Mind, June 4, 2022. https://www.verywellmind.com/can-you-get-addicted -to-dopamine-5207433.

Rogers, Kristen. "Why a Food Addiction Many Americans Say They Struggle with Is One Experts Can't Agree On." CNN, June 15, 2023. https://www.cnn.com/2023/06/15/health/food-addiction-help -symptoms-wellness.

Rosen, Robert H. Just Enough Anxiety: The Hidden Driver of Business Success. Portfolio, 2008.

Rosen, Bob, and Emma-Kate Swann. Conscious: The Power of Awareness in Business and Life. John Wiley & Sons, Inc., 2018.

Schmidt, Nicole. "Signs of a Sex Addict." WebMD, December 18, 2022. https://www.webmd.com/mental-health/addiction/signs-sex-addict.

Steinberg, Alan J. "What is Pleasure?" The Meditating Mind (blog). Psychology Today, March 12, 2022. https://www.psychologytoday.com /us/blog/the-meditating-mind/202203/what-is-pleasure.

Stossel, Scott. My Age of Anxiety: Fear, Hope, Dread, and the Search for Peace of Mind. Alfred A. Knopf, 2014.

Stuart, Annie. "Caffeine Myths and Facts." WebMD, June 12, 2021. https://www.webmd.com/diet/caffeine-myths-and-facts.

Turnbridge. "10 Key Tips for Recovery from Addiction." Accessed August 21, 2024. https://www.turnbridge.com/news-events/latest-articles/tips-for-addiction-recovery.

University of Pennsylvania Health System. "The Pursuit of Pleasure: The Normal Versus Addicted Brain." Accessed August 21, 2024. https://www.uphs.upenn.edu/addiction/berman/neuro/dopamine.html.

Villa, David. "Getting Comfortable with Being Uncomfortable." *Forbes*, February 10, 2021. https://www.forbes.com/sites/forbesagencycouncil/2021/02/10/getting-comfortable-with-being-uncomfortable.

Weil, Andrew. *Healthy Aging: A Lifelong Guide to Your Physical and Spiritual Well-Being.* Alfred A. Knopf, 2005.

Wysociki, Scott. "19 Potential Negative Effects of Technology." *Digital Detox* (blog), accessed August 22, 2023. https://www.digitaldetox.com/blog/the-19-negative-effects-of-technology-in-2019.

Yale Medicine. "How an Addicted Brain Works." May 25, 2022. https://www.yalemedicine.org/news/how-an-addicted-brain-works.

Chapter 8: The Attachment to Youth

Achenbach, Joel, and Dan Keating. "New CDC Life Expectancy Data Shows Painfully Slow Rebound from Covid." *Washington Post*, November 29, 2023. https://www.washingtonpost.com/health/2023/11/29/life-expectancy-2022-united-states.

Attia, Peter, and Bill Gifford. *Outlive: The Science and Art of Longevity.* Harmony Books, 2023.

Brooks, Arthur C. *From Strength to Strength: Finding Success, Happiness, and Deep Purpose in the Second Half of Life.* Portfolio/Penguin, 2022.

Buettner, Dan. *The Blue Zones Secrets for Living Longer: Lessons from the Healthiest Places on Earth.* National Geographic, 2023.

The Cigna Group Newsroom. "Vitality: The Next Generation Measure of Health." Accessed August 22, 2024. https://newsroom.thecignagroup .com/index.php?s=34155.

Crowley, Chris, and Henry S. Lodge. *Younger Next Year: Live Strong, Fit, and Sexy—Until You're 80 and Beyond.* Workman Publishing, 2005.

Dean, Jeremy. "The Youthful Personality Traits Linked To Long Life." *Personality* (blog). *PsyBlog,* January 13, 2023. https://www .spring.org.uk/2023/01/youthfu.php.

Edwards, Erijka. "There Are at Least 4 Different Ways of Aging." *NBC News,* January 13, 2020. https://www.nbcnews.com/health/aging /there-are-least-4-different-ways-aging-scientists-say-n1112796.

Fisher, Marc. "Older Americans are Dominating Like Never Before, but What Comes Next?" *Washington Post,* October 24, 2023. https:// www.washingtonpost.com/nation/2023/10/24/older-americans -working-longer-aging-impact.

Gilbert, Daniel. *Stumbling on Happiness.* Alfred A. Knopf, 2006.

Goldstein, Dana. "The U.S. Population Is Older than It Has Ever Been." *New York Times,* June 22, 2023. https://www.nytimes.com /2023/06/22/us/census-median-age.html.

Gupta, Sanjay. "Dr. Sanjay Gupta: It's Time to Rethink What We Call 'Old Age'." CNN, June 20, 2023. https://www.cnn.com/2023/06/20 /health/gupta-aging-chasing-life-podcast-wellness.

Harrar, Sari. "7 Super Secrets of the Super Agers." *AARP Bulletin,* November 10, 2023. https://www.aarp.org/health/healthy -living/info-2023/super-ager-secrets.

Heller, Karen. "'Aging is a Disease': Inside the Drive to Postpone Death Indefinitely." *Washington Post,* November 6, 2023. https://www .washingtonpost.com/style/of-interest/2023/11/06/longevity-aging -disease.

Jonas, Laurie. "10 Changes for More Youthful Energy." Living Marvelously, January 14, 2019. https://livingmarvelously.com/10-changes -for-youthful-energy.

Kam, Katherine. "Scientists Study the Wise Brain." *Washington Post*, April 27, 2023. https://www.washingtonpost.com/wellness/2023/04/27/wisdom-science-brain.

Know Your Archetypes. "What is a Youthful Personality Type?" Accessed August 23, 2024. https://knowyourarchetypes.com/personality-types-list/youthful-personality.

Koren, Leonard. *Wabi-Sabi for Artists, Designers, Poets & Philosophers*. Stone Bridge Press, 1994.

Laber-Warren, Emily. "Negative Thoughts About Aging Can Be Harmful. Here's How to Reduce Them." *Washington Post*, August 17, 2023. https://www.washingtonpost.com/wellness/2023/08/17/internalized-ageism-health-effects-solutions.

LaMotte, Sandee. "These 8 Habits Could Add up to 24 Years to Your Life, Study Says." CNN, July 24, 2023. https://www.cnn.com/2023/07/24/health/habits-live-longer-wellness.

Levine, Hallie. "Most Strokes Are Preventable. Follow These 6 Steps to Reduce Your Risk." *Consumer Reports*, October 23, 2023. https://www.washingtonpost.com/wellness/2023/10/23/stroke-prevention-diet-exercise-lifestyle.

Levine, Hallie. "Sleep Problems Can Increase as You Age." *Consumer Reports*, October 16, 2023. https://www.washingtonpost.com/wellness/2023/10/16/sleep-napping-aging-circadian-clock.

Levy, Becca. *Breaking the Age Code: How Your Beliefs About Aging Determine How Long and Well You Live*. William Morrow, 2022.

Lewis, Katherine Reynolds. "Young Adults Suffer from Anxiety, Depression Twice as Often as Teens." *Washington Post*, October 24, 2023. https://www.washingtonpost.com/wellness/2023/10/24/anxiety-depression-young-adults.

Marill, Michele Cohen. "Is This Normal Aging or Not?" WebMD, May 4, 2022. https://www.webmd.com/healthy-aging/features/normal-aging-changes-and-symptoms.

Markey, Kristin. "What to Expect During the 4 Phases of Retirement?" *RunawayWidow* (blog), March 2, 2023. https://runawaywidow .blog/2023/03/what-are-the-4-phases-of-retirement.

Mastoianni, Adam. "Your Brain Has Tricked You into Thinking Everything Is Worse." *New York Times,* June 20, 2023. https:// www.nytimes.com/2023/06/20/opinion/psychology-brain-biased -memory.html.

Mayo Clinic. "Aging: What to Expect." September 20, 2023. https:// www.mayoclinic.org/healthy-lifestyle/healthy-aging/in-depth/aging /art-20046070.

McDowell, Jeanne Dorin. "Celebrating What's Right with Aging: Inside the Minds of Super Agers." *AARP Bulletin*, November 10, 2023. https://www.aarp.org/health/brain-health/info-2023/minds -of-super-agers.html.

Meyer, Cyn. "How to Get Over Your Fear of Aging and Death." Second Wind Movement. Accessed August 23, 2024. https://secondwind movement.com/fear-of-aging.

National Institute of Aging. "Understanding the Dynamics of the Aging Process." National Institutes of Health, accessed August 23, 2024. https://www.nia.nih.gov/about/aging-strategic-directions-research /understanding-dynamics-aging.

Rosen, Bob. *Calm in Chaos: How to Thrive in the New World of Work.* Healthy Companies, 2023.

Searing, Linda. "Adopting 8 Therapeutic Habits Can Add Decades to Your Life, Study Says." *Washington Post,* August 21, 2023. https:// www.washingtonpost.com/wellness/2023/08/21/health-lifestyle -habits-live-longer.

Selig, Meg. "Do You Have 'FOGO?' Taming the Fear of Getting Old." *Changepower* (blog). *Psychology Today,* June 29, 2021. https:// www.psychologytoday.com/us/blog/changepower/202106/do-you -have-fogo-taming-the-fear-getting-old.

Senior Allies. "Aging is Real: 10 Ways Your Body Changes After 60." *Senior Allies* (blog), September 11, 2019. https://www.medicare allies.com/senior-insurance-blog/aging-is-real-10-ways-your-body -changes-after-60.

Weil, Andrew. *Healthy Aging: A Lifelong Guide to Your Physical and Spiritual Well-Being.* Alfred A. Knop, 2005.

Weissbourd, Richard, Milena Batanova, Joseph McIntyre, et al. "On Edge: Understanding and Preventing Young Adults' Mental Health Challenges." Harvard Graduate School of Education, 2023. https:// mcc.gse.harvard.edu/reports/on-edge.

Zilca, Ran. "Why Your Late Twenties Is the Worst Time of Your Life." *Harvard Business Review*, March 7, 2016. https://hbr.org/2016/03 /why-your-late-twenties-is-the-worst-time-of-your-life.

Zweig, Connie. *The Inner Work of Age: Shifting from Role to Soul.* Park Street Press, 2021.

Chapter 9: The Attachment to Self

Abelli, Heidi. "The 5 Soft Skills Needed to Succeed in an AI-Dominated Workplace." *Fast Company*, November 18, 2023. https://www.fast company.com/90975351/the-5-soft-skills-needed-to-succeed-in -an-ai-dominated-workplace.

Blum, Dani. "How the Language of Therapy Took Over Dating." *New York Times*, February 11, 2023. https://www.nytimes.com/2023/02 /11/style/therapy-speak-dating.html.

Brooks, Arthur C. *From Strength to Strength: Finding Success, Happiness and Deep Purpose in The Second Half of Life.* Portfolio/Penguin, 2022.

Brooks, David. *How to Know a Person: The Art of Seeing Others Deeply and Being Deeply Seen.* Random House, 2023.

Brooks, Mike. "Hold On Loosely: Why Attachment Is a Double-Edged Sword." *Tech Happy Life* (blog). *Psychology Today*, March 1, 2022. https://www.psychologytoday.com/us/blog/tech-happy-life/202203 /hold-loosely-why-attachment-is-double-edged-sword.

Brown, Brené. *Braving the Wilderness: The Quest for True Belonging and the Courage to Stand Alone.* Random House, 2017.

Carpenter, Shannon. "The Male Loneliness Epidemic and How It Affects Fathers." CNN, September 18, 2023. https://www.cnn.com /2023/09/18/health/male-loneliness-epidemic-wellness.

Chapman, Gary. *The 5 Love Languages: The Secret to Love That Lasts.* Northfield Publishing, 2015.

Chopra, Deepak. *Abundance: The Inner Path to Wealth.* Harmony Books, 2022.

Cummins, Eleanor, and Andrew Zaleski. "If Loneliness Is an Epidemic, How Do We Treat It?" *New York Times*, July 14, 2023. https://www .nytimes.com/2023/07/14/opinion/treating-loneliness.html.

Diamond, Stephen A. "The Psychology of Neurotic Romantic Attraction. Are You Repeatedly Attracted To Inappropriate Romantic Partners?" *Evil Deeds* (blog). *Psychology Today*, November 3, 2013. https://www.psychologytoday.com/us/blog/evil-deeds/201311/the -psychology-neurotic-romantic-attraction.

Formica, Michael J. "The Neurotic Complement in Relationships. Fitting Together Like a Lock and a Key." *Enlightened Living* (blog). *Psychology Today*, January 12, 2019. https://www.psychologytoday .com/us/blog/enlightened-living/201901/the-neurotic-complement -in-relationships.

Friedman, Thomas L. *Hot, Flat, and Crowded: Why We Need a Green Revolution—and How It Can Renew America.* Farrar, Straus and Giroux, 2008.

Gottman, John M., and Nan Silver. *The Seven Principles for Making Marriage Work: A Practical Guide from the Country's Foremost Relationship Expert.* Harmony Books, 2015.

Grogan, Jessica. "Improving Relationships Is Hard. A Couples Therapist Recommends These Books." *Washington Post*, November 26, 2023. https://www.washingtonpost.com/books/2023/11/26/couples-therapist-recommends-books-about-relationships.

Holcombe, Madeline. "Why Most Men Don't Have Enough Close Friends." CNN, November 17, 2023. https://www.cnn.com/2022/11/29/health/men-friendships-wellness/index.html.

Kaur, Harmeet. "The Four Attachment Styles and How They Affect Your Relationships." CNN, August 29, 2023. https://www.cnn.com/health/attachment-styles-types-relationships-wellness-cec/index.html.

Mandriota, Morgan. "Here is How to Identify Your Attachment Style." PsychCentral, October 13, 2021. https://psychcentral.com/health/4-attachment-styles-in-relationships.

McGee, Michael. "Self-Centeredness." *Dr. Michael McGee* (blog), March 17, 2018. https://drmichaelmcgee.com/self-centeredness.

McPhillips, Deidre. "Suicide Deaths Reached a Record High in the US in 2022, Despite Hopeful Decreases Among Children and Young Adults." CNN, November 29, 2023. https://www.cnn.com/2023/11/29/health/suicide-record-high-2022-cdc/index.html.

Miser, Andrew L. *The Partnership Marriage. Creating the Life You Love . . . Together.* CreateSpace Independent Publishing Platform, 2014.

Ni, Preston. "7 Predictors of Long-Term Relationship Success." *Communication Success* (blog). *Psychology Today*, February 14, 2013. https://www.psychologytoday.com/us/blog/communication-success/201302/7-predictors-long-term-relationship-success.

Nicioli, Taylor. "The Loneliness Epidemic: Nearly 1 in 4 Adults Feel Lonely, New Survey Finds." CNN, October 24, 2023. https://www .cnn.com/2023/10/24/health/lonely-adults-gallup-poll-wellness /index.html.

Rogers, Kristen. "Loneliness or Social Isolation Linked to Serious Health Outcomes, Study Finds." CNN, June 19, 2023. https://www .cnn.com/2023/06/19/health/loneliness-social-isolation-early-death -risk-wellness/index.html.

Rosen, Bob. *Calm in Chaos: How to Thrive in the New World of Work*. Healthy Companies, 2023.

Rosen, Bob. *Grounded: How Leaders Stay Rooted in an Uncertain World*. Jossey-Bass, 2014.

Rosen, Bob, and Emma-Kate Swann. *Conscious: The Power of Awareness in Business and Life*. John Wiley & Sons, Inc., 2018.

Rosen, Robert H. *The Healthy Company: Eight Strategies to Develop People, Productivity, and Profits*. Jeremy P. Tarcher, 1991.

Schoichet, Catherine E., and Parker Leipzig. "More Baby Boomers Are Living Alone. One Reason Why: 'Gray Divorce'." CNN, August 5, 2023. https://www.cnn.com/2023/08/05/health/boomers-divorce -living-alone-wellness-cec/index.html.

Schwantes, Marcel. "What's the Best Sign of Success, Emotional Intelligence or IQ? Turns Out, It's Something Else." *Inc.*, October 21, 2023. https://www.inc.com/marcel-schwantes/what-s-the-secret-to -success-turns-out-it-s-neither-emotional-intelligence-or-iq.html.

Seltzer, Leon F. "Self-Absorption: the Root of All (Psychological) Evil? Here's What You Should Know About Obsessing, Ruminating, and Self-Centeredness." *Evolution of the Self* (blog). *Psychology Today*, August 24, 2016. https://www.psychologytoday.com/us/blog/evolution-the -self/201608/self-absorption-the-root-all-psychological-evil.

Upjourney. "Selfish vs Self-Centered vs Self-Absorbed vs Narcissist. What Is the Difference?" December 1, 2023. https://upjourney.com /selfish-vs-self-centered-vs-self-absorbed-vs-narcissist.

Williams, Ashley. R. "A Record-High Number of 40-Year-Olds in the US Have Never Been Married, Study Finds." CNN, July 1, 2023. https://www.cnn.com/2023/07/01/us/record-number-of-40-year -olds-never-married-trnd/index.html.

Chapter 10: The Attachment to Life

Aswani, Romina. "The Law of Detachment: What Does Buddhism Teach Us? Hard Times Build Determination and Inner Strength." *The Apeiron Blog. Medium*, January 29, 2021. https://theapeiron .co.uk/the-law-of-detachment-what-does-buddhism-teach-us -395f090f6a40.

Brach, Tara. *Radical Acceptance: Embracing Your Life with the Heart of a Buddha*. Bantam Books, 2003.

Brain Balance. "Gratitude and the Brain: What is Happening?" *Brain Balance* (blog), accessed August 23, 2024. https://www.brainbalance centers.com/blog/gratitude-and-the-brain-what-is-happening.

Carroll, Lewis. *Alice's Adventures in Wonderland*. MacMillan, 1865.

Clifton, John. *Blind Spot: The Global Rise of Unhappiness and How Leaders Missed It*. Gallup Press, 2022.

Dass, Ram, and Mirabai Bush. *Walking Each Other Home: Conversations on Loving and Dying*. SoundsTrue, 2018.

DuLong, Jon. "Is There Such a Thing as Too Much Gratitude? Turns Out Sometimes Less Is More." CNN, November 26, 2023. https:// www.cnn.com/2023/11/26/health/how-gratitude-practices-work -wellness.

Kegan, Robert. *The Evolving Self: Problem and Process in Human Development*. Harvard University Press, 1982.

Kegan, Robert, and Lisa Laskow Lahey. *Immunity to Change: How to Overcome It and Unlock the Potential in Yourself and Your Organization*. Harvard Business Press, 2009.

Kitazawa, Emily. "Death is a Natural Part of Life—And That's a Happy Thought." *Shortform* (blog), October 22, 2022. https://www.short form.com/blog/death-is-a-natural-part-of-life.

Koren, Leonard. *Wabi-Sabi for Artists, Designers, Poets & Philosophers*. Stone Bridge Press, 1994.

Leshgold, Wendy, and Lisa McCarthy. *Fast Forward: 5 Power Principles to Create the Life You Want in Just One Year*. Matt Holt Books, 2023.

Lyubomirsky, Sonja. *The Myths of Happiness: What Should Make You Happy, but Doesn't, What Shouldn't Make You Happy, but Does*. Penguin Books, 2013.

Meier, JD. "How to Be an Adult: The 5 Stages of Adult Development." Sources of Insight, accessed August 23, 2024. https://sourcesofinsight .com/5-stages-of-adult-development.

Rosen, Bob. *Grounded: How Leaders Stay Rooted in an Uncertain World*. Jossey-Bass, 2014.

Rosen, Bob, and Emma-Kate Swann. *Conscious: The Power of Awareness in Business and Life*. John Wiley & Sons, Inc., 2018.

Schwantes, Marcel. "The Path to Lifelong Happiness Comes down to 7 Simple Choices." *Inc.*, August 30, 2023. https://www.inc.com/marcel -schwantes/the-path-to-lifelong-happiness-comes-down-to-7-simple -choices.html.

Sloman, Steven, and Philip Fernbach. *The Knowledge Illusion: Why We Never Think Alone*. Riverhead Books, 2017.

Zweig, Connie. *The Inner Work of Age: Shifting from Role to Soul*. Park Street Press, 2021.

Living a More Fulfilling Life

Jeste, Dilip, and Scott LaFee. *Wiser: The Scientific Roots of Wisdom, Compassion, and What Makes Us Good.* Sounds True, 2020.

Rosen, Bob, and Emma-Kate Swann. *Conscious: The Power of Awareness in Business and Life.* John Wiley & Sons, Inc., 2018.

Stillman, Jessica. "World's Happiest Country Finland Offered a Master Class on How to Be Happy. These Are the 3 Biggest Takeaways." *Inc.*, December 21, 2023. https://www.inc.com/jessica-stillman /world-happiest-country-finland-offered-masterclass-how-be-happy -3-biggest-takeaways.html.

INDEX

ABOUT THE AUTHOR

 Photo by Annie Gensheimer

Dr. Bob Rosen is a world-renowned thought leader on healthy people and healthy organizations. As a psychologist, *New York Times* best-selling author, researcher, and business adviser, his work in personal and organizational change is recognized worldwide. Each year he speaks to thousands of people worldwide and appears regularly in the international media.

Bob founded Healthy Companies in 1988 and has interviewed or advised more than 600 CEOs of world-class companies—an effort launched with a six-year multimillion-dollar grant from the John D. & Catherine T. MacArthur Foundation.

Bob's innate curiosity about people drives his work. Why do some of us succeed while others fail? What is it that holds some people back as others forge ahead? How does our thinking help or hinder our ability to be happy? To achieve our goals? To feel joy and fulfillment?

Over the years, Bob has written eight books, including *Grounded, Conscious, The Catalyst, Just Enough Anxiety, Leadership Journeys, Global Literacies,* and *The Healthy Company.*

To contact Bob Rosen, go to www.bobrosen.com.

DETACH

Services and Resources

Detach Speaking: Bring Bob Rosen and his message to your organization. As a sought-after keynote speaker and best-selling author, Bob offers a powerful talk on *Detach: Ditching Your Baggage to Live a More Fulfilling Life* and its impact on well-being, happiness, engagement, and performance.

Detach Assessment: Get a profile of how detached you are by assessing your ten attachments and ten aspirations. Use this framework to gain practical advice for self-improvement toward living a happier, more successful life.

Detach Discussion Guide: Make use of a practical interactive guide for individuals and groups about the power of *Detach* at home, school, or work. Perfect for team meetings, book clubs, and networks of friends and family.

Detach Community: Become a member of our global learning network of like-minded people who value Western and Eastern thinking and believe that who you are drives what you do and that self-awareness drives fulfillment and success.

Bob Rosen's Books: Enjoy Bob's best-selling books, including *Detach* (book, e-book, audiobook), *Grounded* (*New York Times* bestseller), *Conscious* (*Washington Post* bestseller), and *Just Enough Anxiety*.

Visit www.BobRosen.com for more information.